DOCUMENTS ON CHRISTIAN UNITY

THIRD SERIES

DOCUMENTS ON CHRISTIAN UNITY

THIRD SERIES
1930–48

Edited by

G. K. A. BELL
BISHOP OF CHICHESTER

GEOFFREY CUMBERLEGE
OXFORD UNIVERSITY PRESS
London New York Toronto
1948

Oxford University Press, Amen House, London E.C. 4
GLASGOW NEW YORK TORONTO MELBOURNE WELLINGTON
BOMBAY CALCUTTA MADRAS CAPE TOWN
Geoffrey Cumberlege, Publisher to the University

PRINTED IN GREAT BRITAIN
AT THE UNIVERSITY PRESS, OXFORD
BY CHARLES BATEY PRINTER TO THE UNIVERSITY

PREFACE

THE first two Series of these *Documents on Christian Unity* cover the period 1920–30. They are in themselves striking evidence of the steady growth of the movement towards the reunion of Christendom. This Third Series marks a still further advance during the years 1930 to 1948. The opportunity has also been taken to add certain earlier documents concerning the Malines Conversations (Nos. 149, 150) and the Syrian Orthodox Jacobite Church (Nos. 161–4). The documents included start with the Lambeth Conference, 1930, and deal, as before, mainly with negotiations and conferences between particular Churches. But the present volume affords still more remarkable illustrations of the way in which the Oecumenical movement generally is developing. The World Conferences at Edinburgh, Oxford, and Tambaram are all represented, as well as the World Council of the Churches in preparation for the First Assembly at Amsterdam, August 22–September 5, 1948.

In spite of the difficulties of book production in present circumstances it is hoped that most of the principal documents of these years will be found in this volume. One important document has had to be omitted—that is the *Proposed Scheme of Church Union in South India*, Seventh Edition (Revised), 1942. This makes a small book in itself, and inquiries of the publishers (United Society for Christian Literature) show that an adequate number of copies are readily available in the ordinary way. But certain resolutions and other documents bearing on this Scheme of Union, which are not so easily procured, will be found in the South India section.

Once again I should like to thank all those who have contributed in various ways to the preparation of this volume. I thank the following in particular: the Rev. Dr. B. J. Kidd (No. 149); Dom Lambert Beauduin (No. 150); Mr. A. C. F. Beales (Nos. 151–5); the Bishop of Albany, U.S.A. (No. 170); the Rev. Dr. Hugh Martin and the Student Christian Movement Press (No. 172); the Rev. H. T. Wigley, General Secretary of the Free Church

Federal Council (No. 177); Bishop Macleavy (No. 178); the Very Rev. Dr. E. J. Hagan (No. 181); Dean Zabriskie and Canon Theodore Wedel (Nos. 196–8); the Rev. Dr. W. B. Pugh (No. 199); the late Archbishop of Toronto, Dr. Owen (Nos. 200–1); the Bishop of Newcastle, Australia (No. 202); the Bishop of Chota Nagpur (No. 203); Bishop F. J. Western (Nos. 204–8); Dr. J. H. Oldham and Messrs. George Allen & Unwin (No. 210); Professor Leonard Hodgson, General Secretary of the World Conference on Faith and Order (Nos. 211–16); the Rev. Norman Goodall, Secretary of the International Missionary Council (No. 217); Dr. W. A. Visser 't Hooft, General Secretary of the World Council of Churches (Nos. 218–19 and 221, and in many other ways); Mrs. William Temple (No. 219); Archbishop Godfrey, Apostolic Delegate to Great Britain (No. 220); the Rev. Dr. A. F. Smethurst and the Rev. H. R. Wilson, for much help with regard to the text of resolutions adopted respectively by the Convocations of Canterbury and York; and the Rev. H. M. Waddams, Secretary of the Church of England Council on Foreign Relations, in connexion with documents concerning foreign Churches generally. I also thank my Chaplain, the Rev. J. R. Porter, and my Secretary, Miss Mary Balmer, for valuable assistance in the organization and arrangement of the documents. A final word of special appreciation is due to the Oxford University Press for the great trouble taken both in printing and in publishing this book in good time.

GEORGE CICESTR:

January, 1948.

CONTENTS

I. THE LAMBETH CONFERENCE 1930

AUGUST 1930

145. *Resolutions on the Unity of the Church*

31. THE Conference records, with deep thanks to Almighty God, the signs of a growing movement towards Christian unity in all parts of the world since the issue of the Appeal to All Christian People by the Lambeth Conference in 1920.

The Conference heartily endorses that Appeal and reaffirms the principles contained in it and in the Resolutions dealing with Reunion adopted by that Conference.

The Malines Conversations

32. Believing that our Lord's purpose for His Church will only be fulfilled when all the separated parts of His Body are united, and that only by full discussion between the Churches can error and misunderstanding be removed and full spiritual unity attained, the Conference expresses its appreciation of the courage and Christian charity of Cardinal Mercier in arranging the Malines Conversations, unofficial and not fully representative of the Churches though they were, and its regret that by the Encyclical, *Mortalium animos*, members of the Roman Catholic Church are forbidden to take part in the World Conference on Faith and Order and other similar Conferences.

The Eastern Orthodox Church

33. (*a*) The Conference heartily thanks the Oecumenical Patriarch for arranging in co-operation with the other Patriarchs and the Autocephalous Churches for the sending of an important Delegation of the Eastern Orthodox Church under the leadership of the Patriarch of Alexandria, and expresses its grateful appreciation of the help given to its Committee by the Delegation, as well as its sense of the value of the advance made through the joint meetings in the relations of the Orthodox Church with the Anglican Communion.

(*b*) The Conference requests the Archbishop of Canterbury to appoint representatives of the Anglican Communion and to invite the Oecumenical Patriarch to appoint representatives of the Patriarchates and Autocephalous Churches of the East to be a Doctrinal Commission, which may, in correspondence and in consultation, prepare a joint statement on the theological points about which there is difference and agreement between the Anglican and the Eastern Churches.

(*c*) The Conference not having been summoned as a Synod to issue any statement professing to define doctrine, is therefore unable to issue such a formal statement on the subjects referred to in the *Résumé* of the discussions between the Patriarch of Alexandria with the other Orthodox Representatives and Bishops of the Anglican Communion, but records its acceptance of the statements of the Anglican Bishops contained therein as a sufficient account of the teaching and practice of the Church of England and of the Churches in communion with it, in relation to those subjects.

34. The Conference expresses its sympathy with the Church of Russia in its persecution and sufferings, and prays that God, in His mercy, may give liberty and prosperity once more to that Church, that it may again take its place with greater freedom and power of self-expression among the other great Churches of Christendom.

The Old Catholic Church

35. (*a*) The Conference heartily thanks the Archbishop of Utrecht and the Bishops of the Old Catholic Church associated with him for coming to consult with its members on the development of closer relations between their Churches and the Anglican Communion, and expresses its sense of the importance of the step taken.

(*b*) The Conference requests the Archbishop of Canterbury to appoint representatives of the Anglican Communion, and to invite the Archbishop of Utrecht to appoint representatives of the Old Catholic Churches to be a Doctrinal Commission to discuss points of agreement and difference between them.

(*c*) The Conference agrees that there is nothing in the Declaration of Utrecht inconsistent with the teaching of the Church of England.

The Separated Eastern Churches

36. (*a*) The Conference thanks Bishop Tourian for taking counsel with one of its committees on the relations between the

[Armenian] Church and the Anglican Communion, and assures him of its deep sympathy with the sufferings of his nation.

(*b*) The Conference expresses its deep sympathy with the Armenian, East Syrian (Assyrian), and West Syrian Christians in the hardship and suffering which they have endured since the war, and earnestly prays that they may be given strength and courage in their efforts for self-preservation, as well as that their rights may be fully secured as religious or racial minorities in the territories in which they live.

(*c*) The Conference welcomes the development of closer relations between the Anglican Communion and the Separated Churches of the East which is recorded in its Committee's Report, and earnestly desires that these relations may be steadily strengthened, in consultation with the Orthodox Church, in the hope that in due course full intercommunion may be reached.

The Church of Sweden

37. The Conference thanks the Church of Sweden for the visit of the Bishop of Lund and expresses its hope that the existing fraternal relations with that Church will be maintained, and that relations may also be strengthened with the other Scandinavian Churches with a view to promoting greater unity in the future.

The Church of Finland

38. The Conference requests the Archbishop of Canterbury, as soon as seems advisable, to appoint a committee to investigate the position of the Church of Finland and its relations to the Church of England.

The Moravians (Unitas Fratrum)

39. The Conference is grateful to the Moravian Church for sending so important a body of representatives to confer with their committee, and respectfully requests the Archbishop of Canterbury to appoint a new committee to confer with a committee of the Moravian Church.

South India

40. (*a*) The Conference has heard with the deepest interest of the proposals for Church union in South India now under consideration between the Church of India, Burma, and Ceylon, the South

India United Church, and the Wesleyan Methodist Church of South India, and expresses its high appreciation of the spirit in which the representatives of these Churches have pursued the long and careful negotiations.

(*b*) The Conference notes with warm sympathy that the project embodied in the Proposed Scheme for Church Union in South India is not the formation of any fresh Church or Province of the Anglican Communion under new conditions, but seeks rather to bring together the distinctive elements of different Christian Communions, on a basis of sound doctrine and episcopal order, in a distinct Province of the Universal Church, in such a way as to give the Indian expression of the spirit, the thought, and the life of the Church Universal.

(*c*) We observe further, as a novel feature in the South Indian Scheme, that a complete agreement between the uniting Churches on certain points of doctrine and practice is not expected to be reached before the inauguration of the union; but the promoters of the scheme believe that unity will be reached gradually and more securely by the interaction of the different elements of the united Church upon one another. It is only when the unification resulting from that interaction is complete that a final judgement can be pronounced on the effect of the present proposals. Without attempting, therefore, to pronounce such judgement now, we express to our brethren in India our strong desire that, as soon as the negotiations are successfully completed, the venture should be made and the union inaugurated. We hope that it will lead to the emergence of a part of the Body of Christ which will possess a new combination of the riches that are His. In this hope we ask the Churches of our Communion to stand by our brethren in India, while they make this experiment, with generous goodwill.

(*d*) The Conference thinks it wise to point out that, after the union in South India has been inaugurated, both ministers and lay people of the united Church, when they are outside the jurisdiction of that Church, will be amenable to the regulations of the Province and Diocese in which they desire to officiate or to worship, and it must be assumed that those regulations will be applied to individuals in the same manner as they would now be applied to similarly circumstanced individuals, unless any Province takes formal action to change its regulations.

(*e*) The Conference, fully assured in the light of the Resolutions of the General Council of the Church of India, Burma, and Ceylon adopted in February, 1930, that nothing will be done to break the fellowship of the Churches of the Anglican Communion, confidently leaves in the hands of the Bishops of that Church the task of working out in detail the principles which are embodied in the Proposed Scheme.

(*f*) The Conference gives its general approval to the suggestions contained in the Report of its Committee with regard to the Proposed Scheme for Church Union in South India, and commends the Report to the attention of the Episcopal Synod and General Council of the Church of India, Burma, and Ceylon.

The Church in Persia

41. The Conference has heard with deep sympathy of the steps towards union which have been proposed in Persia; it desires to express its sincere appreciation of the missionary zeal of the Church in Persia, and it generally approves the sections in the Report of its Committee dealing with this subject.

Special Areas

42. The Conference, maintaining as a general principle that intercommunion should be the goal of, rather than a means to, the restoration of union, and bearing in mind the general rule of the Anglican Churches that 'members of the Anglican Churches should receive the Holy Communion only from ministers of their own Church', holds, nevertheless, that the administration of such a rule falls under the discretion of the Bishop, who should exercise his dispensing power in accordance with any principles that may be set forth by the national, regional, or provincial authority of the Church in the area concerned. The Bishops of the Anglican Communion will not question the action of any Bishop who may, in his discretion so exercised, sanction an exception to the general rule in special areas, where the ministrations of an Anglican Church are not available for long periods of time or without travelling great distances, or may give permission that baptized communicant members of Churches not in communion with our own should be encouraged to communicate in Anglican churches, when the ministrations of their own Church are not available, or in other special or temporary circumstances.

The Conference adopted the following explanatory note.—In view of the dangers of misconception, we think it desirable to say that in recognizing that a Bishop of the Anglican Communion may under very strict regulations and in very special circumstances permit individual communicants to join with members of other Christian bodies in their Services of the administration of the Lord's Supper, we felt bound to consider the difficulties created by present conditions, especially in some parts of the Mission Field. But we would point out that the very special circumstances and the very strict regulations specified in this Resolution of themselves show that we are not departing from the rule of our Church that the minister of the Sacrament of Holy Communion should be a priest episcopally ordained.

The Church of Scotland

43. The Conference expresses its gratitude to the distinguished members of the Church of Scotland[1] who accepted the invitation to confer with its Committee. It hopes that an invitation may soon be issued to the now happily united Church of Scotland to enter into free and unrestricted conference with representatives of the Anglican Communion on the basis of the Appeal to All Christian People issued in 1920.

Evangelical Free Churches of England

44. The Conference cordially thanks the influential Delegation from the Federal Council of the Evangelical Free Churches of England[2] for attending one of the Sessions of its Committee, and for the help of that Delegation in defining the issues which have still to be resolved before further advance towards organic union is possible. The Conference notes with satisfaction and gratitude the great measure of agreement on matters of faith reached at the Conferences held from 1921 till 1925 between representatives of the Church of England and representatives of the Federal Council of Evangelical Free Churches, and hopes that at an early date such Conferences may be resumed with a view to ascertaining whether the Proposed Scheme of Union prepared for the Churches in South

[1] The Very Rev. John White, D.D., and the Hon. Lord Sands, Senator of the College of Justice.

[2] The Rev. A. E. Garvie, D.D., the Rev. M. E. Aubrey, M.A., the Rev. J. T. Barkby, the Rev. S. M. Berry, D.D., the Rev. D. Brook, D.C.L., the Rev. Charles Brown, D.D., the Rev. J. Scott Lidgett, D.D., the Rev. W. L. Robertson, D.D., the Rev. P. Carnegie Simpson, D.D., the Rev. H. J. Taylor, and Bishop Arthur Ward.

India, or other proposals which have been put forward, suggest lines on which further advance towards agreement on questions of order can be made, and that similar conferences may be held elsewhere.

Schemes of Reunion

45. In view of the various schemes of Reunion and other projects and advances towards union and intercommunion which have been the subject of discussion or negotiation, the Conference reminds the Church that it is a paramount duty to seek unity among Christians in every direction, and assures all who are working for this end of its cordial support in their endeavours; it also reminds the Church that until full and final schemes are set out and terms of intercommunion are definitely arranged, the expression of final judgements on individual schemes is premature.

Co-operation in Evangelism

46. Meanwhile the Conference urges the desirability of organizing and participating in efforts of Evangelism in co-operation with Christians of other Communions, both as a means of bearing effective witness to the multitudes who are detached from all forms of organized Christianity, and as a means of expressing and strengthening that sense of unity in the Gospel which binds together in spiritual fellowship those who own allegiance to different Churches.

Unity among Anglicans

47. The Conference calls upon all members of the Anglican Communion to promote the cause of union by fostering and deepening in all possible ways the fellowship of the Anglican Communion itself, so that by mutual understanding and appreciation all may come to a fuller apprehension of the truth as it is in Jesus, and more perfectly make manifest to the world the unity of the Spirit in and through the diversity of His gifts.

146. The Historic Episcopate

Extract from the Report of the Committee on 'The Unity of the Church'

When we speak of the Historic Episcopate, we mean the Episcopate as it emerged in the clear light of history from the time when definite evidence begins to be available. It is, indeed, well known that the origin of episcopacy has been much debated. Without entering into the discussion of theories which divide scholars, we may affirm shortly that we see no reason to doubt the statement made in the Preface to our Ordinal that 'from the Apostles' time there have been these Orders of Ministers in Christ's Church: Bishops, Priests and Deacons'. Whatever variety of system may have existed in addition in the earlier age, it is universally agreed that by the end of the second century episcopacy had no effective rival. Among all the controversies of the fourth and fifth centuries the episcopal ministry was never a subject of dispute. We may therefore reasonably claim that it is 'historic' in a sense in which no other now can ever be. The Episcopate occupies a position which is, in point of historic development, analogous to that of the Canon of Scripture and of the Creeds. In the first days there was no Canon of New Testament Scripture, for the books afterwards included in it were still being written. For a time different Churches had different writings which they regarded as authoritative. The Canon was slowly formed, and the acceptance of a single Canon throughout the Church took several generations. So, too, the Apostles' Creed is the result of a process of growth which we can in large measure trace. If the Episcopate, as we find it established universally by the end of the second century, was the result of a like process of adaptation and growth in the organism of the Church, that would be no evidence that it lacked divine authority, but rather that the life of the Spirit within the Church had found it to be the most appropriate organ for the functions which it discharged.

In the course of time the Episcopate was greatly affected by secular forces, which bent it to many purposes alien to its true character, and went far to obscure its spiritual purpose. It is hard to recognize the successors of the Apostles in the feudal Prelates of the medieval Church, or in the 'peers spiritual' of eighteenth-century England. Moreover, the essential character of the Episcopate was distorted by the development of the Papal Supremacy. Such deviations from its true principle are mainly responsible for the general abandonment of Episcopacy by the Protestant Churches. The Historic Episcopate as we understand it goes behind the perversions of history to the original conception of the Apostolic Ministry.

For it is not a mere fact, but an institution fulfilling certain purposes. As an institution it was, and is, characterized by succession in two forms: the succession in office and the succession of consecration. And it had generally recognized functions: the general superintendence of the Church and more especially of the Clergy; the maintenance of unity in the one Eucharist; the ordination of men to the ministry; the safeguarding of the faith; and the administration of the discipline of the Church. There have been different interpretations of the relation of these elements in the Historic Episcopate to one another; but the elements themselves are constant. When, therefore, we say that we must insist on the Historic Episcopate but not upon any theory or interpretation of it, we are not to be understood as insisting on the office apart from the functions. What we uphold is the Episcopate, maintained in successive generations by continuity of succession and consecration, as it has been throughout the history of the Church from the earliest times, and discharging those functions which from the earliest times it has discharged.

We readily agree that there are other elements in the full life of the Church, and we hold that the episcopate should be 'constitutional' in the sense that provision should be made for the due co-operation of the presbyterate and the congregation of Christ's faithful people in the ordering of the Church's life. Indeed, this is already secured in varying degrees in all parts of the Anglican Communion by the revival of Diocesan and Provincial Synods, or by other similar means. We recognize that in this respect we have much to learn and to gain from the traditions and customs of the non-episcopal Churches. But our special responsibility as an episcopal Church is to bring into the complete life of the united Church those elements which we have received and hold in trust. Chief among these, in the matter of Order, is the Historic Episcopate.

In laying this emphasis on our own inheritance, we emphatically declare that we do not call in question the spiritual reality of the ministries now exercised in non-episcopal communions. On the contrary, we reiterate the declaration of the Lambeth Conference of 1920, that 'these ministries have been manifestly blessed and owned by the Holy Spirit as effective means of grace'. But when we consider the problem which must be paramount in all our discussions, namely, the restoration of the broken unity of Christ's Body and the drawing together of the separated groups of His followers, we realize that one necessary element in that visible fellowship must be a ministry universally acknowledged. Thus considered, there is, at present, no ministry which fully corresponds with the purpose of God. Yet we are persuaded that the historic continuity of the episcopal ministry provides evidence of the Divine intention in this respect such as to constitute a stewardship which we are bound to discharge. . . .

But while we thus stand for the Historic Episcopate as a necessary element in any union in which the Anglican Communion can take part, and have given our reasons for so doing, we do not require of others acceptance of those reasons, or of any one particular theory or interpretation of the Episcopate as a condition of union. We recognize as fully the gifts of the one Spirit entrusted to those others, and their equal responsibility to maintain their several trusts; and we are content to believe that the acceptance of the Episcopate itself, in its continuity of succession and consecration, and in the discharge of its historic functions, will bring to the united Church those gifts of Grace which, as we believe, the Providence of God has associated with it.

147. The South India Scheme

Extract from the Report of the Committee on 'The Unity of the Church'

IT is with reference to the principles we have already set forth that we have considered the Proposed Scheme of Union affecting the southern dioceses of the Church of India, Burma, and Ceylon, the South India United Church, and the South India Province of the Wesleyan Methodist Church.

First it is important to make clear the way in which this scheme came before the Lambeth Conference. It was not submitted for acceptance or rejection. The Lambeth Conference has no constitutional authority to accept or reject such proposals; the responsibility for action lies with the Church of India, Burma, and Ceylon.[1] That Church has throughout fully recognized this fact. But before exercising its responsibility it has desired, in the spirit of fellowship, to ascertain the views of the Bishops belonging to other Provinces of the Anglican Communion, inasmuch as the whole of that Communion may be greatly concerned in and affected by what takes place. Accordingly, the Episcopal Synod of the Church of India, Burma, and Ceylon submitted the Proposals to the Lambeth Conference, together with certain Resolutions of the General

[1] Cf. Resolution 11 of the Lambeth Conference of 1920: 'The Conference recognizes that the task of effecting union with other Christian Communions must be undertaken by the various national, regional or provincial authorities of the Churches within the Anglican Communion.'

Council and certain expressions of its opinion on special points by which it desires that its own delegates may be guided at future meetings of the Joint Committee of the uniting Churches, in order that the assembled Bishops might offer their advice. The Episcopal Synod further asked for such advice with reference to four specific points and communicated one other on which the General Council desired to obtain the opinion of the Conference.

Secondly, it should be plainly understood that 'the scheme is frankly an outline'. In its present form it is the work of a joint committee on which representatives of the Churches concerned have been serving since 1920. It is an endeavour to state the central points on which agreement is necessary for union, for presentation to the Governing Bodies of the Churches concerned in India and elsewhere. No final conclusions have been reached on these central points by any of the Churches concerned. And, as the Joint Committee itself declares, even after agreement on the central points many details would still remain to be worked out.

One very important fact, however, as to the general position of the united Church[1] is impressed upon our minds at the start. We find in the proposed scheme a conception which is alike bold and new. The Joint Committee definitely intend that the Church in which the uniting bodies are to converge shall be autonomous in the fullest sense. It is to be free from any control legal or otherwise of any Church or society external to itself. The Anglican dioceses concerned are to be no longer a part of the Church of India, Burma, and Ceylon. The suggestion that the united Church should form a new province of that Church is rejected, on the ground that such an arrangement would have the appearance, and even something of the reality, of the absorption of the South India United Church and of the Wesleyan Church of South India in the Church of India, Burma, and Ceylon. Those dioceses will therefore not be Anglican dioceses in which we are asked to recognize elements foreign to the Anglican system; they would go forth from the Anglican Communion in order to make their own distinctive contribution to the faith and order of the new united Church. Moreover, the Church in which those dioceses are to be embraced will be itself 'a distinct province of the Universal Church', with a rule and character of its own. It is understood on all sides and is recognized in the scheme

[1] The phrase 'united Church' is used to denote the Church that will exist if the Proposed Scheme of Union becomes operative, but it must not be taken to be the name by which that Church will be called.

itself that no province of the Universal Church is free to act according to its own choice in contravention of the faith once for all delivered to the Saints or without regard to the preservation of the fellowship of the Church Universal.

From the position thus frankly stated follow certain results. The Anglican Communion consists of various Provinces and Dioceses in full communion with the Church of England. At the present time the Lambeth Conference is the visible bond which unites the different portions of the Anglican Communion to one another. It consists of Bishops in full communion with the Church of England and exercising oversight over Anglican dioceses. But the united Church in South India will not be a part of the Anglican Communion.

This does not, however, involve anything in the nature of schism, for even though the united Church will not be an integral part of the Anglican Communion, the fact of the formation of the united Church will not deprive any members of the united Church, whether Bishops, Clergy, or Laity, of any privilege of communion which they have hitherto enjoyed with the Church of England and with the Churches in communion with it.

Though the representatives of the Anglican Communion assembled in this Conference are not ready to express approval of every detail of the scheme, they are (we believe) desirous that the venture should be made and the Union inaugurated, and they hope that it will lead to the emergence of a part of the Body of Christ which will possess a new combination of the riches which are His. In this hope they wish to stand by the Church of India while she makes this experiment with generous goodwill.

We should hope that when the inauguration of the Union takes effect, the united Church will at once enjoy communion with the Churches of the Anglican Communion in the following ways:

(1) No censure should attach to any member, ordained or unordained, of a Church of the Anglican Communion who may be in South India or go thither, if he communicates with the united Church or takes work of any kind in it.

(2) No Church of the Anglican Communion should establish churches or congregations in the area of the union apart from the united Church.

(3) If communicant members or ordained ministers of the united church should go into any diocese of the Anglican Com-

munion, the Church of that diocese should receive them to communion whenever this can be done consistently with the regulations of each Province or extra-Provincial diocese, and episcopally ordained ministers of the united Church should be qualified, at the discretion of the Bishop, to officiate, subject to the regulations of the diocese for its own ministers.

These provisions represent certain restrictions upon full communion, that is to say, upon complete interchangeability of ministers and complete mutual admissibility to communion. We hope that when the unification within the united Church, contemplated in the Proposed Scheme, is complete, full communion in that sense will be secured between the united Church and the Churches of the Anglican Communion.

We proceed to offer the comments and advice for which we have been asked.

We rejoice that those who have combined to draw up the Proposed Scheme have endeavoured to follow the method of incorporating the distinctive elements of all the uniting bodies, for we are convinced that this method alone corresponds to the facts of the situation.

We associate ourselves with the General Council of the Church of India, Burma, and Ceylon, when it declares that it 'recognizes with great thankfulness that the Joint Committee has been guided by Almighty God to base the Scheme of Union upon the acknowledgement of essential truths and principles of the Christian Religion which the Church has ever held; namely, the doctrine of the Holy Trinity, and of the Incarnation of the Son of God, the authority of the Holy Scriptures, the Creeds as witnessing to and safeguarding the Faith, the two Sacraments of Baptism and the Holy Communion, and Christ's gift of the Ministry of His Church'; and also when it declares that 'it observes with equal thankfulness that the Committee has been guided to seek the achievement of union by unifying the Ministry through adoption of the rule of episcopal ordination; and it desires to express its grateful appreciation of the service which has been rendered to the common cause by those who have been willing to change their customs in order to make this possible'.

We therefore thank the Episcopal Synod and General Council of the Church of India, Burma, and Ceylon for the courage and wisdom which they have shown in sanctioning the negotiations at various times. We know how closely they have studied the needs of the Church, and the local circumstances in which the union is projected. We are impressed by the very careful consideration which they have given to the Proposed Scheme in its present form, and are in general accord with the opinions and instructions which they have furnished to their delegates. We are prepared to encourage the General Council and the Bishops to continue to seek union, on the lines which their own Resolutions suggest, without committing ourselves to particular propositions or provisions in the Proposed Scheme. And we trust that under the guidance of the Holy Spirit such a union may result as may fulfil the desire of those concerned in the negotiations 'so to organize the Church in South India that it shall give the Indian expression of the spirit, the thought, and the life of the Church Universal'.

In giving our general endorsement to the Resolutions passed by the General Council, and the Opinions expressed by it with reference to the Proposed Scheme, we desire to call special attention to the following points:

(1) We assent to the provision that those who unite in acceptance of the Episcopate with the functions assigned to it in the Scheme should not be required to accept any one particular interpretation of it.

(2) We approve the method of proceeding towards union by means of a pledge given in mutual trust, to respect the long-established traditions and conscientious convictions of the uniting Churches. Among such long-established traditions of our own we number the Preface to the Ordinal, and therefore understand this pledge to secure that the rule which the Anglican Church has inherited, that an episcopally ordained ministry is within our Church required for the due administration of Holy Communion, will be preserved for those congregations which have in the past been bound by that rule.

(3) We welcome the principle of the Scheme, which is that of uniting the Churches through unification of ministries so that eventually every minister exercising a permanent ministry in the united Church will be an episcopally ordained minister, and inasmuch as the actual words in the Scheme dealing with this point have been challenged as indecisive, we hope they may be so modified as to put an end to all doubt. Similarly we suggest that the words referring to possible exceptions after the period of

thirty years, which are left to the judgement of the united Church at that time, should be so modified as to make it clear that the intention is to reach finality in the unification of the ministry of the united Church.

(4) We approve the method by which it is sought to commend the use of Confirmation; we assent to the provision that the acceptance of Confirmation should not be insisted on as a prerequisite term of union; but we most earnestly commend the use of it, both because of its association from the time of the Apostles with the gift of the Holy Spirit, and also because of the benefit which it has bestowed on individual members of our Church and the enrichment which it brings to the pastoral ministry of the Bishop.

Certain matters were specifically referred to us by the General Council or by the Episcopal Synod of the Church of India, Burma, and Ceylon. With regard to these we offer the following advice:

(1) It is pointed out to us that if the united Church comes into being on the basis of the Proposed Scheme, which includes the provision 'that none of the existing Churches should cease to enjoy such privileges of fellowship with other Churches as they enjoyed before the Union', an anomalous situation will arise; the Anglican Communion will, at least to the extent already described, be in communion with the united Church, which will itself be in communion with bodies not in communion with the Anglican Communion. There is no doubt that this is anomalous. But we hold that as part of a movement towards general and complete union, to which the Proposed Scheme looks forward, such a situation may be covered by the principle of 'economy'.[1] Accordingly we are agreed that the situation described by the General Council constitutes no bar to the Church of India taking such action as it may think right.

(2) On the question of Consecration *per saltum*,[2] our view is that while undesirable in the normal course of the Church's life, such Consecration is not invalid and in the special circumstances of the inauguration of the united Church is justifiable.

(3) With reference to the question whether Confirmation is

[1] 'Economy' is a technical term representing administrative action to meet a temporary situation without prejudice to any principle of ecclesiastical order.

[2] i.e. Consecration to the Episcopate without previous ordination by a Bishop to the diaconate and priesthood.

a necessary prerequisite of Ordination, we wish to say that the prevailing custom of the Anglican Communion is to require Confirmation before Ordination, and we desire to commend this custom. But, inasmuch as there has been great variety of practice in the Church with regard to Confirmation, and it has not always been regarded as an indispensable preliminary to Ordination as Priest or Consecration as Bishop,[1] we do not see sufficient ground for urging the Episcopal Synod to insist upon it as a necessary part of the initial agreement.

(4) With reference to the participation of Presbyters in the Laying-on of Hands at the Consecration of Bishops our advice is as follows:

(*a*) We regard as legitimate the proposal that, in the inaugural service of Consecration, Presbyters should take part in the Laying-on of Hands, as we think that this would symbolize the full concurrence of the uniting Churches, the passing on to the Episcopate of the authority which Presbyters have hitherto exercised in their own communions to confer Ordination, and the coming together in the ministry of the united Church of the spiritual blessings previously enjoyed by the ministries of the several Churches in separation.

(*b*) With regard to subsequent Consecrations, we hold that the participation by Presbyters in the Laying-on of Hands could not, in any way, affect the validity of the Consecration, provided, of course, that three Bishops take part in the Laying-on of Hands; but we prefer that it be not adopted lest it should tend to confusion, and we would urge that, if it be adopted, care should be taken to make it plain that the Presbyters do not take part as Consecrators.[2]

(5) With regard to the question whether it is in order for Bishops to grant authorizations to non-episcopally ordained ministers, we suggest that the difficulty might be avoided if the existing ministers of the uniting Churches who will continue to minister in the united Church 'provided that they assent to the Basis of Union and accept the Constitution of the united Church' are not required to receive any fresh authorization or licence for

[1] Cf. S. Thomas Aquinas, *Summa Theologica*, Pt. III, *Supp*. Q. xxxv. A. 4.

[2] This would, as we understand, conform to the practice and principle of the Church of Sweden, which has missions in the area of the proposed union in South India.

that purpose, and if non-episcopally ordained ministers who are received during the period of thirty years are at the request of the Church or Society entitled to send them received without episcopal authorization or licence, the ministers in both cases agreeing to work under the 'pastoral oversight' of the Bishop; but the Committee is unwilling to condemn the action of the Church of India, Burma, and Ceylon if with its consent Bishops of South India give such authorization or licence to non-episcopally ordained ministers after the inauguration of a union agreed to by the Church, and in consequence of the exceptional circumstances created by the Union.

Having thus offered the counsel asked of us, we thank God for the signs of the guidance of His Holy Spirit as manifested by the degree and nature of the agreement already reached with regard to the Proposed Scheme of Union; we pray that the Bishops and other members of the General Council of the Church of India, Burma, and Ceylon may still receive that guidance in the decisions which they will be responsible for making in this regard, and that in the result the united Church of South India may by God's blessing be brought into existence to His glory and the extension of His Kingdom.

148. A Résumé of the Discussions between the Patriarch of Alexandria, with other Orthodox Representatives, and Bishops of the Anglican Communion at Lambeth Palace

JULY 15–18, 1930

Extract from the Report of the Committee on 'The Unity of the Church'

1. It was agreed that a Joint Commission of Orthodox and Anglicans should be appointed for the consideration of questions of Doctrine.

2. It was agreed by the Anglican Bishops that the 'Terms of Intercommunion suggested between the Church of England and the Churches in Communion with her and the Eastern Orthodox Church', published under the auspices of the Archbishop of Canterbury's Eastern Churches Committee in 1921, though not officially communicated to the different Provinces of the Anglican

Communion, are not inconsistent with the mind and doctrine of the Anglican Church.

3. It was agreed by the Orthodox Delegation that the suggested 'Terms of Intercommunion', though they had not yet been officially considered, would form a useful basis of discussion with certain modifications.

4. It was stated by the Anglican Bishops that in questions of faith the authentic decision would be given in the Anglican Communion by the whole body of Bishops without, however, excluding the co-operation of clergy and laity during the discussions.

5. It was stated by the Orthodox Delegation that the final authority in matters of Doctrine in the Orthodox Church lies with the whole body of Bishops in Synod, without excluding the expression of opinion by clergymen and laymen.

6. It was stated by the Anglican Bishops that in the Anglican Communion the Bishop has jurisdiction in questions of discipline through his own court in the first instance, with due provision for appeal to the Provincial Court or a similar body.

7. It was stated by the Orthodox Delegation that in the Orthodox Church spiritual causes are tried in spiritual courts, sentence being given in the case of a Bishop by a court of Bishops, in the case of other clergymen by the Bishop through his own court.

8. It was stated by the Anglican Bishops that in the Anglican Communion Ordination is not merely the appointment of a man into a particular post, but that in Ordination a special *charisma* is given to the person ordained, proper to the Order, and that the nature of the special gift is indicated in the words of Ordination, and that in this sense Ordination is a *mysterion*.

9. It was stated by the Anglican Bishops that the Preface to the Ordinal declares 'that from the Apostles' time there have been these Orders of ministers in Christ's Church: Bishops, Priests and Deacons', and that to preserve unbroken succession the rules regarding Ordination have been framed 'to the intent that these Orders may be continued, and reverently used and esteemed, in the Church of England'.

10. The Orthodox Delegation stated that they were satisfied with regard to the maintenance of the Apostolic Succession in the Anglican Church in so far as the Anglican Bishops have already accepted Ordination as a *mysterion*, and have declared that the Doctrine of the Anglican Church is authoritatively expressed in the Book of Common Prayer, and that the meaning of the XXXIX Articles

must be interpreted in accordance with the Book of Common Prayer.

11. It was stated by the Anglican Bishops that in the Sacrament of the Eucharist 'the Body and Blood of Christ are verily and indeed taken and received by the faithful in the Lord's Supper', and that 'the Body of Christ is given, taken, and eaten in the Supper only after an heavenly and spiritual manner', and that after Communion the consecrated elements remaining are regarded sacramentally as the Body and Blood of Christ; further, that the Anglican Church teaches the doctrine of Eucharistic sacrifice as explained in the Answer of the Archbishops of Canterbury and York to Pope Leo XIII on Anglican Ordinations; and also that in the offering of the Eucharistic Sacrifice the Anglican Church prays that 'by the merits and death of Thy Son Jesus Christ, and through faith in His blood, we and all Thy whole Church may obtain remission of our sins, and all other benefits of His passion', as including the whole company of faithful people, living and departed.

12. It was stated by the Orthodox Delegation that the explanation of Anglican Doctrine thus made with regard to the Eucharistic Sacrifice was agreeable to the Orthodox Doctrine, if an explanation were to be set out with all clearness.

13. It was stated by the Anglican Bishops that in different parts of the Anglican Communion, Anglican Clergy, at the request of Orthodox Clergy, provide sacramental ministrations to Orthodox laity, who are out of reach of their own Church's ministrations; that such clergy always desire to keep the Orthodox to whom they minister faithful to the Orthodox Church and are ready to teach them the Orthodox faith and to notify Orthodox Bishops or priests of persons thus receiving their ministration or instruction.

14. It was stated by the Orthodox Delegation that the whole question of arrangements in such circumstances is to come up for discussion at the forthcoming Synod of the whole Orthodox Church.

15. It was stated by the Orthodox Delegation that it is the practice of the whole Orthodox Church not to re-baptize after Anglican Baptism.

16. It was stated by the Orthodox Delegation that in its forthcoming Pro-Synod the Orthodox Church would probably not object to recognizing the Baptism of children and their instruction from Orthodox books by Anglican clergy, or to marriage, or any other rites being performed by Anglican clergy (in case of need and where no Orthodox priest is available), provided that all persons

baptized or married are properly registered as Orthodox, and their names notified as soon as possible to the competent Orthodox authority.

17. It was stated by the Orthodox Delegation with regard to the Holy Eucharist that, pending a formal decision by the whole Orthodox Church and therefore without giving the practice official sanction, for which it has no authority, it is of opinion that the practice of the Orthodox receiving Holy Communion from Anglican priests in case of need and where no Orthodox priest was available, might continue, provided that an Orthodox authority did not prohibit such a practice.

✠ ARCHBISHOP OF THYATEIRA, G. A. C. GLOUCESTR:

II. THE ROMAN CATHOLIC CHURCH

THE MALINES CONVERSATIONS 1921–5

149. 'The Church of England United not Absorbed' Memorandum by a Canonist read by Cardinal Mercier

[This Memorandum was read aloud by Cardinal Mercier on May 19, 1925, at the fourth and last Conversation, as the work of an anonymous canonist. Its title was *L'Église Anglicane unie non absorbée*. It is printed in *The Conversations at Malines, 1921–1925, Original Documents*, ed. by Lord Halifax (Philip Allan, 1930). The canonist was Dom Lambert Beauduin. It aroused deep interest at the time of reading, but was not discussed in detail. The Report of the Committee of the Lambeth Conference, 1930, on 'The Unity of the Church' contains this reference to it: 'They regret also that in the Encyclical (*Mortalium Animos—vide supra*, Document 113) the method of "complete absorption" has been proposed to the exclusion of that suggested in the Conversations, as, for example, in the paper read at Malines, *L'Église Anglicane unie non absorbée*. There are difficulties greater than perhaps were realized in the scheme proposed, but it has the great merit of attempting to recognize to some extent at any rate the autonomy which might be possible in a united Church.' (*The Lambeth Conference, 1930*, p. 131.)]

INTRODUCTION

1. If we only consider divine right, all Bishops are equal among themselves. One alone, the successor of St. Peter, Bishop of Rome, is constituted the supreme head of the episcopal body and of the whole Catholic Church. His episcopal jurisdiction is extended to all individual Churches without exception—he is *Episcopus catholicus*.

2. But human law, whether by ancient custom or by actual precept, has set up a hierarchy of jurisdiction among bishops, which implies relationships of superiority and subordination between patriarchs, primates, archbishops, and suffragans. To be legitimate and in accordance with divine right, these different powers must be established explicitly, or admitted implicitly, or recognized *post factum* by the supreme power mentioned above.

3. These two principles have been exactly applied in the development and history of the Anglican Church during the first ten centuries of its existence (594–1537). On the one hand the Church had an autonomous organization through the dependence of the bishops on the very real and extensive power of the Patriarch of Canterbury. On the other hand there was the most explicit recognition both in theory and practice of the jurisdiction of the Roman

Pontiffs, and the clear subordination of the patriarchal power of Canterbury to the See of Peter, which made the Church of England the most thoroughly Roman of all the Churches of East and West.

4. In other words, the Anglican Church stands throughout its history not as an assembly of scattered dioceses attached to Rome and without any real hierarchic unity, but as a strongly organized body, as a compact whole united under the authority of the successors of St. Augustine, an organization in accordance with the aspiration of a self-governing and island race, where splendid isolation was an ideal.

On the other hand there is no Church so Roman in its origin, in its traditions, spirit, and history; there is no Church so strongly bound to the Apostolic See, to that Church, Mother and Mistress of all the others, so much so that after four centuries of separation a writer has been able to say 'England is a Catholic Cathedral occupied by Protestants'.

5. A large measure of self-government and fidelity to the Roman See, such are the two marks of its history, and such are perhaps the lines of reconciliation. This statement takes into account these two aspects.

I. First Section: Historical evidence of these two characteristics; the approach from History.

II. Second Section: The possibility of a Catholic basis in modern times for the Anglican Church on these historic lines: the approach from Canon Law.

III. Conclusion.

I. *Historical Approach*

1. From the beginning, St. Augustine of Canterbury was made head of the Church of England by St. Gregory the Great and invested by him with the pallium, the insignia of patriarchal powers—'We concede to you the use of the pallium to be used only in solemnities' (Letter to Augustine quoted in Bede's *Ecclesiastical History, P.L.*, vol. xcv, col. 69). This conferred effective jurisdiction over all the bishops both present and future of the English Kingdom—'We commit the care of all bishops of the Britons to your Fraternity, that the ignorant may be instructed, the weak strengthened by persuasion, and the perverse corrected by authority' (Letter to Augustine, *P.L.*, vol. lxxvii, col. 1192).

2. There is no doubt possible as to the reality of this Patriarchal

jurisdiction. In fact, St. Augustine wished to obtain more precise instructions and asked if his power covered at the same time the bishops of Gaul whom he doubtless visited on his journeys to Rome. St. Gregory writes to him: 'We grant you no authority over the bishops of Gaul because from the days of our predecessors the Bishop of Arles received the pallium and we must not deprive him of the authority he has received. . . . You cannot of your own authority judge the bishops of Gaul, save by persuading, encouraging, and showing them your good works as an example . . . but we commit the charge of all the British bishops to your Fraternity, &c. . . .' There is no question then of a mere precedence of honour or of a fraternal influence; the Bishop of Arles in Gaul and the Bishop of Canterbury in Great Britain enjoy Patriarchal powers over all the Churches of their respective countries.

3. This Patriarchal jurisdiction is conferred by a symbol that is at once venerable and significant, the imposition of the pallium; and in order to understand the documents used in this study it is necessary to realize fully the exact meaning of this rite of investiture to which was formerly attached so much importance. The pallium is a garment, a broad scarf of wool, that covered the neck and shoulders. The pallium of the popes soon took on a higher meaning; it symbolized the power of the Good Shepherd Who takes the lost sheep on His shoulders and holds it clasped round His neck. Then in order to pass on to a bishop a share in the power of the chief Pastor, what was more natural than to clothe him with the symbolic robe of the Successor of Peter, the pallium, that is, pontifical investiture? This symbol was already ancient in the time of St. Gregory the Great, as is shown by the letter to St. Augustine already quoted (*ab antiquis temporibus*), and was held in great veneration in the Middle Ages. It was made out of lambs' wool solemnly offered at the altar, and was blessed by the pope in the Vatican Basilica on the Feast of St. Peter, being afterwards placed over the Confession of the Prince of the Apostles until it was given. It is asked for, delivered, and imposed in three successive ceremonies; it is the sign of the investiture of a power beyond that of a bishop which can only have as its origin the tomb in possession of the successor of Peter, *in quo est plenitudo pontificalis officii cum archiepiscopalis nominis appellatione*.

Thus in imposing the pallium upon St. Augustine, St. Gregory said to him: 'Your Fraternity shall have subject to yourself by the authority of Our Lord Jesus Christ, not only the bishops ordained by you, nor only those ordained by the Bishop of York, but all the bishops of Britain.' (Bede's *Eccl. Hist.*, Lib. l, c. 29, *P.L.*, vol. xcv, col. 69.)

4. In the Records of the Archbishop of Canterbury we find frequent mention of the patriarchal power of Canterbury: 'Elfsin . . . going to Rome for the pallium . . . died.' (959.) Quoted from Mabillon, *Annales*, lib. 46, Lucca (1739), vol. iii, p. 518.

The account of the Life of his successor Dunstan begins thus: 'Dunstan, setting out for Rome for sake of the pallium . . .'. From Augustine to Cranmer all the archbishops of Canterbury received their pallium from the Sovereign Pontiffs; most of them even, according to the ancient rule, made the journey to Rome in person to receive it at the hands of the pope himself. Before receiving investiture the archbishop had no patriarchal rights; the pallium imposed by the pope is as it were the consecration of his supra-episcopal jurisdiction. Thus an archbishop who had received the pallium from an anti-pope was not received in England as Patriarch. (Edwin Burton, *Catholic Encyclopaedia*, vol. iii, p. 301.)

5. This patriarchal power of Canterbury conferred by St. Gregory on St. Augustine became later the unifying principle of the Anglican Church. In 668 Pope Vitalian nominated to this See Theodore, an Eastern monk of Tarsus in Cilicia, who had passed many years in Rome, and who was famed for his sacred and humanistic learning. According to his famous contemporary the Venerable Bede (675–735) (cf. *Hist. Eccl. Anglorum*, Lib. iv, *P.L.*, vol. xcv, col. 171) he was for more than a quarter of a century (668–90) one of the greatest archbishops of Canterbury and firmly established the patriarchal power. He set up new dioceses, nominated or dismissed bishops, held visitations of the dioceses, and summoned to his patriarchal council the different ecclesiastical provinces. In short, he organized the very real and very extensive jurisdiction of the Patriarch on the model of the Eastern Churches and with the constant support of Rome.

6. Two centuries later Pope Formosus III (896) in a famous letter addressed to the Bishops of England solemnly confirms these patriarchal powers and threatens with ecclesiastical penalties the bishops who might try to claim exemption from this perfectly legitimate jurisdiction. (Allusion to the Archbishop of York who would have liked to withdraw his metropolitan see from this jurisdiction.) Seeing the importance of this document it is necessary to quote the principal passage:

'Who amongst you should hold the first place, and which episcopal see has power before all others and holds the primacy, is well known from ancient times. For as we learn from the writings of Blessed Gregory and his successors the metropolitan and first episcopal see of the kingdom of the English is in the city of Canterbury, over which our venerable brother Plegmund (890–914) now presides. On no account do we permit the honour of his high office to be diminished, but we ordain him to carry out all things as with Apostolic Authority. As Blessed Pope Gregory ordained first to your nation that all the bishops of the English should be subject to Augustine, so we to the forenamed brother the Archbishop of Canterbury and his lawful successors confirm the same dignity. We ordain and decree, by the authority of God and of Blessed Peter Prince of the Apostles, that all should obey his canonical decisions, and that no one should violate whatever has been granted to him and to his successors by Apostolic Authority.' (*Bullarium*, Editio Taurinensis, 1857, vol. i, p. 369.)

7. In the following century, at the Council of Brandanford in 964, all the bishops approve the decree of King Edward putting an end to the persecution of his predecessor, and recalling St. Dunstan to the see of Canterbury:

'That the Church of Christ in Canterbury shall be the mother and mistress of the other Churches of our kingdom . . . .' (Mansi, vol. xviii A, col. 476.)

8. All the life of St. Anselm (d. 1109) bears witness to this same truth. The whole English episcopate is present at his consecration in 1093 and proclaims him Primate of All Britain, *totius Britanniae primatem*. It will be seen that this is not merely a title of honour (cf. Mansi, vol. xx, col. 792).

At the Council of Rockingham in March 1094 (ibid., col. 791), in the speech where St. Anselm explains to the assembly of all the bishops his conflict with the king, he says:

'For when recently I had asked him for permission to visit Urban, the ruler of the Apostolic See, to receive the pallium according to the custom of my predecessors . . . .'

At the Council of Bari (1098) Urban II made Anselm sit beside him and his archdeacon saying, 'Let us put him in our immediate sphere, for he is as it were Pope of the other sphere.' (*Includamus hunc in orbe nostro quasi alterius orbis papam.* Mansi, xx, col. 948.)

A still more significant fact and one which shows the efficacy and extent of this primatial jurisdiction: Gerard, bishop of Hereford, was promoted in 1107 to the metropolitan see of York, the first see in Britain after Canterbury and which sought to be free of its dependence. Anselm wished to obtain from the newly-elect another explicit profession of obedience and submission, not being satisfied with that made by Gerard on entering into possession of the see of Hereford. Hence a conflict in which the king found a satisfactory solution: without making a fresh profession the elect would renew explicitly that made for Hereford:

> 'Anselm agreed, and Gerard, with his hand placed in that of Anselm and his bond placed between, promised that he would show the same subjection and obedience to Anselm and his successors as he had promised when he was to be consecrated Bishop of Hereford.' (Mansi, vol. xx, col. 1229.)

9. Nothing indeed was lacking for the reality of this patriarchal jurisdiction. Numerous ecclesiastical benefices were withdrawn from the dependence of the local bishop and made to depend directly on the see of Canterbury. It is what we would call exemption, but to the advantage of the Patriarch. In the time of St. Anselm there were about 80 benefices exempted in this sense. Many monasteries followed the same law.

10. Under the pontificate of Alexander III (1159–81) the patriarchal rights of the see of Canterbury were strongly attacked by the bishops of York and London, and the king, anxious to humble the Patriarch in order to have a stronger hold on the Church, upheld these claims; just as later on in Russia Peter the Great substituted the Holy Synod for the Patriarch of Moscow. Archbishop Thomas, who was soon to die a victim of his zeal, vindicated the rights of his Church and excommunicated the insubordinate bishops and the king himself. Alexander III confirmed by several bulls all the rights and privileges of the see of Canterbury:

> 'As it is established that your predecessors from the time of St. Augustine have held by the authority of the Apostolic See.' (Mansi, vol. xxi, cols. 871–2.)

These few historical facts that have just been mentioned and that could be multiplied, are surely proof of the two principles mentioned at the outset. A Church strongly unified and organized under the very real patriarchal authority of the Archbishop of Canterbury, the Anglican Church is a Catholic and historic reality constituting one homogeneous whole. She cannot be absorbed and fusioned without losing the proper character of all her history. On the other hand this Church was strongly united from the beginning to the see of Peter. Invested with the symbolic mantle of the prince of the Apostles, the Archbishop of Canterbury shares in the apostolic jurisdiction not only over the faithful but also over the bishops. As once Elisha took on the mantle of his master and found thereby the influence of his spirit, so St. Augustine and all his successors without exception sought at Rome, by the imposition of the pallium, the investiture of their patriarchal jurisdiction. This historical position is so evident that it must in truth be said that an Anglican Church separated from Rome is above all things an historical heresy.

In brief, an Anglican Church ABSORBED by Rome and an Anglican Church SEPARATED from Rome are two conceptions that are equally inadmissible. The true formula must be sought somewhere between, which is the only position based on history, namely, in an Anglican Church UNITED to Rome.

II. *Project of a Catholic Status according to these Data*

According to Western Canon Law of the present day, the title of Patriarch or Primate is purely one of honour and does not imply of itself any special jurisdiction (Can. 271). This was not always the case. Historically, until the twelfth century, and longer still for certain sees, the function of Patriarch or Primate implied effective and very extensive jurisdiction both over different ecclesiastical provinces and dioceses. Had this jurisdiction a share in the power of the Primate of the whole Church of Christ, borne the same name, and more especially had it the same extent in the Latin as in the Byzantine Church? The greater proximity of Rome and the title of Patriarch of the West that the Sovereign Pontiff still uses officially to-day, diminished the utility and importance of the hierarchic rank and gradually brought about its decline. But it is incontestable that, under the different name of Primate, the reality existed in the west as in the east, and more especially, as has been shown, in the Church of England.

Let us first examine from this point of view the present status of the Eastern Churches united to Rome. Then we shall see what application can be made to the Church of England.

i. *The Internal Organization of the United Eastern Churches*

Patriarchal organization is still the practice, as is known, of the Eastern Churches. It can even be said that it is more effective in the Churches united to Rome than in the Separated Churches where the interference of the Civil Power and of the laity often make it illusory.

To take a concrete example, let us examine the patriarchal organization of the Catholic Melkite Church. The jurisdiction of the Patriarch, Mgr. Cadi, includes all the Melkite faithful who were living in the Ottoman Empire in 1894, the date of this concession by Leo XIII.

The Melkite Patriarch of Antioch, who at the same time administers the two patriarchates of Jerusalem and Alexandria, counts in his patriarchate five metropolitan sees and seven bishoprics, in all twelve dioceses, and together about 170,000 faithful.

1. As soon as the synod of bishops has elected the new patriarch, he sends to the Pope a detailed profession of faith and asks him for the patriarchal pallium as a sign of his apostolic investiture. Before he has received this investiture the elect has no patriarchal power.

2. The choice of bishops is made in the following manner. The Patriarch proposes three candidates among whom the secular priests must make their choice. The newly-elect is then confirmed and consecrated by the Patriarch, without any intervention from Rome which is not even informed of the election and consecration. Thus no Eastern bishop is proclaimed in the Consistory. As for the titular bishops, their choice and consecration depend on the Patriarch alone, without Rome interfering or being informed.

3. At certain times the Patriarch convokes the Archbishops and Bishops to the Patriarchal Synod, over which he presides. The decrees and decisions are afterwards submitted for the approval of the Holy See.

4. The Patriarch has a right of inspection and visitation in the different dioceses. For more important measures, as would be the dismissal of a bishop, the approval of the Synod is required.

5. The exemption of certain great monasteries from episcopal jurisdiction means that they are submitted to the Patriarch. They are called stavropegiac and depend directly on the Patriarch. Among the Orthodox Melkites, of 17 monasteries five are stavropegiac.

6. The Patriarchal Churches have their own laws and customs, regulated by the Synods, their own liturgies and their own enterprises; in short, they constitute, under the authority of the Patriarch, autonomous institutions with their own organization; but they are in communion with and depend on Rome.

7. Far from being prejudicial to this autonomous internal or-

ganization, Rome has assured to the Eastern Churches the conservation of this wide autonomy. The first article of the Codex of Canon Law declares that Western legislation does not affect them and that the Catholic East preserves its own Laws and institutions. The same is true of the Liturgy and for the whole ecclesiastical organization. Leo XIII has admirably stated in his encyclical *Praeclara* of June 20, 1894, and in the Constitution *Orientalium Dignitas* of November 30, 1894, the basic line of conduct of the Roman Church: 'The real unity among Christians is that which the Founder of the Church, Jesus Christ, has instituted and willed; it consists in the unity of faith and government. Neither We nor Our successors will ever suppress anything of your Law, nor the privileges of your Patriarchs, nor the ritual customs of each Church. It has always been and will be part of the mind and policy of the Holy See to show itself generous in concessions that affect the traditions and customs of each Church.'

ii. *Application to England*

1. There is then a Catholic formula for the Reunion of the Churches, which is not an absorption but which safeguards and respects the internal autonomous organization of the great historic Churches, while maintaining their perfect dependence towards the Roman Church, the centre of unity for the Universal Church.

2. If any Church by reason of its origins, its history, and the habits of its people, has a right to these concessions of autonomy, it is the Anglican Church. We have shown it in our historical inquiry. The principle affirmed by Leo XIII and applied by him to the Eastern Churches can equally well be applied to the Anglican Church: 'It has always been and will be part of the mind and policy of the Holy See to show itself generous in concessions that affect the traditions and customs of each Church.'

3. In practice, the Archbishop of Canterbury would be re-established in his traditional and effective rights as Patriarch of the Anglican Church. After receiving his investiture from the successor of St. Peter by the traditional imposition of the pallium, he would enjoy patriarchal rights over the whole Church of England. These would include the nomination and consecration of bishops, the convocation and presidency of inter-provincial councils, the inspection of dioceses, and jurisdiction over the chief religious institutes that would be exempt from episcopal jurisdiction. The internal organization of the Anglican Church would be modelled on that sanctioned and maintained by Rome for the united Eastern Churches.

4. The Codex of Canon Law for the Latin Church would not be imposed on the Anglican Church. In an inter-provincial Synod she would establish her own ecclesiastical laws, and these would be submitted for the approval of the Holy See and sanctioned for the Anglican Church. It is well known that the Eastern laws are quite different from the Latin laws, except on matters of the natural or divine law. If by chance it was deemed opportune for the Anglican Church, there should be no hesitation in not imposing celibacy of clergy any more than in the East.

5. The Anglican Church would have its own Liturgy, the Roman Liturgy of the seventh and eighth centuries, as she practised it at that period and as it is found in the Gelasian Sacramentaries. Already at the present time there is a great desire in the Anglican Church to return to the classic beauty of this Roman Liturgy, which has unfortunately been lost by Rome and which the Anglican Church would restore to honour. As the worship of Our Lady and of the Saints is less exuberant in this classic Liturgy than in the present Roman Liturgy, there would thus be a useful means of effecting a transition.

6. Evidently all the historic sees of the Anglican Church would be maintained and the new Catholic sees created after 1851, such as Westminster, Southwark, Portsmouth, &c., would be suppressed. Doubtless that would be a serious measure but it should be remembered that at the time of the Concordat with France, Pius VII suppressed the existing dioceses and demanded the resignation of all those in possession, more than a hundred.

7. An important question as to precedence would be raised: are the Patriarchs to have precedence over Cardinals? A serious question that might compromise and spoil all negotiations unless it is decided according to historical data, as outlined below.

(*a*) Several Oecumenical Councils have solemnly decreed (IVth Constantinople in 869, Can. 21, and IVth Lateran in 1215, Can. 5) that the four effective Patriarchs of Constantinople, Alexandria, Antioch, and Jerusalem had a right to the first four places, in the order indicated, immediately after the Sovereign Pontiff of Rome. If then Canterbury has the fulness of its patriarchal function restored, it would rank in this category and occupy the fifth place among the Patriarchs, immediately after the Pope and before the Cardinals. It should be clear that there is only question here of the great Patriarchs, who had a residence in Rome, and each of whom was attached by name to a Basilica. Thus the Lateran was the residence of the Catholic Patriarch, the supreme and universal Pontiff; St. Peter's was the residence of the Patriarch of Constantinople, St. Paul's of the Patriarch of Alexandria, St. Mary Major's of the Patriarch of Antioch, and St. Lawrence's outside the Walls of the Patriarch of Jerusalem. All these usages from before the Schism should be resumed, and the Archbishop of Canterbury should be assimilated to these four Patriarchs. There can be no doubt that before the Schism the Patriarchs were before the Cardinals.

(*b*) However, in view of the ideas dominant since the eleventh century, it would be difficult to apply these ancient uses. Advantage might then be taken of a rule that has been followed at certain times for princely persons, who ranked after the Dean of the Sacred College. The precedence of the members of the Sacred College was admitted in the person of its Dean.

(*c*) Finally, another system that has prevailed at certain times is for the Patriarchs to rank after the Cardinal Bishops and before the Cardinal Priests and Deacons.

(*d*) A good solution would be to establish an order of Cardinal Patriarchs, as in the eighth century was established the order of Cardinal Bishops, several centuries after the Cardinal Priests and Deacons. This solution has the disadvantage of being new, and in a domain where the Church is very traditional; but in spite of being new the solution respects the lines of tradition.

In any case, it must not be forgotten that these questions of precedence, because of the principles that they symbolize, are most important and must be considered according to traditional principles.

Practical Conclusions

1. Union, not absorption, such would seem to be the formula of reconciliation. On the one hand the Anglican Church, a religious society with its own internal organization and a moral entity enjoying autonomy, its own institutions, laws, and Liturgy, under the authority of its head, the Archbishop of Canterbury, but without the principle of unity and the infallible ground of truth that Christ desires in the Church He founded: *unum ovile et unus Pastor*. On the other hand the Roman Church with her own institutions, laws, and Liturgy, in a word, with her internal Latin organization, but who also especially possesses in her head the principle of unity, the

ground of truth and apostolicity, the unshakable rock on which the whole Church of Christ is founded. It would be necessary, then, if the Anglican Church wished to belong to the unique and visible society of Christ, for her to establish between herself and the Roman Church a link of dependence and submission to the successor of Peter, in other words she must become not Latin but Roman; while preserving all her internal organization, all her historical traditions and her legitimate autonomy, on the model of the Eastern Churches, she would strongly establish this essential link of subordination to the universal Church whose centre of unity is in Rome.

2. If the general principles indicated in this memorandum could serve as a basis for a movement of Reunion of the Churches, it would be necessary to develop this sketch and to establish the historical and canonical positions in a scientific way. In view of the inevitable and probably strong opposition that these unaccustomed ideas would arouse, it would be necessary before their publication to strengthen them with different considerations and developments that would make them theologically and historically unassailable, and it would be necessary to give precisions and details to prevent any uncertainty. Such a work would need the collaboration of several who would be able to produce a complete work.

3. What will Rome think of this plan? It is clear that it suggests a principle of decentralization which is not in accordance with the actual tendencies of the Roman Curia, a principle that could have other applications. Would it not be a good and a great good? Yet would Rome be of this opinion? Nothing can allow us to foresee what would be the answer.

150. Letter from Cardinal Mercier to the Author of 'The Church of England United not Absorbed'

[The following letter was sent to the author of the above Memorandum by Cardinal Mercier before the final Conversation took place. The original French text is given in *Irénikon*, vol. iii, no. 3, June 1927, p. 150.]

ARCHEVÊCHÉ DE MALINES,
15 February, 1925

DEAR AND REVEREND FATHER,

THE truth cannot be believed. In spite of my being so desirous of closely studying your memoir, over which I had cast a rapid glance, it is only on this peaceful morning of Sexagesima, under the protection of the great Apostle, that I have succeeded in according myself leisure for the delight of reading your splendid work at one sitting. How interesting it is, dear friend! For me, as a 'layman', it comes as a revelation and at the same time, as a hope. Up till now, I had never, it is true, put aside the possibility of a reunion of the Anglican Church with the Roman Church, but I did not see, or even glimpse, any concrete formula for realizing it, and I resigned myself to leaving this collective success to the goodness of Providence.

But, now, I see in you an active instrument of this divine Providence.

You know that, at our second Conversation at Malines, our Anglican friends asked us to consider the eventual means of reunion, laying stress on the patriarchate of Canterbury and the Pallium. I confess that they made me smile, because I did not grasp the importance which would be attached to what seemed to me, and is to-day with us, a badge of honour, a sort of pontifical decoration, the Pallium.

Your statement lifts us and shows us a much wider perspective. . . . I have the feeling that this communication would cause an important group of Anglo-Catholics to take a huge step towards 'reunion'. The English, a practical people, attach much more importance to institutions than to ideas. And, truly, one cannot deny that if nationalism in its extreme form is a peril, yet, contained within the bounds of subordination and unity, it is a power. . . . So, dear friend, thanks to you, we emerge from dreams, we enter at last the domain of realities for which one may hope, if not yet of accomplished facts. . . .

✠ D. J. CARD. MERCIER,
Archbishop of Malines.

PRONOUNCEMENTS ON CHRISTIAN CO-OPERATION

EXTRACTS FROM ENCYCLICAL LETTERS AND ALLOCUTIONS OF POPE PIUS XI AND POPE PIUS XII

151. Pius XI. Encyclical ('Divini Redemptoris') on Atheistic Communism

MARCH 10, 1937

BUT in this battle joined by the powers of darkness against the very idea of Divinity, it is Our fond hope that, besides the host which glories in the name of Christ all those—and they comprise the overwhelming majority of mankind—who still believe in God and pay Him homage may take a decisive part.

152. Pius XII. Encyclical on True and False Prosperity, to the Archbishops and Bishops in the U.S.A.

NOVEMBER 1, 1939

It will be a triumph indeed if the American people, with its genius for splendid and unselfish action, should thus lay the foundations of a better world, solving once for all this old and thorny question, and still keeping to the safe paths which the light of the Gospel reveals to us. If this fortunate result is to be achieved, our forces must not be weakened by disunion; we must join them and so add to their effectiveness. It is only by united and concerted action that we can foster great schemes. For that reason We are impelled by charity to invite here the co-operation of those whom Mother Church mourns as separated from her communion. Many of these expressed, personally or by writing, sentiments that were full of respect and of generosity, at the time when Our predecessor had gone to his hallowed rest and We, after a short interval, had been raised by the inscrutable design of Providence to the Throne of Peter. We were fully sensible of that, and We freely confess that it has given Us hopes in their regard which have not since then diminished; Our mind cherishes those hopes as it looks forward into the future, and derives consolation from them amidst all the difficult tasks that confront Us.

153. Pius XII. Christmas Eve Allocution to the Sacred College of Cardinals

DECEMBER 24, 1939

[The Fifth 'Peace Point']

V. But even the best and most detailed regulations will be imperfect and foredoomed to failure unless the peoples and those who govern them submit willingly to the influence of that spirit which alone can give life, authority, and binding force to the dead letter of international agreements. They must develop that sense of deep and keen responsibility which measures and weighs human statutes according to the sacred and inviolable standards of the law of God; they must cultivate that hunger and thirst after justice which is proclaimed as a beatitude in the Sermon on the Mount and which supposes as its natural foundation the moral virtue of justice; they must be guided by that universal love which is the compendium and most general expression of the Christian ideal, and which therefore may serve as a common ground also for those who have not the blessing of sharing the same faith with us.

We are not insensible of the grave difficulties which lie in the way of the achievement of these ends which We have described as needful for establishing and preserving a just peace between nations. But if ever there was an objective deserving the collaboration of all noble and generous minds, if there was ever a spiritual crusade which might assume with a new truth as its motto, 'God wills it', then it is this high purpose, it is this crusade, enlisting all unselfish and great-hearted men in an endeavour to lead the nations back from the broken cisterns of material and selfish interests to the living fountain of divine justice, which alone is able to provide that morality, nobility, and stability of which the need has been so long experienced, to the great detriment of nations and of humanity.

154. Pius XII. Christmas Eve Allocution to the Sacred College of Cardinals

DECEMBER 24, 1941

MAY our blessing be also upon those who, though not belonging to the visible body of the Catholic Church, are near to Us by their faith in God and in Jesus Christ, and are of one mind with Us concerning the peace settlement and its fundamental aims.

155. Pius XII. Allocution on the Anniversary of the War

SEPTEMBER 1, 1944

ACCORDINGLY, to all Our sons and daughters throughout the vast world, and to those who, while not belonging to the Church, feel themselves united with Us in this hour of perhaps irrevocable decision, We address an urgent appeal to weigh the extraordinary gravity of the moment and to consider that, above and beyond all such co-operation with other diverse ideological tendencies and social forces that may perhaps be suggested by purely contingent motives, fidelity to the heritage of Christian civilization and its strenuous defence against atheist and anti-Christian tendencies is the keystone which can never be sacrificed for any transitory advantages or for any shifting combination. This invitation which, We trust, will find a sympathetic welcome from millions of souls throughout the world, looks chiefly to achieve a loyal and effective collaboration in all those fields in which the very idea of Christianity demands the creation of a more exact judicial order. This is especially true of that group of formidable problems which refer to the setting up of an economic and social order more in keeping with the eternal law of God and with the dignity of man. In it Christian thought insists as a substantial element on the regarding of the proletariat. The achievement of this, in a resolute and generous manner, appears to every true follower of Christ not only as a step forward along the path of earthly progress, but also as the fulfilment of a moral obligation.

III. THE EASTERN ORTHODOX CHURCH

156. *Letter from the Patriarch of Alexandria to the Archbishop of Canterbury*

DECEMBER 25, 1930

TO THE MOST REVEREND DR. COSMO LANG, LORD ARCHBISHOP OF CANTERBURY AND PRIMATE OF ALL ENGLAND, GREETINGS IN THE NEW-BORN CHRIST.

THE Feast of the Nativity, according to the Flesh, of the Redeemer of our Souls being a most suitable occasion for us, as it were, to visit your Beatitude, our friend, by means of a letter, we come to you hereby with a heart that is filled alike with joy, that 'unto us is born a Saviour, which is Christ the Lord', and with fervent prayers both for your health and for the peace and stability of the holy Churches of God over which you preside.

At the same time, together with our greetings for the Feast, we send you as our gift the news, which we are sure will be good news, to you, that having derived the greatest gratification from the accounts which it has received both of the marks of honour which were rendered in London, alike by your Grace and by the general body of your Church, to the office which is ours, and also of the happy results which by the favouring breath of the Holy Spirit have emerged from the contact of the Orthodox Delegation with the Lambeth Conference, our Holy Synod of the Metropolitans of the Apostolic and Patriarchal Throne of Alexandria has proceeded to adopt a resolution recognizing the validity, as from the Orthodox point of view, of the Anglican Ministry.

The text of that resolution is as follows: 'The Holy Synod recognizes that the declarations of the Orthodox quoted in the Summary, were made according to the spirit of Orthodox teaching. Inasmuch as the Lambeth Conference approved the declaration of the Anglican Bishops as a genuine account of the teaching and practice of the Church of England and the Churches in communion with it, it welcomes them as a notable step towards the Union of the two Churches. And since in these declarations, which were endorsed by the Lambeth Conference, complete and satisfying assurance is found as to the Apostolic Succession, as to a real reception of the

Lord's Body and Blood, as to the Eucharist being *thusia hilasterios* (Sacrifice), and as to Ordination being a Mystery, the Church of Alexandria withdraws its precautionary negative to the acceptance of the validity of Anglican Ordinations, and, adhering to the decision of the Ecumenical Patriarchate, of July 28th, 1922, pronounces that if priests, ordained by Anglican Bishops, accede to Orthodoxy, they should not be re-ordained, as persons baptized by Anglicans are not rebaptized.'

We rejoice to see the middle wall of partition being thrown down more and more, and we congratulate your Beatitude that under God you have had the felicity of taking the initiative in furthering that work. May the Lord who was born in Bethlehem give to you and to us the happiness of its completion.

In Alexandria upon the Feast of Christ's Nativity, 1930

Your Beatitude's Beloved Brother in Christ

MELETIOS OF ALEXANDRIA

157. *Joint Doctrinal Commission between the Anglican and the Eastern Orthodox Churches. Points of Agreement and Difference*

OCTOBER 1931

[The Commission was appointed under Resolutions 33(*b*) and 33(*c*) of the Lambeth Conference, 1930 (*vide supra*, Document 145). It consisted of nine Anglican and nine Orthodox representatives.

The Orthodox representatives were:
The Metropolitan of Thyateira (Constantinople and Jerusalem)
The Great Archimandrite Michael Constantinides (Alexandria)
The Metropolitan of Tyre and Sidon (Antioch)
The Bishop of Novi-Sad (Yugoslavia)
The Metropolitan of Bukovina (Rumania)
The Metropolitan of Paphos (Cyprus)
The Metropolitan of Trikkes and Stagon (Greece)
Professor Nicholas S. Arseniev (Poland)

The Anglican representatives were:
The Bishop of Gloucester (*Chairman*) [A. C. Headlam]
The Archbishop of Dublin [J. A. F. Gregg]
The Bishop of Northern Indiana [Campbell Gray]
The Bishop of Gibraltar [F. C. N. Hicks]
The Bishop of Fulham [B. S. Batty]
Dr. H. L. Goudge
Dr. L. W. Grensted
Dr. J. A. Douglas
The Rev. Philip Usher (*Secretary*)

The Commission was required to examine the teaching of the two Churches, to register the points on which agreement was found between them, to note any differences which appeared to be of importance, and to report these matters to the respective Churches. The representatives met in London from October 15 to 20, 1931, and discussed six topics, reporting the results as follows. See *Report of the Joint Doctrinal Commission Appointed by the Oecumenical Patriarch and the Archbishop of Canterbury for Consultation on the Points of Agreement and Difference between the Anglican and the Eastern Orthodox Churches*, London, S.P.C.K., 1932.]

1. *The Christian Revelation*

WE accept the Divine Revelation which was delivered once and for all in Our Lord Jesus Christ; and we receive it as it is revealed in the Holy Scriptures, and as it has been made known and handed down from the Apostles in the Tradition of the Church throughout the ages by the operation of the Holy Spirit.

2. *Scripture and Tradition*

We agree that we receive the Divine Revelation in Our Lord Jesus Christ through Scripture and Tradition. By *Scripture* we mean the Canon of Scripture as it is defined by St. Athanasius and as it has been received by the whole Catholic Church. As regards the other books which are sometimes called Deuterocanonical, sometimes *ἀναγινωσκόμενα*, we also accept the teaching of St. Athanasius: 'For greater exactness I add this also . . . that there are other books besides these not included in the Canon but appointed by the Fathers to be read by those who newly join us and wish to be instructed in the word of Godliness. . . . The former books . . . being included in the Canon, the latter being only read.' And the teaching of St. Jerome: 'That the Church may read them for the edification of the people, not for the confirmation of the authority of ecclesiastical dogmas.'

Further, the representatives of the Anglican Church would say: 'Holy Scripture containeth all things necessary to salvation: so that whatsoever is not read therein, nor may be proved thereby, is not to be required of any that it should be believed as an Article of the Faith or be thought requisite or necessary to salvation.' As St. Athanasius says: 'The sacred and inspired Scriptures are sufficient to declare the truth.' And elsewhere: 'These are the fountains of salvation that he who thirsts may be satisfied with the oracles contained in them. In these books alone is proclaimed the doctrine of Godliness. Let not man add to them nor take aught from them.' And as St. Augustine says: 'In those things which are plainly laid down in Scripture all things are found which cover Faith and Morals —namely, Hope and Love.'

The representatives of the Eastern Orthodox Church would say: 'We believe that the Holy Scripture is completed, explained, and interpreted by the Holy Tradition.' As St. Basil says:

> 'Of the dogmas and preachings which are kept in the Church, some are derived from the written doctrine, others we have received by way of Apostolic Tradition as they were secretly transmitted to us, and these two classes are of equal value to piety. No one will dispute this, at all events no one who has had the least experience of ecclesiastical institutions. For if we were to attempt to reject the unwritten customs on the ground that they are therefore of no great importance we should unwittingly inflict a deadly wound on the Gospel, or rather we should make the matter of our preaching a name and nothing more. For example (to mention first the earliest and most common), who taught us in writing to sign with the sign of the Cross those who hope on the name of Our Lord Jesus Christ? What saint was it that bequeathed to us in writing the words of invocation at the showing of the Eucharistic bread and the cup of blessing? For we are not satisfied with what the Apostle or the Evangelist recorded, but we add a preface and an epilogue which we have received from unwritten tradition, and which we consider to be of great import in celebrating the mystery.'

Having made the above statements we agreed upon the following:

Everything necessary for salvation can be founded upon Holy Scripture as completed, explained, interpreted, and understood in the Holy Tradition, by the guidance of the Holy Spirit residing in the Church.

We agree that by Holy Tradition we mean the truths which came down from Our Lord and the Apostles through the Fathers, which are confessed unanimously and continuously in the Undivided Church, and are taught by the Church under the guidance of the Holy Spirit.

We agree that nothing contained in Tradition is contrary to the Scriptures. Though these two may be logically defined and distinguished, yet they cannot be separated from each other nor from the Church.

3. *The Creed of the Church*

We agree in accepting as the Creed of the Catholic Church that which is sometimes called the Nicene, sometimes the Nicaeno-

Constantinopolitan, which was put forth by the Council of Chalcedon and has been accepted by the whole Catholic Church. We accept the following statement of the Council of Chalcedon concerning the Creed: 'These things having been defined by us with all possible accuracy and care, the Holy and Oecumenical Synod has decreed that it is unlawful for any one to present, or compile, or compose, or believe, or teach to others, any other creed.' We recognize, therefore, that it is unlawful for a Church to put forward any other Creed as the teaching of the Catholic Church, or to add to or subtract from the Creed. Yet it is not unlawful for the several Churches to use as their Baptismal Creed some other Creed agreeable to the Tradition of the Church, as in the Western Church that which is called the Apostles' Creed. Nor is it unlawful for a Church to use any other such document in the Services of the Church or for the instruction of the faithful, provided that it is agreeable to Scripture and Tradition.

4. *The Doctrine of the Holy Spirit*

On the difference which has prevailed between the East and the West concerning the doctrine of the Holy Spirit we record the propositions adopted by the Conference held at Bonn in the year 1875. While we reject every proposition or form of expression which implies the existence of two principles or *ἀρχαί* or *αἰτίαι* in the Holy Trinity, we consider as acceptable the teaching of St. John of Damascus and of earlier Greek Fathers that the Holy Ghost proceeds from the Father through the Son.

5. *Variety of Customs and Usages in the Church*

With regard to ecclesiastical Customs or Usages (*ἔθη καὶ νόμιμα*) we distinguish two classes—those which according to St. Photius are based on the authority of a general or catholic decree, and are thus obligatory for the whole Church; and those which have only a local character, which every local Church is therefore free to accept or not. We agree with St. Augustine that every Christian should accept the Customs and Usages of the Church to which he belongs.

6. *The Sacraments*

The representatives of the Orthodox Church say:

'We accept that the two of the seven Sacraments—namely Baptism and the Holy Eucharist—the first as introducing us into the Church, the second as uniting us with Christ, are pre-eminent among the others. But we do not think that the other five are of secondary importance as Sacraments, neither that they are unnecessary to the spiritual life of the Christian and consequently to his salvation. These also as the two first are Holy Services of Divine foundation in which through an outward visible sign the invisible grace of Christ is conveyed.'

The representatives of the Anglican Church say:

'The number of the Sacraments has never been authoritatively fixed either by tradition from the Apostles or any decision of an Oecumenical Council. We recognize that the two Sacraments of Baptism and the Holy Eucharist are pre-eminent above the rest. As regards other Sacraments, while the Eastern Orthodox Church uses the term *mysterion* also of Ordination, Penance, Confirmation or Chrism, Marriage and the Anointing of the Sick; in the Book of Common Prayer of the Church of England the word Sacrament is only used of the two Sacraments Baptism and the Holy Eucharist, inasmuch as these only have an outward visible sign ordained by Christ Himself and are held to be generally, that is universally, necessary for salvation. But it is recognized also in the Anglican Communion that in other Rites there is an outward and visible sign and an inward spiritual grace, and in that sense they may be considered to have the character of Sacraments and are commonly called Sacraments.'

We agree that with regard to the manner of celebration of Sacraments a variety of custom and rite is acceptable, provided that the things essential to the Sacrament are preserved.

As regards the Holy Eucharist and Holy Orders, we desire to hand on to the Synod of the Eastern Orthodox Church and the Convocations and Synods of the Anglican Communion the Résumé and the précis of discussions that were held at Lambeth in 1930.

CONCLUSION

A

We have been able in the time at our disposal to discuss several fundamental questions which concern the Christian Faith. There are others which we have not had time to consider and we hope it may be possible to arrange a further meeting at some subsequent date to continue our discussions. But we would like to say in conclusion that we believe that in spite of differences there is much underlying agreement between our two Churches. We agree that the basis of Intercommunion should be a union of Faith, but we do not think that it is our function to determine what measure of divergence may be considered legitimate. We think that it is a matter which must be determined by the bodies to which we would report—the Holy Synod of the Orthodox Church and the Convocations and Synods or Conventions of the Anglican Communion.

B

The representatives of the Anglican Communion laid before the Commission the Report of the Conference that was held between representatives of the Anglican Communion and the Old Catholic Churches and the Resolutions therein agreed upon. The representatives of the Eastern Orthodox Church agreed to lay this Report and these Resolutions for the consideration of the Synod of the Eastern Orthodox Church. The Resolutions are as follows:

'(1) Each communion recognizes the catholicity and independence of the other, and maintains its own.

'(2) Each communion agrees to admit members of the other communion to participate in the Sacraments.

'(3) Intercommunion does not require from either communion the acceptance of all doctrinal opinion, sacramental devotion, or liturgical practice characteristic of the other; but implies that each believes the other to hold all the essentials of the Christian Faith.'

A. C. GLOUCESTR:
✠ METROPOLITAN OF THYATEIRA, GERMANOS.

158. Report of the Conference between Delegates of the Church of Rumania and the Church of England

JUNE 1935

[In 1935, from June 1 to June 8, a Conference was held, in the Patriarchal Palace at Bucarest, between the Commission of the Rumanian Church upon Relations with the Anglican Communion and a delegation from the Church of England appointed by the Archbishop of Canterbury. The Joint Chairmen were the Bishop of Roman (Rt. Rev. Lucian) and the Bishop of Lincoln (Dr. F. C. Nugent Hicks). The terms of reference were 'to consider the statements exchanged between the Orthodox Delegation to the Lambeth Conference of 1930 and the Committee on Unity of that Conference' (*vide supra*, Document 148). After papers had been read, the following Report was agreed upon. See *Report of the Conference at Bucarest . . . between the Rumanian Commission on Relations with the Anglican Communion and the Church of England Delegation appointed by the Archbishop of Canterbury* (Press and Publications Board of the Church Assembly, 1936).]

REPORT

The Thirty-nine Articles

In answer to an inquiry of the Rumanian Commission the Anglican Delegation stated that:

> 'The Doctrine of the Anglican Church is authoritatively expressed in the Book of Common Prayer, and that the meaning of the XXXIX Articles must be interpreted in accordance with the Book of Common Prayer' [see *Lambeth Conference*, 1930, p. 139],

and that therefore the XXXIX Articles are to be regarded as a document secondary to the Book of Common Prayer.

The Holy Eucharist

A statement was submitted by the Rumanian Commission to the Anglican Delegation concerning the Holy Eucharist and was accepted unanimously by the latter in the following form:

1. At the Last Supper, our Lord Jesus Christ anticipated the sacrifice of His death by giving Himself to the Apostles in the form of bread blessed by Him as meat and in the form of wine blessed by Him as drink.
2. The sacrifice offered (προσενεχθεῖσα) by our Lord on Calvary was offered once for all, expiates the sins as well of the living as of the dead, and reconciles us with God. Our Lord Jesus Christ does not need to sacrifice Himself again.
3. The sacrifice on Calvary is perpetually presented in the Holy Eucharist in a bloodless fashion (ἀναιμάκτως) under the form (Rumanian, *sub chipul*) of bread and wine through the consecrating priest and through the work of the Holy Ghost in order that the fruits of the sacrifice of the Cross may be partaken of by those who offer the Eucharistic Sacrifice, by those for whom it is offered, and by those who receive worthily the Body and Blood of the Lord.

4. In the Eucharist the bread and wine become by consecration (μεταβολή) the Body and Blood of our Lord. How? This is a mystery.
5. The Eucharistic bread and wine remain the Body and Blood of our Lord as long as these Eucharistic elements exist.
6. Those who receive the Eucharistic bread and wine truly partake of the Body and Blood of Our Lord.

Holy Scripture and Holy Tradition

The Conference considered the following statement agreed unanimously at its session at Lambeth in 1931 by the Orthodox and Anglican members of the Joint Doctrinal Commission appointed in pursuance of the recommendation of the Orthodox Delegation to the Lambeth Conference of 1930 and of the Lambeth Conference of 1930 [see *Lambeth Conference* 1930, Resolution 33 (*b*), p. 48[1]].

'Everything necessary for salvation can be founded upon Holy Scripture as completed, explained, interpreted, and understood in the Holy Tradition, by the guidance of the Holy Spirit residing in the Church.

'We agree that by Holy Tradition we mean the truths which came down from our Lord and the Apostles through the Fathers, which are confessed unanimously and continuously in the Undivided Church and are taught by the Church under the guidance of the Holy Spirit.

'We agree that nothing contained in Tradition is contrary to the Scriptures. Though these two may be logically defined and distinguished, yet they cannot be separated from each other nor from the Church.'

The Rumanian Commission agreed unanimously that if the above statement is emended to read as follows, it will be sufficient:

'*The Revelation of God is transmitted through the Holy Scriptures and the Holy Tradition.*[2] Everything necessary for salvation can be founded upon Holy Scripture, as completed, explained, interpreted, and understood in the Holy Tradition, by the guidance of the Holy Spirit residing in the Church. We agree that by Holy Tradition we mean the truths which come down from our Lord and the Apostles and *have been defined by the Holy Councils*

[1] *Vide supra*, Document 145.

[2] The words italicized constitute the emendments by addition or alteration.

or are taught by the Fathers,[1] which are confessed unanimously and continuously in the Undivided Church and are taught by the Church under the guidance of the Holy Spirit.

'We agree that nothing contained in Tradition is contrary to the Scriptures. Though these two may be logically defined and distinguished, yet they cannot be separated from each other nor from the Church.'

The Anglican Delegation concurred unanimously with the Rumanian recommendation.

Divine Mysteries

The Conference compared the two statements upon the Sacraments made respectively and unanimously by the Orthodox and Anglican members of the Joint Doctrinal Commission at its session of October 1931, namely:

(*a*) by the Orthodox:

'We accept that two of the seven Sacraments—namely Baptism and the Holy Eucharist—the first as introducing us into the Church, the second as uniting us with Christ, are pre-eminent among the others. But we do not think that the other five are of secondary importance as Sacraments, neither that they are unnecessary to the spiritual life of the Christian and consequently to his salvation. These also, as the two first, are Holy Services of Divine foundation in which through an outward visible sign the invisible grace of Christ is conveyed.'

(*b*) by the Anglicans:

'The number of the Sacraments has never been authoritatively fixed either by tradition from the Apostles or any decision of an Œcumenical Council. We recognise that the two Sacraments of Baptism and the Holy Eucharist are pre-eminent above the rest. As regards other Sacraments, while the Eastern Orthodox Church uses the term *mysterion* also of Ordination, Penance, Confirmation or Chrism, Marriage, and the Anointing of the Sick; in the Book of Common Prayer of the Church of England the word Sacrament is only used of the two Sacraments Baptism and the Holy Eucharist, inasmuch as these only have an outward visible sign ordained by Christ Himself and are held to be generally,

[1] The words italicized constitute the emendments by addition or alteration.

that is universally, necessary for salvation. But it is recognized also in the Anglican Communion that in other Rites there is an outward and visible sign and an inward spiritual grace, and in that sense they may be considered to have the character of Sacraments and are commonly called Sacraments.'

While hesitating to revise the above Anglican statement and while considering that before a final and complete agreement is reached, a further Conference is desirable, the Anglican Delegation agreed unanimously to recommend for consideration the following formula:

'We agree that Baptism and the Holy Eucharist, the first as introducing us into the Church, the second as uniting us with Christ and through Him with the Invisible Church, are pre-eminent among the Divine Mysteries. We agree that because Holy Scripture and Tradition witness to their origin, Confirmation, Absolution, the Marriage Blessing, Holy Orders, and the Unction of the Sick are also Mysteries in which, an outward visible sign being administered, an inward spiritual grace is received.'

The Rumanian Commission agreed to recommend this formula to the Holy Synod of Rumania for consideration.

Justification[1]

The Orthodox Commission and the Anglican Delegation agreed unanimously upon the following statement:

'By the redeeming action of our Lord Jesus Christ, mankind has become reconciled to God. Man partakes of the redeeming grace through faith and good works, and reaches through the working of the Holy Ghost, the Lord and Giver of Life, sanctification by means of the Church and the Holy Sacraments.'

[1] This section was explained by Dr. Hicks in the debate on the Report in the Upper House of the Convocation of Canterbury on May 27, 1936, and in a statement later the same year. He said that the title did not really agree with the text of the section, which dealt with Sanctification and not only with Justification. The Anglican representatives had in mind both Article XI and Article XII of the Thirty-nine Articles. Article XII said that good works 'do spring necessarily out of a true and lively faith: insomuch that by them a lively faith may be so evidently known as a tree discerned by its fruit'. That meant that if a man had the real faith which justified, he would have the works that spring necessarily from it. It was in that sense that the Anglican Delegation felt able to include the words 'and good works' in the agreed statement.—Ed.

The Validity of Anglican Orders

The Rumanian Commission made the following Declaration:

'Having considered the conclusions of the papers on the Apostolic Succession, Holy Orders, Holy Eucharist, Holy Mysteries in general, and Tradition and Justification,

'And having considered the declarations of the Anglican Delegation on these questions, which declarations are in accordance with the Doctrine of the Orthodox Church,

'The Rumanian Orthodox Commission unanimously recommends the Holy Synod (of the Rumanian Orthodox Church) to recognise the validity of the Anglican Orders.'

The Anglican Delegation received the Declaration with due acknowledgement.

Note:

The following Resolution was carried in both Houses of the Convocation of Canterbury in January 1937. In the course of the debate in the Upper House, the Archbishop of Canterbury explained that, while he personally would have preferred the expression 'permissible interpretation', he did not think there was any real difference in meaning between that and 'legitimate interpretation'.

'That inasmuch as the Report of the Conference at Bucarest between the Rumanian Commission on Relations with the Anglican Communion and the Church of England Delegation appointed by the Archbishop of Canterbury is consonant with Anglican formularies and a legitimate interpretation of the Faith of the Church as held by the Anglican Communion, this House accepts and approves of the Report.'

159. *Resolution of the Holy Synod of the Rumanian Orthodox Church*

MARCH 20, 1936

THE PATRIARCH, HIS BEATITUDE MIRON CRISTEA, *presiding*. *Secretary:* BISHOP VENIAMIN

HIS All Holiness the Patriarch of Constantinople having notified the Holy Synod that he had recognized the Validity of Anglican Orders, and having requested our Holy Synod to examine that question and to inform him in reply of its opinion:

1. Accordingly, the Holy Synod of the Orthodox Church of Rumania replied in 1925:

(*a*) That from the historical point of view no obstacle exists to the recognition of the Apostolic succession of Anglican orders.

(*b*) That from the dogmatic point of view the validity of Anglican orders depends upon the Anglican Church itself and especially upon whether or not that Church recognizes Holy Orders to be a Mystery (Sacrament).

In order to explain the doctrine of the Anglican Church concerning Holy Orders, a Delegation of four bishops and six theologians was sent to Bucarest by the Archbishop of Canterbury (Dr. Cosmo Lang) and from June 1 to 8, 1935, made such explanations to the Commission of Bishops and of expert professors of our faculties in theology appointed by our Holy Synod.

The Rumanian Commission set before the Anglican Delegation a statement of Orthodox doctrine concerning the Mystery of Holy Orders.

In view of the fact that the Anglican Delegates accepted without reservation the doctrine of the Orthodox Church in regard to the Sacrament of Holy Orders after the Rumanian Commission had expressed it in all its points of importance and in its full sacramental character as one of the Seven Mysteries:

The Holy Synod of the Orthodox Church of Rumania resolved the adoption of the recommendations of the Commission, viz.:

'Having considered the conclusions of the papers on the Apostolic Succession, Holy Orders, Holy Eucharist, Holy Mysteries in general, and Tradition and Justification;

'And having considered the declarations of the Anglican Delegation on these questions, which declarations are in accordance with the Doctrine of the Orthodox Church;

'The Rumanian Orthodox Commission unanimously recommends the Holy Synod (of the Rumanian Orthodox Church) to recognise the validity of Anglican orders.'

It is to be understood that the above resolution will become definitive as soon as the final authority of the Anglican Church ratifies all the statements of its delegation concerning the Mystery of Holy Orders in regard to the points of importance comprised in the doctrine of the Orthodox Church.

2. This decision is to be communicated to His All Holiness the

Oecumenical Patriarch of Constantinople and the Archbishop of Canterbury, the Primate of the Anglican Church.

3. At the same time the Holy Synod of the Orthodox Rumanian Church expresses its great joy inasmuch as Divine Providence prepared the way that the representatives of the Anglican Church might be able to show us what effective and definitive steps have been taken towards establishing clearly their teaching to be in harmony with that of the Orthodox Eastern Church which is the faithful depository of the Christian Faith in all its Apostolic purity.

May this approach be of great use in the path shown by our Common Saviour Jesus Christ in His words: 'That they all may be one.'

4. In conclusion the Rumanian Church prays from its soul that such exploratory meetings may be continued in the future until the Holy Spirit pour out His Grace to make clear the doctrines of the Anglican Church to be in complete agreement with the doctrines of the Orthodox Oecumenical Church.

In confirmation the Seal of the Holy Synod of the Orthodox Church of Rumania.

HIEROMONK CALLIST RADULESCU

160. Resolution of the Holy Synod of the Church of Greece

SEPTEMBER 21, 1939

THE Holy Synod has decided that it intends as before to follow in each individual case that may arise of the adherence of an Anglican cleric to Orthodoxy the practice of the Church and the unanimous conclusions of the Theological Faculty of the University of Athens, that 'The Orthodox Church recognizes as valid without qualifications only those Sacraments which she has herself administered, but that nevertheless the Church, in so far as she considers it proper and useful, in particular cases, after previous investigation of the current circumstances, recognizes by Economy the Ordination of those who come over to Orthodoxy'.

The Holy Synod appreciates the desire expressed by His Grace the Archbishop of Canterbury to send a delegation of Anglican theologians under the chairmanship of the Right Reverend Bishop of Gloucester for common discussion of questions of interest. It remembers in this connexion the bonds of affection which have long united the two Churches, and realizes that every opportunity of strengthening these contacts should be welcomed, and that every contact and interchange between the two Churches serves to strengthen their friendship and *rapprochement*. The Holy Synod will therefore look forward to welcoming the arrival of such a delegation after the difficulties caused by the present war are resolved, and will appoint a corresponding delegation to represent our Church.

Finally the Holy Synod expresses its warmest thanks to the theologians for their memoranda. . . .

IV. THE LESSER EASTERN CHURCHES

THE SYRIAN ORTHODOX JACOBITE CHURCH

[In 1921, the Chaplain of the Crimean Memorial Church, Constantinople (the Rev. R. F. Borough), reported that the Syrian Orthodox Patriarch of Antioch, Mar Ignatios Elias III, of his own motion asked him to ascertain on what conditions the Syrian Orthodox (Jacobites) resident in the West, and especially in America, when unable to obtain the ministrations of their own clergy, might resort to the ministrations of the Anglican clergy. A similar inquiry had previously been made in 1908 by the former Patriarch, Mar Ignatios Abdullah. The resolutions of the Lambeth Conferences of 1908 and 1920 (quoted in the Archbishop of Canterbury's letter of June 21, 1922, to Mar Ignatios Elias) outline the general conditions. Personal interviews between Mar Ignatios and the Rev. R. F. Borough took place at Constantinople in August 1921 and January 1922, Mr. Borough being accompanied on the latter occasion by Sir Samuel Hoare (now Viscount Templewood), then treasurer of the Eastern Churches' Committee. Mar Ignatios said he would prefer to answer specific questions regarding the doctrine of the Incarnation, rather than affirm a formula such as the Athanasian Creed, which had not been accepted by his Church. The questions were duly prepared and answered. The Oecumenical Patriarch expressed himself as viewing the correspondence with satisfaction, and in due course the Archbishop of Canterbury's letter reached Mar Ignatios, who had by then left Constantinople for Dar-es-Saffran, by way of Jerusalem. Mar Ignatios's reply was in turn transmitted to the Archbishop.]

161. Questions authorized for submission to Mar Ignatios

APRIL 24, 1922

1. Is it believed that, when One (and only One) of the Three Persons in the Holy Trinity—to wit, God the Word—became Incarnate, He took Flesh, mortal, of the Virgin Mary?

2. Is it believed that, by the Incarnation of God the Word, Manhood and Deity (each remaining perfect and complete) became for ever the One Indivisible Christ?

3. Is it believed:

(*a*) That, in the One indivisible Christ, the Manhood has the qualities proper to manhood, and the Deity the qualities proper to Deity?

(*b*) That each—the Manhood as well as the Deity—is therein active according to its proper qualities?

162. Reply of Mar Ignatios to the Questions

MAY 5, 1922

1. WE believe that the Second Person of the Holy Trinity, God the Word, became Incarnate by the Holy Ghost, took mortal flesh from the Immaculate Virgin Mary, that is to say, He became man like us in every sense, except sins.

2. We believe that by the Incarnation of God the Word, His Deity became united with our humanity, a union without confusion, change, division, mixture, transformation, or separation; from this admirable and inscrutable union became the One Indivisible Christ.

3. We believe:

(*a*) That in the One Indivisible Christ, the manhood has the qualities proper to manhood and the Deity has the qualities proper to Deity.

(*b*) That our Lord Jesus Christ being perfect Deity and perfect Man, His Deity as well as His Manhood each acts according to the properties which are peculiar to them, except sins; He accomplished miracles, as God, and He suffered, as Man; the Venerable Simeon carried Him in his arms, as man, and he asked Him to let him go in peace, being God.

163. Letter from the Archbishop of Canterbury to Mar Ignatios

JUNE 21, 1922

[The course of action proposed in the following letter was described to the Oecumenical Patriarch, Meletios II, at Constantinople, in a letter of the same date from the Archbishop of Canterbury, and received his approval.]

LAMBETH PALACE, S.E.1.
21st June 1922.

MOST REVEREND AND DEAR BROTHER,

I HAVE followed with great hope and interest the correspondence which has taken place between Your Holiness and the Committee sitting under Bishop Gore's presidency in this country, on Relations between the Anglican Church and the Churches of the East. This correspondence includes the inquiry made by Your Holiness last summer as to the terms on which intercommunion could be established between the Anglican Church and the Orthodox Syrian Church.

It was with great satisfaction that I received from that Committee a Report that the Statement made by Your Holiness respecting the Faith of your Church concerning the Person of our Lord and Saviour Jesus Christ furnishes a complete and satisfactory reply to the questions which the Committee had the privilege of forwarding to you, and of which I enclose a copy.

It is now my privilege in consequence of these communications to authorize those recognized members of the Orthodox Syrian Church who, being prevented from access to their own clergy, desire to receive the Holy Communion, or to have their children baptized, or their marriage solemnized, to avail themselves of the ministrations of our clergy.

There may be cases also of a special kind in which members of the Syrian Orthodox Church may for special reasons desire to communicate with us, though not actually deprived of Holy Communion through isolation. In these cases, too, I shall be glad if recognized communicant members of your Church were in this special way to communicate with us.

This authorization is in complete accord with the Resolutions of the Lambeth Conference of 1908 and 1920, as follows:

Resolutions of the Lambeth Conference 1908

The Conference would welcome any steps that might be taken to ascertain the precise doctrinal position of the ancient separated Churches of the East with a view to possible inter-communion, and would suggest to the Archbishop of Canterbury the appointment of Commissions to examine the doctrinal position of particular Churches, and (for example) to prepare some carefully framed statement of the Faith as to our Lord's Person, in the simplest possible terms, which should be submitted to each of such Churches, where feasible, in order to ascertain whether it represents their belief with substantial accuracy. The conclusions of such Commissions should in our opinion be submitted to the Metropolitans or Presiding Bishops of all the Churches of the Anglican Communion.

In the event of doctrinal agreement being reached with such separate Churches, the Conference is of opinion that it would be right (1) for any Church of the Anglican Communion to admit individual communicant members of those Churches to communicate with us when they are deprived of this means of grace through isolation, and conversely, for our communicants to seek the same privilege in similar circumstances; (2) for the Churches of the Anglican Communion to permit our communicants to communicate on special occasions with these Churches, even when not deprived of this means of grace through isolation, and conversely, that their communicants should be allowed the same privileges in similar circumstances.

We consider that any more formal and complete compact between us and any such Church, seeing that it might affect our relations with certain other Churches, should not take place without previous communication with any other Church which might be affected thereby.

Resolutions of the Lambeth Conference 1920

The Conference has received with satisfaction its Committee's report of the investigations that have been made during the last twelve years with regard to the present doctrinal position of the Separated Churches of the East; and, without expressing an opinion as to the past, believes that these investigations have gone far towards showing that any errors as to the Incarnation of our Lord which may at some period of their history have been attributed to them, have at any rate now passed away.

The Conference repeats the proposals made by the Conference of 1908 that, when any of the Separated Churches of the East desire closer relations with us and wish for the establishment of occasional intercommunion, and give satisfactory assurances as to their faith, such relations should at once be established.

The Conference respectfully requests the Archbishop of Canterbury to take advantage of any opportunity that may arise to enter into friendly relations with these Churches, and to inform the authorities of the Orthodox Eastern Church of any steps that may be taken in the direction of intercommunion with them. Similar action should be taken with regard to informing Metropolitans of our own Communion.

I have only to add that in the case of such of Your Holiness's people as require their children to be baptized, or their wedding to be solemnized by Anglican clergy, it would be, I presume, desirable that you or some other authority of your Church should in each case be formally notified.

I shall be glad to know your mind as to any procedure which you might wish to be observed in regard to this matter.

Conversely it will be a great satisfaction to me also if in similar emergencies on our side your clergy were willing on request to provide similar ministrations to recognized communicant members of the Anglican communion who are prevented from access to Anglican clergy, or, on special occasions, desire to communicate with your Church.

I should be glad to hear from Your Holiness that you would be willing that the ministrations of your own clergy may be available for our people.

In conclusion I desire to assure Your Holiness that the Church of England and the different Provinces of the Anglican communion will welcome this opportunity of rendering brotherly help and hospitality to your people, and will pray that by this step the Reunion of Christendom for which we hope may be in some degree furthered.

With all brotherly greeting and much respect,

I am

Your Holiness's faithful brother and servant in our Lord Jesus Christ

(Sgd.) RANDALL CANTUAR:

His Holiness Mar Ignatios Elias.

164. Letter from Mar Ignatios to the Archbishop of Canterbury

SEPTEMBER 27, 1922

PATRIARCAT SYRIEN D'ANTIOCHE.

MOST REVEREND AND DEAR BROTHER,

WITH great pleasure I have received your letter dated 21st June, 1922, and have read all that you wrote concerning our correspondence presented to the respected Committee of Lambeth. It pleases me very much to hear from Your Eminence that you thought the faith of our Church in the Lord Jesus Christ is correct, and that the Lambeth Conference begged Your Eminence to allow the communicants of your Church to have communion with us and that our communicants can do the same. The achievement of this result gives great joy, because it is the first step for peace in the Church, and nothing could please me more than for the Churches to become united, and of such a blessed event the result would be great joy in heaven and earth.

Our Church does not prevent those who wish it from receiving the Sacraments, but a man must first confess his sins according to the rules of the Church and then the Church will let him receive the communion.

With regard to the reception of the Sacraments reciprocally, before a meeting of the Council of our Metropolitans and Bishops and telling them about these discussions between myself and the Lambeth Conference, I cannot proclaim this arrangement, and the meeting of this Council is not possible, because the Metropolitans and Bishops belong to different governments. But my hope is that when peace comes in the Near East I may ask them to meet me, to study with them this question of union; for which purpose I wish you to tell me what that union can be, and by what means it can be attained, and I hope the result will be good.

As I pray for the success of this good matter so I hope Your Eminence will pray for the same purpose; and the success is from God. Through Your Eminence I send my Christian salutations to the Committee of the Lambeth Conference. And in conclusion please accept my kind regards.

The grace of God be with us for ever.

Your Eminence's brother in Our Lord Jesus Christ

IGNATIOS ELIAS

Syrian Patriarch of Antioch.

Jerusalem the 27th September 1922.

To His Eminence the Archbishop of Canterbury.

THE MAR THOMA SYRIAN CHURCH

[A Committee of the Episcopal Synod of the Church of India, Burma, and Ceylon, under the chairmanship of Bishop E. A. L. Moore, then Bishop of Travancore, was appointed in 1933 with a view to establishing closer relationships with the Mar Thoma Syrian Church of Travancore. As a result of the Committee's Report, negotiations commenced with the authorities of the Mar Thoma Church, and reached a satisfactory conclusion. Rules of comity were agreed between the two Churches, and the Metropolitan of Calcutta solemnly promulgated an authorization of occasional intercommunion between them in St. Paul's Cathedral, Calcutta, on April 4, 1937.]

165. *The Assembly of the Mar Thoma Syrian Church Resolution adopted at its Session of May 5 and 6, 1936*

In view of the measure of intercommunion that has already existed between the Mar Thoma Church and the Church in India, Burma, and Ceylon (formerly known as the Church of England in that territory), and in view of a unanimous finding of a joint committee appointed by the authorities of the two Churches that there is no bar in respect of the orders, doctrine, and worship of either Church to the formal establishment of the measure of intercommunion between them which is known as occasional intercommunion, this *sabha*, believing that the unity of the Church is the will of God, records its approval of such occasional intercommunion being now established and requests the Metropolitan in agreement with the Metropolitan of the Church of India, Burma, and Ceylon formally to authorize it.

[A note is appended defining occasional intercommunion in terms identical with the definition contained in Resolution 64 of the Lambeth Conference 1908.]

166. *Rules of Comity agreed upon between the Mar Thoma Syrian Church and the Church of India, Burma, and Ceylon in the Diocese of Travancore and Cochin*

APRIL 4, 1937

(i) Persons seeking to change their membership from the Mar Thoma Church to the Anglican Church or vice versa shall in no case be admitted to such new membership, until they produce a certificate signed both by the pastor of the congregation and by the Bishop of the Church to which they have belonged hitherto. Such certificate shall not ordinarily be issued until a period of at least three months has elapsed after it has been applied for.

(ii) The same procedure shall be followed in the case of those who may seek admission into the Anglican or Mar Thoma Church even from any other Church, if they were members of the Anglican or Mar Thoma Church at any period within three years before applying for such admission. In issuing certificates of admission the Bishops will require information on this point.

(iii) Subject to rule (iv) below, the Pastors of either Church shall have authority and discretion to admit to the Holy Communion communicant members of good standing in the other Church in places where they have no access to the ministrations of the Church to which they belong.

(iv) Members of either Church desiring to avail themselves of this privilege shall previously give notice of their intention to the Pastor concerned and shall produce to him a certificate from their own pastor as to their communicant status and good standing in the Church to which they belong. No member of either Church shall be allowed to avail himself of this privilege on more than one occasion without producing such a certificate.

(v) Even in places where a member has access to the ministrations of his own Church he may in exceptional cases be allowed to communicate in the other Church. In such cases the procedure laid down in rule iv shall be followed, but the certificate to be produced in such cases must state not only that the member is a communicant of good standing in his own Church, but also that his own pastor approves of his being admitted to the Holy Communion in the other Church.

(vi) The existing rules obtaining between the two Churches regarding marriages (*Deshakuri*, *Pasaram*, &c.) shall continue to be observed until altered by mutual consent.

V. THE OLD CATHOLIC CHURCHES

[In accordance with Resolution 35 of the Lambeth Conference 1930 a Joint Doctrinal Commission was appointed by the Archbishop of Canterbury and the Archbishop of Utrecht, with the consequences noted in the following documents. See *Report of the Meeting of the Commission of the Anglican Communion and the Old Catholic Churches held at Bonn on Thursday, July 2, 1931*, S.P.C.K.]

167. Statement agreed between the representatives of the Old Catholic Churches and the Churches of the Anglican Communion at a Conference held at Bonn

JULY 2, 1931

1. EACH Communion recognizes the catholicity and independence of the other and maintains its own.

2. Each Communion agrees to admit members of the other Communion to participate in the Sacraments.

3. Intercommunion does not require from either Communion the acceptance of all doctrinal opinion, sacramental devotion, or liturgical practice characteristic of the other, but implies that each believes the other to hold all the essentials of the Christian Faith.

Signed:

A. C. GLOUCESTR:
[A. C. Headlam]
STAUNTON FULHAM.
[B. S. Batty]
A. S. DUNCAN-JONES.
N. P. WILLIAMS.
J. A. DOUGLAS.
G. F. GRAHAM-BROWN.
C. B. MOSS.
C. L. GAGE-BROWN.

J. H. DEVENTER.
ADOLF KÜRY.
GEORG MOOG.
A. RINKEL.

168. Letter from the Archbishop of Utrecht to the Archbishop of Canterbury

SEPTEMBER 1931

TO THE MOST REVEREND THE LORD ARCHBISHOP OF CANTERBURY

In response to your letter of August 26, I have the honour to inform you that the Episcopal Synod of the Old Catholic Churches at its meeting on September 7 at Vienna discussed the Report of the Conference of the Anglican Communion and the Old Catholic Churches held at Bonn on Thursday July 2, 1931, and in particular the three resolutions printed on page 27. The Synod declared itself well satisfied with the discussions, approved of the spirit which animated the members of the two Commissions, and adopted the following resolutions: (1) The Synod assembled in Vienna on September 7, 1931, of the Old Catholic Bishops united in the Union of Utrecht, on the basis of the recognition of the validity of Anglican Ordinations, agrees to intercommunion with the Anglican Communion. (2) Intercommunion consists in the reciprocal admittance of the members of the two Communions to the Sacraments. (3) Intercommunion does not require from either Communion the acceptance of all doctrinal opinion, sacramental devotion, or liturgical practice characteristic of the other, but implies that each believes the other to hold all the essentials of the Christian Faith. With the confident belief that Your Grace will be satisfied with this result, I remain your brother in Jesus Christ,

FRANÇOIS KENNINCK,
Archbishop of Utrecht.

169. Convocation of Canterbury. Resolutions of both Houses

JANUARY 20 AND 22, 1932

UPPER HOUSE

THAT this House approves of the following statements agreed on between the representatives of the Old Catholic Churches and the Churches of the Anglican Communion at a Conference held at Bonn on July 2, 1931:

1. Each Communion recognizes the catholicity and independence of the other and maintains its own.
2. Each Communion agrees to admit members of the other Communion to participate in the Sacraments.
3. Intercommunion does not require from either Communion the acceptance of all doctrinal opinion, sacramental devotion, or liturgical practice characteristic of the other, but implies that each believes the other to hold all the essentials of the Christian Faith.

And this House agrees to the establishment of Intercommunion between the Church of England and the Old Catholics on these terms.

LOWER HOUSE

That this House concurs with the establishment of Intercommunion between the Church of England and the Old Catholics on the terms of the Resolutions sent down by the Upper House.

Note: Both Houses of York Convocation also passed similar Resolutions in January 1932. Intercommunion was established on the same terms with the Episcopal Church in Scotland (1932); the Church of India, Burma, and Ceylon (1932); the Church in China (1933); the Church of the Province of the West Indies (1933); the Church of England in Canada (1934); the Protestant Episcopal Church in U.S.A. (1934); the Church of the Province of South Africa (1935); and the Church in Wales (1936).

THE POLISH NATIONAL CATHOLIC CHURCH

170. *The Polish National Catholic Church and the Protestant Episcopal Church in the United States of America: Resolutions of the Committee on Intercommunion*

JUNE 27, 1947

[The Polish National Catholic Church in America, officially in communion with the See of Utrecht, ratified the terms of the Bonn agreement in October 1946. As a consequence, intercommunion with the Protestant Episcopal Church followed. The two Churches appointed Committees on Intercommunion, 'to confer on questions arising from their new relationship', which met on June 27, 1947, and agreed on terms of official relations.]

Official Relations

It was agreed that each Church would furnish the other with lists of clergy and of parishes. Notices of depositions or suspensions will be sent by the authorities of each Church to the Prime Bishop or to the Presiding Bishop of the other Church.

There was unanimous agreement that at every General Synod of either Church an official representative of the other Church be invited to attend and to bring a message of brotherly greeting. A similar invitation at Diocesan Synods is also desirable. It was also recommended that on such occasions opportunity should be given if possible for intercelebration, a Bishop or priest of the other Church being invited to celebrate at the altar. It was explained that the Diocesan Synods of the Polish National Catholic Church meet every five years, and the General Synod every ten years, the next one being in 1956; while in the Episcopal Church, Diocesan Conventions meet annually and the General Convention every three years, the next being in 1949.

Particular care, it was agreed, must be taken by each Church to respect the disciplinary actions of the other Church, both as to clergy and as to laity. In the case of mixed marriages, the conditions required by both Churches shall be observed.

It was unanimously the view of both Committees that this closer relationship should lead in both Churches to a strengthening of loyalty. Thus it is expected that requests for transfer of membership would need to be considered only rarely, under very special conditions. In the case of clergy, transfer would be permissible only for one in good standing, and then only with the full agreement of the respective Bishops of both Churches. In the case of lay persons, the request should first be submitted to the Bishop of the Church to which that family belongs for his official approval; no pastor should receive members of the other Church without prior notice of such approval by the applicant's Bishop.

The relationship between the Churches, it was agreed, is one of *inter*communion—that is, sacramental communion between two autonomous Churches, each respecting the independence and jurisdiction of the other, and avoiding any actions that would tend to weaken the faith or loyalty of those in its sister Church, while seeking to cultivate all suitable means for increasing mutual acquaintance and fellowship. This is clearly stated in the terms of the Bonn Agreement, which is the basis on which both Churches have entered into the new relationship. In all doubtful matters, the pastors shall seek the counsel of their diocesan Bishops and shall abide by their decisions.

VI. THE CHURCH OF ENGLAND

171. Convocation of Canterbury: Upper House. Resolutions on Resolution 42[1] *of the Lambeth Conference 1930*

JANUARY 18, 1933

[A tentative version of these Resolutions was approved by the Upper House in June 1931, and sent to the Lower House for its consideration and comment.]

THAT this House, having considered Resolution 42 of the Lambeth Conference (1930), is of opinion

(1) that, so far as it concerns permission for Anglicans to receive Holy Communion at the hands of Ministers other than those of the Anglican Churches, the resolution has no application in this Province, inasmuch as the conditions contemplated in it do not exist within the Province;

(2) that, so far as it concerns permission to encourage persons who do not belong to the Anglican Communion to receive the Holy Communion in Anglican Churches, in temporary circumstances or on special occasions, the giving or withholding of such permission is in the discretion of the Diocesan Bishop, who should be guided by the following considerations:

(*a*) Where a baptized communicant member of a Church not in communion with our own is cut off by distance from the ministrations of his own Church, he may be welcomed to communion by the incumbent. But if such person becomes a habitual communicant over a long period, the claim of the Church to full conformity with its requirements should be pressed upon his conscience.

(*b*) In school or college chapels where services are conducted according to the rite of the Church of England, a member of the society who, being baptized, has the status of communicant in his own denomination, may be admitted to communion at the discretion of the Ordinary.

(*c*) On special occasions, if and when they arise, when groups of members of the Church of England or of other Christian denominations are joined together in efforts definitely in-

[1] *Vide supra*, Document 145, Resolution 42.

tended to promote the visible unity of the Church of Christ, the Bishop if requested may approve of the admission of baptized communicant members of these other denominations to Holy Communion according to the Anglican rite.

Note. The Lower House offered its comments on the Tentative Resolutions of 1931; and the Upper House made certain modifications incorporated in the final Resolutions as above. The Prolocutor read the above document to the Lower House of the Convocation of Canterbury on January 19, 1933, for its information. And the following note of the Prolocutor's statement appears in the *Chronicle*, January 19, 1933, No. 1, p. 160:

'It would be seen that the Bishops had in the main accepted the suggestions made in the Report of the Lower House with some slight verbal modifications, and that the main drift of the Resolutions of the Upper House which he had now read to them was to leave the matter of administration in the hands of the Diocesan Bishop, subject to the general Rules, and to avoid the further step of making these Rules part of anything like canonical legislation. Therefore His Grace the President had asked him to say that, having laid these Rules before this House for its information, no concurrence was asked for on the part of the Lower House.'

172. *Convocation of York: Upper House. Resolutions on Resolution 42*[1] *of the Lambeth Conference 1930*

JUNE 1931 AND JANUARY 1933

[The text below is as adopted in June 1931, and subsequently, in January 1933, slightly modified in the opening words of 2 (*c*), as a result of discussions in the Lower House.]

'THAT this House, having considered Resolution 42 of the Lambeth Conference, is of opinion:

(1) that, so far as it concerns permission for Anglicans to receive the Holy Communion at the hands of ministers other than those of the Anglican Churches, the resolution has no application in this province, inasmuch as the conditions contemplated in it do not exist within the province;

(2) that, so far as it concerns permission to encourage persons who do not belong to the Anglican Communion to receive the Holy Communion in Anglican churches in temporary circum-

[1] *Vide supra*, Document 145, Resolution 42.

stances or on special occasions, the giving or the withholding of such permission is in the discretion of the Diocesan Bishop, who should be guided by the following considerations:

(*a*) Where a baptized communicant member of a Church not in communion with our own is cut off from the ministrations of his own Church, we recommend that he should be admitted to communion;

(*b*) In school or college chapels where services are conducted according to the rite of the Church of England, members of the society who, being baptized, have the status of communicant in their own body, may be regarded as falling within the scope of this resolution;

(*c*) Or on occasions where groups of workers engaged in joint evangelistic efforts desire to express and confirm their aspiration towards unity, it seems legitimate to approve the holding of a corporate communion according to the Anglican rite subject to the requirements of Resolution 42 as regards those who are admissible.'

JANUARY 1933

'With reference to the resolutions adopted by the Upper House on June 3, 1931, and laid before the Lower House on January 21, 1932, and the consequent action of the Lower House taken on June 2, 1932, the Upper House:

1. expresses its very cordial gratitude to the members of the Lower House for the care and thoroughness with which they have discussed and considered these matters and for the counsel which they have offered;

2. assures the members of the Lower House that it has considered most carefully the valuable memorandum which they adopted and which they have submitted to its consideration and informs them that it has modified one of its resolutions in the light of that memorandum;

3. is of opinion that it is not at present desirable that its resolutions should be made Declarations or Acts of the Provincial Synod but that the giving or withholding of permission to persons who do not belong to the Anglican Communion to receive the Holy Communion in Anglican churches in temporary circumstances or on special occasions should be left to the discretion of the Diocesan

Bishop guided by the considerations set forth in the resolutions mentioned above and in the memorandum submitted by the Lower House.'

173. Convocation of Canterbury: Upper and Lower Houses. Resolutions on Interchange of Preachers

MAY 27, 1943

1. That this House is of the opinion that while the questions of Faith and Order which at present divide the Churches of the Anglican Communion from non-Episcopal Communions within Christendom are still unresolved, no general interchange of preachers is practicable, and there should be adherence on the part of the Church of England, with respect to the ministry of the Word no less than with respect to the ministry of the Sacraments, to the principles laid down in the Preface to the Ordinal and in the formula accompanying the delivery of the Bible to the recipient of the Order of Priesthood.

2. That this House, acknowledging that the divisions within Christendom have the nature of sin for which all concerned have a measure of responsibility, affirms that it is the duty of all Members of the Church of England to reach out in penitence, charity, and friendship towards those who at present are separated from them by ecclesiastical barriers.

Accordingly:

3. This House is of the opinion that in particular circumstances, namely:

(*a*) when joint services are held in connexion with conferences and meetings designed to promote Christian reunion, or

(*b*) in connexion with inter-denominational campaigns concerned either with the application of Christian principles to the ordering of life in Society, or with the promotion of Christian evangelism at home or with the work of Christian missions overseas, or

(*c*) at services on an interdenominational basis on special occasions of national or local prayer and thanksgiving or of national humiliation or in commemoration of the fallen in war or of the victims of disaster, or (*d*) when, in the Bishop's judgement, the giving of such permission would set forward the ideal of union which was generally approved at the Lambeth Conferences of 1920 and 1930

a Bishop should be free to give permission for a minister or duly accredited preacher of another Christian denomination to give an address in an Anglican church at services other than Holy Communion; so also the Bishop should be free to give approval for a minister of the Church of England to give an address in a place of worship belonging to some other denomination. Such permissions should be exceptional and without prejudice to the normal maintenance of the recognized rules of Church order. Before giving any such permission the Bishop shall first be satisfied by inquiry that his proposed action will be acceptable alike to the clergy and to the laity in the parish or parishes concerned.

4. This House is further of the opinion that it is legitimate to make use of the Parish Church, at times other than those of the regular and appointed services, for the holding of informal gatherings for united prayer on the part of Christian people: that the promotion and holding of such gatherings is greatly to be desired; and that on such occasions ministers and members of other Christian communions may with the Bishop's permission be invited either to speak or to lead in prayer.

Note: The Upper House of the Convocation of York in May 1946 passed a similar Resolution to that of the Upper House of Canterbury, but defined the 'circumstances in which permission may be given' as follows:

(*a*) When joint services are held in connexion with conferences or meetings designed to promote Christian reunion (or on a special occasion for the purpose of promoting Christian reunion), in accordance with the Lambeth Resolutions, *or*

(*b*) in connexion with interdenominational (as distinguished from undenominational) campaigns for the affirmation of the Christian doctrine of God and man and its implications for individual and corporate life, or with the Christian mission in the world, *or*

(*c*) at services held on national, local, or civic occasions of prayer, thanksgiving, or commemoration.

174. Convocation of York: Upper House. Resolution on Unitarians

JUNE 1934

[The Rev. L. Redfern, a Unitarian minister, had, as Chaplain to the Assize, preached in Liverpool Cathedral at the Assize Service on Sunday morning, October 22nd, 1933.]

(*a*) THAT this House has heard with satisfaction the statement of the Bishop of Liverpool to the effect that he neither sanctioned nor approved the invitation issued to a Unitarian minister to preach in Liverpool Cathedral at an ordinary service of the congregation, and that he has taken steps to secure that no such invitation shall be issued in future.

(*b*) That, with regard to addresses delivered at gatherings in churches or cathedrals other than gatherings of the congregation for the regular worship of the Church, this House reaffirms its resolution of 15th February, 1922, and recognizes that a wider liberty may reasonably be permitted on such occasions than is appropriate in connexion with the ordinary service of the Church, but it desires to make plain:

(i) that by a *Christian Communion*, as the words are used in that resolution, the House understands a communion which holds the Faith described in the report on *The Church's Common Confession of Faith* and unanimously received by the World Conference on Faith and Order at Lausanne in 1927 as the 'common Christian Faith, which is proclaimed in the Holy Scriptures, and is witnessed to and safeguarded in the Œcumenical Creed, commonly called the Nicene, and in the Apostles' Creed, which Faith is continuously confirmed in the spiritual experience of the Church of Christ';

(ii) that this House accepts the definition of the visible Church implicit in the opening words of the Appeal issued by the Lambeth Conference of 1920, viz.:

'We acknowledge all those who believe in our Lord Jesus Christ, and have been baptized into the name of the Holy Trinity, as sharing with us membership in the Universal Church which is His Body.'

Accordingly this House is of opinion that, in the exercise of discretion approved in 1922 with regard to invitations to preachers at special services, the Bishop should not extend such invitation to any person who does not hold, or who belongs to a denomination which does not hold, 'the common Christian Faith' in Jesus Christ as 'Very God of Very God Who for us men and for our salvation came down from heaven and was made man'.

Note: In the Lower House it was agreed:

That this House requests the Prolocutor to express to his Grace the President the thanks of the House for his solemn communication to this House of the results of the discussion in the Upper House on the Bishop of Durham's resolutions.

VII. THE FREE CHURCHES IN ENGLAND

175. *Outline of a Reunion Scheme for the Church of England and the Free Churches in England*

FEBRUARY 1938

[The Joint Conferences which were suspended in 1925 were resumed after the Lambeth Conference of 1930, which Conference expressed the hope of resumption 'with the definite aim of ascertaining whether the proposed scheme of union prepared for the Churches of South India suggests lines on which further advance on questions of order can be made'. The Joint Conference in 1936 issued *A Sketch of a United Church*, which Canterbury Convocation commended to the attention of the Church. It continued its work, and in 1938 issued three documents, viz.: *Outline of a Reunion Scheme*, *The Practice of Intercommunion*, and *1662 and To-day* —of which the *Outline* is much the most important.]

PREFACE

THE 'Conversations' between Anglicans and Free Churchmen, which have been carried on for several years, have a twofold value. Probably their chief value consists in the growing understanding and appreciation on both sides; this arises at first in those who share the conversations, but as these are leaders in their several denominations it spreads beyond them to those whom they influence. But this process is assisted by the documents which are prepared by the Committee of the Joint Conference and passed on by it for the consideration of the Churches. At its last session the Joint Conference thus received and generally commended three such documents, of which this is one. We invite for it wide attention, because we believe that it is calculated both to dispel prejudices and to point the way to fuller agreement and so at last to the union for which we pray.

COSMO CANTUAR:
A. E. GARVIE.

THE JOINT CONFERENCE

THE ARCHBISHOP OF CANTERBURY [Cosmo Gordon Lang] (*Chairman*)

Representatives of the Church of England

The Archbishop of York [William Temple] (*Convener*)
The Bishop of Chelmsford [H. A. Wilson]
The Bishop of Chichester [G. K. A. Bell]
The Bishop of Coventry [Mervyn Haigh]
The Bishop of Gloucester [A. C. Headlam]
The Rev. Professor H. L. Goudge, D.D.
The Bishop of Lichfield [E. S. Woods]
The Bishop of London [A. F. Winnington-Ingram]
The Bishop of Manchester [Guy Warman]
Bishop E. J. Palmer, D.D.
The Rev. Canon O. C. Quick, D.D.
The Bishop of Wakefield [J. B. Seaton]
The Bishop of Winchester [C. F. Garbett]
The Bishop of Worcester [A. W. T. Perowne]
The Dean of York [H. N. Bate]

Representatives of the Federal Council of the Evangelical Free Churches

The Rev. A. E. Garvie, D.D. (*Convener*)
The Rev. M. E. Aubrey, C.H., M.A.
The Rev. Sidney M. Berry, D.D.
The Rev. Charles Brown, D.D.
The Rev. Benjamin Gregory, D.Litt.
The Rev. E. Griffith-Jones, D.D.
The Rev. J. D. Jones, C.H., D.D.
The Rev. Gilbert Laws
The Rev. J. N. Libbey, M.A.
The Rev. J. Scott Lidgett, C.H., D.D.
The Rev. J. Lineham, Ph.D.
The Rev. W. F. Lofthouse, D.D.
Sir Henry Lunn, M.D.
The Rev. Hugh Martin, M.A.
The Rev. H. G. Meecham, Ph.D.
The Rev. James Reid, D.D.
The Rev. P. Carnegie Simpson, D.D.
The Rev. Jacob Walton

INTRODUCTORY NOTE

THE scheme set out in the following pages was drafted in this form by the Committee of the Joint Conference of Anglicans and Free Churchmen and is now submitted by that Conference to its appointing authorities, namely, the Archbishop of Canterbury and the Federal Council of Evangelical Free Churches, in the hope that they will commend it to the careful consideration of the Churches represented in the Joint Conference.

The Committee responsible for the final draft was fortunate in having before it an earlier draft which was the work of the Research Group of Friends of Reunion, representing all the Churches concerned. Apart from this preliminary work, the Committee would probably not have been able, in the amount of time that its members are able to spare for this purpose, to draw up so complete a scheme, and those who thus took over the fruit of so much labour wish gratefully to acknowledge their indebtedness.

None of those who have been responsible for the preparation of the scheme in its various stages expects that it will be carried into effect in this form. Further discussion is bound to produce important alterations in it, but discussion is only fruitful where it is concentrated on some definite proposal. There can be but little valuable discussion of reunion in England until a scheme is suggested. It is hoped that what is now presented may prove a useful basis for further work towards the attainment of reunion.

The scheme gives a general outline of the kind of Church in which the Churches represented in the conference might find themselves united without loss of what is specially valuable in their distinctive traditions. It embodies in substance and often in the original form all the agreements hitherto reached in the Joint Conferences since the issue of the Lambeth Appeal in 1920, and much also from the scheme of union under discussion in South India. But little is said in it of the interim arrangements which would be necessary between any decision of the Churches to unite and the final achievement of the united Church. It is fully recognized that these are of primary importance, but they belong to the stage of actual negotiation which has not yet been reached. There is, however, a definite recommendation on this subject at the close of the document.

REFERENCES

Reports of Joint Conferences between the Church of England and the Evangelical Free Churches in *Documents on Christian Unity*. 2 vols. Edited by G. K. A. Bell. Oxford University Press [1924 and 1930]. Referred to as *Bell*. [*Vide supra*, *First* and *Second Series* of this collection.]

A Sketch of a United Church. S.P.C.K. [1936.] Referred to as *Sketch*.

Proposed Scheme of Union. Christian Literature Society for India. 1934 edition. Referred to as *South India*.

A reference does not necessarily imply verbal quotation.

I. *The Purpose of the Scheme*

1. This scheme is drafted in the belief that it is the will of God that in this world the spiritual unity of His Church should be

manifested in a visible society, holding the one faith, having its recognized ministry, using God-given means of grace and inspiring all its members to the world-wide service of the Kingdom of God. (*Bell*, i. 1.)

2. It rests upon the conviction that the unity of the Church is involved in the Christian Doctrine of God, and is demanded for the manifestation and achievement of His purpose. As there is one Lord, one Faith, one Baptism, one God and Father of us all, so there must be one Body, one fellowship of the people of God on earth, seen of all men; for it is the purpose of God not only to reconcile all men through Christ to Himself, but also to unite them to one another in the Body of Christ.

3. The divisions among Christian people everywhere disable them from serving God according to the will of Christ and obstruct His purpose to win and rule over men.

This disunion debars us from giving our torn and distracted world effective witness to the truth that the Gospel of Christ is the one basis of enduring fellowship among men and nations. Similarly it confuses and weakens the presentation and imperils the acceptance of our Christian message, especially in the mission field. The continuance of this disunion involves a waste which is sinful, inasmuch as it hinders the work of God.

4. Our ideal of reunion is one of unity with variety. It does not mean absorption by any existing body, nor would it involve a flat and meagre uniformity; rather it would conserve, and make more widely available, the spiritual treasures at present cherished in separation. The spiritual vitality of each section suffers through isolation in organization from the rest. While the value of the present varieties of emphasis in Christian faith and experience must be preserved, these very varieties should be varieties within the life of one Body.

This scheme makes its own the ideal set forth by the Lambeth Conference of 1920, and reaffirmed by the Lambeth Conference of 1930:

> 'The vision which rises before us is that of a Church, genuinely Catholic, loyal to all Truth, and gathering into its fellowship all "who profess and call themselves Christian" within whose visible unity all the treasures of faith and order, bequeathed as a heritage by the past to the present, shall be possessed in common, and made serviceable to the whole Body of Christ. Within this unity

Christian communions now separated from one another would retain much that has long been distinctive in their methods of worship and service. It is through a rich diversity of life and devotion that the unity of the whole fellowship will be fulfilled.' (*Bell*, i. 2, 2 [Document 1].)

5. In every effort to bring together divided members of Christ's Body the final aim must be the union in the Universal Church of all who acknowledge Christ as Lord, and the test of all local schemes of union is that they should express locally the principle of the great catholic unity of the Body of Christ. (Cf. *South India*, 22.)

The united Church of England (*a*) desires in no way to impair the fellowship and communion which the constituent bodies from which it has been formed have previously enjoyed in England and throughout the world, and (*b*) will continually work towards the goal of the full union in one body of all parts of the Church of Christ.

II. *The Membership of the Church*

1. The Body of Christ, the One Church, consists of all the redeemed in Christ, in this world and in the world beyond our sight. The visible Church on earth was constituted by Christ as a fellowship of men and women united with Him and in Him with one another to be His witnesses and the servants of His Kingdom on earth. (*Bell*, i. 147 [Document 44].)

2. Those only shall be members of the united Church of England who have by Baptism been admitted to Christ's Church visible on earth.[1] Baptism may be administered in infancy or upon profession of faith. Where baptism is administered in infancy communicant status shall be attained only upon a profession of faith following upon due instruction and sealed in a public service of confirmation, or such other service of attaining communicant status as shall be agreed upon. The privilege of participating in the government of the united Church shall be confined to communicants who have attained the age of eighteen years.

3. It is the duty and privilege of every member to realize his

[1] No one who believes that Jesus Christ commanded His disciples to baptize or that His first disciples from the very beginning did so, could consent to any other rule of membership in His Church, but when the Church in unity has that wisdom which it lacks in its divisions, it will have to consider what fellowship it can give to devoted followers of Christ like the Friends who do not use sacraments, supposing that they on their part desire fellowship with the Church which provides sacraments, and with its members who use them.

sonship in the family of God and to rejoice in his salvation through Jesus Christ, in whom we have forgiveness of sins; and further through the gift of the Spirit to continue in that salvation by being diligent in prayer and in the reading of the Scriptures; by attendance at public worship and Holy Communion; by contribution of his time and substance to the pastoral and evangelistic work of the Church; and by manifesting a Christian temper and practice in all his intercourse with his fellow men, and especially by helping those who are in need, sickness, or distress; and by seeking to bring all personal and social relationships under the rule of Christ. (*South India*, 36.)

4. All persons who have been confirmed or have been admitted as communicants by any of the services of admission which were in use in any of the uniting Churches before union shall be recognized as communicants throughout the united Church of England. (*South India*, 36–7.)

III. *The Faith of the Church*

1. The united Church of England holds the Faith which the Church has ever held in Jesus Christ, the Redeemer of the world, in whom men are saved by grace through faith; and in accordance with the revelation of God which He made, being Himself God incarnate, it worships one God in Trinity and Trinity in Unity. (*South India*, 23.)

It accepts as the supreme standard of the Faith the revelation of God contained in the Holy Scriptures of the Old and New Testaments and summed up in Jesus Christ. (*Bell*, i. 150 [Document 44].)

2. It accepts the Apostles' Creed and the Creed commonly called the Nicene, as witnessing to and safeguarding that Faith, which is continuously verified in the spiritual experience of the Church and its members, and as containing a sufficient statement thereof for a basis of union. (*South India*, 23.)

This acceptance of the Creeds does not imply that they are regarded as a complete expression of the Christian Faith. They are accepted as agreeable to the Word of God contained in the Holy Scriptures, and as historic affirmations of essential elements in the Christian Faith. This acceptance of the Holy Scriptures and of the Creeds does not exclude reasonable liberty of interpretation.

The united Church also recognizes fully and thankfully the continued teaching of the Holy Spirit, and emphasizes its duty to keep its mind free and ready to receive from Him in each day and generation ever-renewed guidance in the apprehension and expression of the truth. (*Bell*, i. 151.)

IV. *The Sacraments*

1. The united Church of England accepts the sacraments of Baptism and the Holy Communion as of divine appointment, as means of grace, and as expressing and strengthening the corporate life of the whole fellowship in, and with, Christ. (*Bell*, i. 3.)

2. It is a rule of order in the united Church that the celebration and administration of the Holy Communion or the Lord's Supper should be entrusted to those who have received authority thereto. (*Sketch*, 16.)

(*Note.*—It is already the accepted practice of all Churches that only one called and authorized by the Church to do so may celebrate the Holy Communion. The mode of authorization varies according to the constitution of the Church concerned. Thus if the local congregation be regarded as holding the full authority of the Church in that place, the authorization is given by the local congregation through its own proper channels. In Episcopal and Presbyterian Churches, the authorization is given in ordination; in Episcopal Churches it is given in no other way; in some Presbyterian Churches the Presbytery may occasionally authorize one who is not an ordained minister to supply the Sacrament to people who could not otherwise receive it—though probably this would be an elder and therefore in that sense an ordained person. In actual practice it is usual in all denominations for an ordained minister to celebrate the Eucharist, though celebration by a duly authorized layman is in some not infrequent. Consequently a general rule of order that authorization should be by ordination would continue the most familiar practice of all the uniting Churches. But there is need to reach (1) fuller agreement about the universality of this rule, and (2) fuller understanding of the views held with regard to its underlying principle. For the rule determining the proper minister of the sacraments cannot be left unsettled in any actual scheme of union, but it can only be settled by official representatives of Churches which have entered upon negotiations for union.)

3. In connexion with Baptism there should be (whether immediately or, in the case of persons baptized in infancy, after an interval of some years) a service of prayer for the fuller gifts of

the Holy Spirit, to which, following Apostolic custom, we desire the laying on of hands to be joined, the bestowal of the Spirit being sought, and by God's goodness vouchsafed, as at once the source of the new life in grace and of continual increase of its strength.

(*Note.*—In Western Christendom this service has come to be associated with an age at which the person concerned can exhibit repentance and faith, and can be prepared by instruction in the doctrines, privileges, and duties of the Church. Among the Baptists the 'baptism of believers' is understood to include these elements. Where infant-baptism is practised a rite is needed which supplies elements not in that case associated with Baptism. Among Anglicans this function is fulfilled by Confirmation. In all cases the completion of Baptism, whether immediate or deferred, should lead to the full spiritual privileges of the Christian life, though not necessarily to participation in the government of the Church. This rite connected with and completing Baptism should be administered either by the bishop or by presbyters authorized for the purpose.) (*Sketch*, 17.)

4. Responsibility for presenting candidates for Confirmation may be exercised by the presbyter-in-charge of a congregation either alone, or in consultation with responsible lay members. The bishop (or the presbyter) must himself be satisfied of the fitness of the candidate.

(*Note.*—For the word 'presbyter', as used in this scheme, see section X below. Presbyter-in-charge is used where necessary to distinguish the minister in chief charge of a congregation from other presbyters who may be assisting him.)

V. *The Ministry* (*Bell, i. 148–9* [Document 44])

1. The ministry of the Word and Sacraments is a divine gift to the Church, and has been since the days of the Apostles an integral part of its organic life. It is a ministry within the Church exercising in the Name and by the authority of the Lord who is the Head of the Church, powers and functions which are inherent in the whole life of the Church.[1]

[1] The relation of the Ministry to the Church is in the New Testament expressed from two points of view. In 1 Cor. xii and Rom. xii the Church, as the Body of Christ, receives the divine gift of the Spirit in its fullness, and within the Body various 'members' are specialized to particular functions, which include those of the apostolate, the prophetic and teaching ministries, and Church

2. No man can take this ministry upon himself. There must be not only an inward call of the Spirit, but also an outward and visible call and commission by the Church, acting through those who have authority given to them in the Church to confer it.

3. It is in accordance with Apostolic practice and the ancient customs of the Church, that this commission should be given through ordination, with prayer and the laying on of hands. We believe that through ordination, together with the commission to minister, Grace is given through the Holy Spirit in response to faith and prayer, for the fulfilment of the charge so committed.

4. Means should be provided whereby the ministry of the united Church may be acknowledged by every part thereof as possessing the authority of the whole Body.

In view of the fact that the Episcopate was accepted from early times and for many centuries, and by the greater part of Christendom is still accepted, as the means whereby the authority of the whole Church is given, we agree that it ought to be accepted as such for the united Church of England. We think it fitting that presbyters should be associated with the bishop in the ceremony of ordination, and that the laity should have a share in the process by which a candidate is approved for ordination. (*Bell*, i. 148–9 [Document 44].)

5. The acceptance of episcopal ordination for the future would not imply the disowning of past ministries of Word and Sacrament otherwise received, which have, together with those received by episcopal ordination, been used and blessed by the Spirit of God. It would allow for various theories regarding the origin and character of the Episcopate. It would imply the continuity of the Episcopate of the united Church with the Historic Episcopate in its

government. Such ministries therefore may be rightly described as God-given organs *of* the Church. In Eph. iv the ministries of apostle, prophet, evangelist, pastor, and teacher are given by the glorified Lord to the Church for the upbuilding of the Body of Christ. The Ministry, therefore, may be rightly described as a gift of God *to* the Church. These two views are complementary and not contradictory. In the view of 1 Cor. and Romans, the Ministry is not created by the Church but by the Spirit, whose divers *charismata* mark out this man and that for special functions. God appoints ministers (1 Cor. xii. 28). The Church in Corinth is bidden to recognize, discipline, and correlate the gifts and activities of different kinds of ministers (1 Cor. xiv. 26–33, cf. xvi. 15). In Ephesians again, no less than in 1 Cor. and Romans, the one Body is the recipient of the one Spirit, and the *charismata* of the Ministry are specialized forms of gifts which the Church as a whole possesses through possessing the Spirit. The statement in the text is intended to recognize both aspects of the truth.

succession from ancient times. It neither affirms nor excludes the view that Apostolic Succession determines the validity of the Ministry and Sacraments. (*Bell*, i. 150 [Document 44]; *Sketch*, 12.)

VI. *Forms of Worship*

1. The united Church will aim at conserving for the common benefit whatever good has been gained in the separate history of those Churches from which it has been formed, and therefore in its public worship will retain for its congregations freedom either to use historic forms or not to do so, as in their judgement may best conduce to the worship of God in spirit and in truth.

No forms of worship which have been in use in any of the uniting Churches shall be forbidden in the united Church unless on the ground that they are not congruous with the fundamental principles of the Church of Christ, nor shall any wonted forms be changed, or new forms introduced into the worship of any congregation without the agreement of the presbyter-in-charge and congregation. This shall not be interpreted as necessarily precluding the whole Church in the course of time from determining new, and withdrawing old, forms of worship. (See also VI, 5.) (*South India*, 27–8.)

Subject to these conditions, and to the provisions of this constitution and any special regulations which may hereafter be issued by the Assembly under the constitution with regard to the services of ordination and consecration, and the essential elements or central parts of other services, especially those of Baptism, Holy Communion, and Marriage, every presbyter-in-charge and congregation shall have freedom to determine the forms of their public worship. (*South India*, 62–3.)

2. *Holy Communion.* As the Church grows in unity of mind and spirit, and experiences closer fellowship in worship, it may develop a common form or forms of the Service of Holy Communion.

The following shall be constituent parts of every Communion Service, the word 'service' being understood to mean either a single service, or two services, of which the former (whether held on the same or on a previous day) forms one whole with the actual Communion Service, and will be attended by those who will be communicants. The particular order of the elements in the service noted below is not intended to be binding.

i. *Introductory Worship.*

ii. *The Ministry of the Word*, including readings from the Scriptures, which may be accompanied by preaching.

iii. *The Preparation of the communicants* by a general confession of sin, and the declaration of God's mercy to penitent sinners, whether in the form of an absolution or otherwise, and such a prayer as 'The Prayer of Humble Access'.

(*Note.*—Portions, or even the whole of these three sections, may be incorporated in a previous service, provided that the communicants attend the service.)

iv. *The offering to God of the gifts of the people.*

v. *The Thanksgiving*, for God's glory and goodness and the redemptive work of Christ, leading to a reference to His institution of the Sacrament, in which His own words are rehearsed, and to the setting apart of the bread and wine to be used for the purpose of the Sacrament with prayer that we may receive that which our Lord intends to give us in this Sacrament.

vi. *An Intercession for the Whole Church*, for whom and with whom we ask God's mercy and goodness through the merits of the death of His Son.

vii. *The Lord's Prayer.*

viii. *The Administration of the Communion* with words conformable to Scripture indicating the nature of the action.

ix. *A Thanksgiving for the Grace received in the Communion* with which should be joined the offering and dedication of ourselves to God, unless this has been included earlier in the service.

3. *Baptism.*

i. The administration of Baptism shall include a profession of faith and promise of loyalty made by each candidate, or, in the case of an infant, by sponsors being parents or godparents on his behalf. This profession and promise shall be made in such forms of words, or in either of such alternative forms of words, as the Assembly of the united Church shall direct, provided that, if the profession of faith be in the form of assent to the Apostles' Creed, a simpler alternative form or profession shall also be permitted.

ii. In administering Baptism, the presbyter shall either immerse each candidate in water or pour water on his head and openly declare, in regard to each candidate severally, that he baptizes him in the name of the Father, the Son, and the Holy Spirit.

iii. The presbyter shall also use a form of words, to be authorized by the united Church, declaring that the candidate ought either immediately or in due course to seek communicant status, and that, as having this provision in remembrance, he is received into the congregation of Christ's flock. (See further II, 2, and IV, 3.)

iv. Subject to any regulations which may be issued by the Assembly of the united Church, responsibility for accepting candidates for infant Baptism shall rest with the presbyter-in-charge. (See also IV, 3.) The candidates shall normally be baptized, and always be received, in the face of the congregation.

The united Church shall decide how many witnesses, and in the case of infants, how many sponsors, shall be required, and what person or persons may thus act.

The united Church will also decide the age, or ages, above which a person may not be presented for Baptism as an infant.

4. *The Creeds.* (*South India*, 63–4.) The use of the Creeds in worship is an act of adoration and thanksgiving towards Almighty God for His nature and for His acts of love and mercy, as well as a joyful remembrance of the faith which binds together the worshippers.

In the ordinary congregational worship of any congregation no authority of the Church shall forbid the use of the Creeds or impose it against the will of the congregation. But in services in which the whole Church is concerned, as, for instance, consecrations or ordinations, the Assembly may issue regulations on the matter.

5. *Alterations in forms of worship.* (*South India*, 64.) Acting subject to the provisions of this constitution, a presbyter-in-charge of any congregation, after consultation with the elders and due notice to the congregation, may introduce experimentally the use of a form of worship different from that to which they have been accustomed.

He shall thereafter consult members of the congregation on the matter, and if any six members so desire, he shall after two months consult a general meeting of the communicant members of the congregation, after due notice has been given, as to whether the use of the altered or new form shall be continued; and it shall not be continued unless at least two-thirds of those present at such meeting desire its continuance. The advice of the bishop of the diocese should be sought in any case of difficulty or serious division of opinion. In some cases where the new form is not adopted for general use in the congregation, it may be agreed that it should be used occasionally.

VII. *Relation to the Secular Authority* (*Sketch*, 11)

The spiritual actions and decisions of all Councils, Courts, or Assemblies of this Church, and particularly those of the highest available authority—the General Assembly—in respect to faith, worship, morals, discipline, and government, must be free from the control of, or reversal by, any secular authority.

On the other hand, the Church acknowledges the jurisdiction of the civil courts in such matters as property, endowments, and the like.

Such freedom in spiritual matters from the control of the State does not necessarily exclude some form of State *recognition* of the Church as the expression for the nation of its religious allegiance. The possibility of retaining what is valuable in the State connexion calls for further examination.

VIII. *Organization*

1. In the Church of God the one and only ultimate authority is that of Jesus Christ Himself, the Head of the Body, who is 'the same yesterday, to-day and for ever', on whom the Church may rely to-day as fully as in any generation of the past for the guidance of His Spirit.

To Him all assemblies owe allegiance. They also bear responsibility towards the whole Body of the Church, of which the members on earth at any time form but a portion, and they should therefore pay due regard to the tradition of the Church wherein its continuous life finds expression. (*Sketch*, 8.)

2. Need will be found in the united Church of England for at least three organs of government: the General Assembly, the Diocesan Synod, and the Congregational Council. (These names are tentative and employed only for convenience in reference.) Each Synod or Council should accept the authority of the wider fellowship in those respects which seem to that fellowship to be essential; and this wider fellowship will bring gifts of the Spirit to the local Church as truly as the local Church to the wider fellowship. (*Sketch*, 9.)

(*Note.*—Since one of the dangers of the united Church will be unwieldiness of national organization, decentralization of administration should be sought so far as possible. The Diocesan Synod will perform a very important function. It is likely, however, that the Church may find it convenient to divide England into Provinces for certain administrative purposes, in which division the archiepiscopal Sees of Canterbury and York would retain their status.

Provincial Synods would then be required which might be composed of members of the General Assembly in the Province. They could be summoned when desired by the Archbishop of the Province, or at the request of a specified number of members. They might meet three months before the annual meeting of the General Assembly for preliminary consideration of matters of exceptional importance, or matters affecting only the Province, or matters referred to the Province by the Assembly.)

3. In the sphere of legislation the ultimate authority of the united Church resides in the harmony of bishops, presbyters, and laity. Neither should the Episcopate be able to impose regulations on either presbyters or laity without their consent, nor should presbyters or laity be able to compel a bishop to administer a rule disapproved by the Episcopate. In the case of Ordination, for example, the bishop should not be able to ordain any man contrary to the judgement of presbyters or people, in whatever way or degree they are called to execute that judgement, nor should they be able to compel the bishop to ordain any candidate of whose fitness he is not satisfied. (*Sketch*, 12.)

4. A legislative change affecting the worship or doctrine of the Church should require a majority of bishops and of presbyters and of laity in the General Assembly.

Though on such a matter they would thus vote 'by Houses', it is much to be desired that they should conduct their discussion, at least largely, in open session where all three are present together.

(*Note.*—A vote 'by Houses' means that the proposal in question must be carried in each 'house'; each 'house', therefore, has a veto, and the laity can veto what is desired by both bishops and presbyters no less than either of these can veto what is desired by one or both of the other two.) (*Sketch*, 9, 10.)

5. The General Assembly (see XIV), which would comprise, together with the bishops, duly elected representatives both of clergy and laity, would be the supreme conciliar authority of the

national Church, and, subject to its allegiance to Christ and its responsibility towards the mind of Christendom and towards the tradition of the Church as a whole, would legislate for the national Church, and would exercise supervision over other conciliar authorities and over administration generally therein. (*Sketch*, 9.)

6. The Diocesan Synod (see XIII), the functions and limitations of which would be determined by the Assembly, would have charge of, and responsibility for, administration, together with some legislative authority, within its area. (*Sketch*, 9.)

7. The Congregational Council (see XII) would exercise authority—except as regards the rights and responsibilities of the presbyter-in-charge—over the practice of the congregation in worship, as well as over finance, property, &c. (*Sketch*, 9.)

8. The people should have an effective voice in the selection of the presbyter-in-charge of the congregation, whether this be expressed through the Congregational Council or through a meeting of communicant members of the congregation. In some cases the congregation would call the presbyter subject to ratification by the Synod; in others a bishop, Synod, Assembly, or other authorized person or body would appoint subject to consultation with the congregation, who might, if they wished, refer the question to some body of advisers established for that purpose. (*Sketch*, 9.)

IX. *The Episcopate*

1. In an episcopal Church the position of the bishop is ideally that of the father in a family. The bishop, in addition to the spiritual and administrative functions which are recognized under this constitution as belonging to his office, and those which may be entrusted to him by the Assembly, exercises a representative function in two ways. In the Councils of the Church, whether national or universal, he represents his diocese, and in his diocese he represents the Church as a whole. For this reason both the diocese and the wider fellowship of the Church should have a share in the selection of a bishop, which should not be the responsibility of any secular authority. (*Sketch*, 10.)

(*Note.*—There is no reason why the episcopate should not, if circumstances at first so require, be exercised by more than one person in a diocese. In the initial stage it is probable that each of the uniting Churches would be represented in each diocese in a college of bishops. Perhaps one ex-Anglican and one ex-Free Church bishop would be sufficient in some dioceses. With the progress of the process of growing together, the unification of congregations, &c., the need for a number of diocesan bishops would probably lessen though suffragans might be desirable.

While at the outset the existing diocesan boundaries should probably be retained, an increase in the number of dioceses might later prove desirable.)

2. In the Diocesan Synod the bishop would take his place along with the presbyters and representatives of the laity. His place is naturally that of president; but there may be occasions when a deputy should take his place.

In any case, the bishop would not have any final authority in administration apart from the presbyters and laity, except so far as this might be committed to him by the General Assembly. (*Sketch*, 10.)

3. *Pastoral Oversight.* The bishop has the general pastoral oversight of the diocese and more particularly of the presbyters. It is his duty to minister as occasion may serve the rite of Confirmation, or to preside when desired at similar services (see IV, 3) in which admission is given into communicant membership of the Church, and he is responsible for doing all that he can to foster the spiritual unity and welfare of the diocese.

4. *Teaching.* The office of a bishop is also essentially a teaching office, and he should do all that is in his power for the edification of the presbyters and congregations over whom he has oversight by instructing them or providing for their instruction concerning the truths of the Christian faith.

On each bishop in his own diocese, and on the bishops of the Church as a body, is laid the responsibility of publicly stating, as need may from time to time arise, the doctrine of the Church Universal and its application to the problems of the age and of the country. But no such statement shall have any force as a rule of the Church unless and until it be adopted by the Assembly as such. (*South India*, 38.)

5. *Worship.* The bishop of the diocese, acting in accordance with the rules laid down in this Scheme, shall acquaint himself with the various methods of worship used in the diocese, shall advise the presbyters and congregations in this matter, and shall cause to be prepared and shall issue special services and prayers as they may be

required. He shall have authority in the case of grave irregularities in public worship to forbid their continuance, and any such prohibition shall remain in force pending any action which the Executive Committee of the Assembly of the Church may take thereon. (*South India*, 39.)

6. *Ordination*. For the distinctive function of the bishop in ordination see V, 4.

7. *Discipline*. For the distinctive function of the bishop in the administration of discipline see XV.

8. *General Assembly*. For the position of the bishop in the General Assembly see VIII, 4, and XIV.

9. *Permanence of Appointment*. The bishop of a diocese shall remain bishop of that diocese until he resign, or accept the charge of another diocese, or depart permanently from the diocese or be deprived of his charge by sentence of the Court of the Assembly, or be adjudged to be mentally, physically, or otherwise incapable of discharging the duties of his office, or until he die. (*South India*, 40–1.)

10. *The Election, Appointment, and Consecration of Bishops*. (*South India*, 42 *ff*.)

Provision is made for four stages in the appointment of bishops.

Both the Executive Committee of the Assembly and the Diocesan Synod shall have the right of making nominations for the election of a diocesan bishop.

Some such procedure as the following might be adopted: From the combined list of nominations the Diocesan Synod, or an electoral body appointed by the Synod, shall, in consultation with the Executive Committee, elect not less than two and not more than four persons, each of whom must be supported as being an acceptable candidate by not less than two-thirds of the number of the members of the Diocesan Synod or electoral body present and voting, and shall submit the list of those thus selected to a board consisting of the President and six members appointed by the Executive Committee of the Assembly. This board shall appoint a bishop for the diocese from among the names submitted. (See Appendix.)

11. The Assembly will prescribe a form of consecration of bishops, in which, while provision may be made for extempore prayer and variation in the details of the service, there shall be

certain invariable parts; these to include at least (i) the solemn presentation of the person to be consecrated to the bishops who are taking part in the consecration by two presbyters of the diocese to which he is to be appointed; (ii) a prayer of consecration, asking that the person to be consecrated may receive the gift of God's Holy Spirit for the office and work of a bishop in His Church; and (iii) the laying on of hands by the bishops (who shall be at least three in number) and with whom shall normally be associated the two presbyters referred to above, as further symbolizing and expressing the concurrence of the Church of the diocese in the act of consecration. (*South India*, 45.)

12. No person may be consecrated as bishop unless he is already a presbyter and has attained the age of thirty years.

X. *The Ordained Ministry of the Church—Presbyters and Deacons or Probationers*

Presbyters (*South India*, 46–9)

1. It is the special duty of a presbyter:

(i) To watch over the flock committed to him; to build up all its members in their most holy Faith; to teach, to encourage, to warn, and to rebuke; and to maintain the doctrine and discipline of the Church with all fidelity.

(ii) To preach the Word of God, to declare God's forgiveness to penitent sinners, to administer Baptism and the Holy Communion, to pronounce God's blessing upon those who are married according to His Word, to conduct the other services of the Church; and in general to lead the worship of the congregation.

(iii) To instruct the young and to prepare candidates for Baptism and Confirmation, and for admission to communicant membership, and where authorized under IV, 3, to admit approved candidates to communicant membership.

(iv) To visit the congregation and especially the sick and the erring; to strive to bring sinners to repentance and forgiveness both by public and private ministry; to encourage the exercise by the laity of their various ministries in the Church; and to forward all efforts directed to the establishment of righteousness and the removal of wrong in the community.

(v) To use every opportunity to preach the Gospel and to

bring all men to the knowledge of Christ and into the fellowship of His Church.

(vi) To these ends, to be diligent in private study and prayer.

2. It is the duty of all presbyters, when summoned, to attend a meeting of the Diocesan Synod, and meetings which may be convened by the bishop from time to time to discuss with them matters concerning their ministry and the faith, order and discipline of the Church, or to advise them upon such topics.

3. Men will be ordained to the presbyterate who, believing themselves called of God to that office, are recognized by the Church as giving evidence of that call through their possession of gifts appropriate to their calling, and have been given due training for the work of the ministry. Men will be ordained only in view of a definite sphere of work awaiting them.

4. Subject to the provisions of this scheme and in accordance with such general rules as shall be laid down by the Assembly, each Diocesan Synod shall make rules for the selection of candidates, for their training and for the final approval and presenting for ordination of those who have received training.

Rules with regard to these matters made by Diocesan Synods shall be submitted to the Assembly to ensure that they are in accordance with the standards accepted by the Church.

Such rules shall provide that at one stage or another there shall be recommendation by, or consultation with, the congregation to which the candidate belongs, and also acceptance of the candidate both by the bishop and by representatives of the Diocesan Synod of the diocese in which he is to serve.

5. The Assembly will prescribe a form of ordination for presbyters, in which, while provision may be made for extempore prayer and variations in the details of the service, there shall be certain invariable parts; these to include at least (*a*) the presentation of the candidate by lay representatives of the congregation in which he is to minister; (*b*) the assent of the congregation assembled at the ordination service, signified by their answer to a question from the bishop; (*c*) a prayer of ordination asking that those about to be ordained may receive the gift of God's Holy Spirit for the office and work of presbyters; and (*d*) the laying on of hands by the bishops and by presbyters.

6. Every person about to be ordained or admitted to any new

office in the Church is required to affirm his sincere acceptance of the Christian Faith as revealed in Holy Scripture and witnessed to by the Nicene Creed in the sense expressed in section III of this scheme, and his acceptance of the doctrinal truths included in any other statement of doctrine which the Church may have drawn up.

Further, every person who is being ordained presbyter, and every presbyter who is to receive authority to exercise ministry in the Church, shall before receiving authorization from the bishop of the diocese, declare his acceptance of the constitution of the Church and of its rules of discipline.

Deacons and Probationers. (See footnote to XI, 2.) (*South India*, *49–50*)

7. So far as the diaconate is continued in the united Church in the form in which it is familiar in the Church of England, such provisions as the following would be required:

Persons who have been selected as candidates for the presbyterate shall, after undergoing the necessary theological course, receive ordination to the diaconate, and undertake the duties outlined below as part of their training for the presbyterate.

8. The functions of deacons shall include the following: assisting the presbyter in the administration of the Lord's Supper and in other services of the Church; administering of Baptism; ministering in the temporalities of the Church; giving succour to the poor, the needy, and the sick; instructing children and catechumens in the Faith; and generally giving assistance in pastoral and evangelistic work.

9. The Assembly will prescribe a form of ordination for deacons or probationers, in which, while provision may be made for extempore prayer and variations in the details of the service, there shall be certain invariable parts; these to include at least (*a*) a prayer of ordination asking that those about to be ordained may receive the gift of God's Holy Spirit for the office and work of deacon or probationer, and (*b*) the laying on of hands by the bishop.

10. *Deaconesses.* Women may be ordained or set apart to a special ministry after due examination and training.

(*Note.*—The whole question of the position of women in the ministry calls for further consideration, especially in view of the varying beliefs and practices in the uniting Churches.)

XI. *The Ministry of the Laity* (*South India, 50–1*)

1. To the whole Church of God and to every member of it belongs the duty and privilege of spreading the good news of the Kingdom of God, and the message of salvation through Jesus Christ. The united Church, therefore, welcomes, and will provide for the exercise by lay persons, both men and women, of such gifts of prophecy, evangelization, teaching, healing, and administration as God bestows upon them. In particular the laity are called upon to function as members of disciplinary courts and as representatives to Councils, Synods, and Assembly. Women shall be eligible for membership of the Council, Synod, and Assembly, and any other administrative or governing bodies.

2. *Elders.* Elders are lay persons set apart to assist the presbyter-in-charge in the spiritual and administrative work of the congregation and in its discipline. They shall be elected by the Congregational Council and shall be set apart at a service conducted by the bishop or the presbyter-in-charge.[1]

3. *Lay Preachers.* Lay persons of suitable gifts and Christian character who are communicant members of the Church may be authorized to preach in the public services of the Church.

[1] The Presbyterian Delegates at the World Conference on Faith and Order a Edinburgh contributed to its Report (page 25) a note on the constitution of their Churches, in which it is said that 'the functions of the diaconate in the New Testament have been performed not only by those named deacons, but also in some measure by the lay eldership, which in addition to a responsible share in the government and discipline of the Church in all its courts, assists in the dispensing of charity, the visitation of the people, and the distribution of the elements at Holy Communion'. In the Congregationalist and Baptist Churches the deacons have much the same functions (but their appointment is purely local, and does not carry with it a qualification to serve as deacon in any other place). The diaconate in the primitive Church was an office of help to the poor, the sick, and the ignorant, discharged as a spiritual ministry by men of good report, full of 'the Spirit and of wisdom', ordained for this duty. It was a substantive office, held for life, from which men were sometimes promoted to the episcopate, rarely, if ever, at first, to the presbyterate. In the Western Church, for at least four centuries before the Reformation, this office had been practically lost, and the diaconate had come to be a probationership for the presbyterate, as it is in the Church of England at the present day. In view of the power of the primitive diaconate and the strength given to Presbyterian, Congregational, and Baptist Churches by its modern revivals, negotiators of reunion authorized by the Churches might well consider framing proposals which would revive the former and preserve the values of the latter. They might also consider whether persons who had been selected with a view to ultimate ordination to the presbyterate might be ordained deacon in order to serve that office for a time as part of their training for the presbyterate.

4. *Church Stewards or Wardens.* These may be appointed as stewards of Church funds, and administrators or trustees of Church property.

XII. *The Congregational Council*

See VIII, 7, 8

1. The Congregational Council shall be composed of:

(*a*) The presbyter-in-charge and the assistant presbyters and deacons, if any;

(*b*) The elders;

(*c*) The Church stewards or wardens (if any);

(*d*) One member for every   communicants to be elected at an annual meeting of the communicant members of the congregation.

2. It shall summon an annual meeting of all the communicant members of the congregation for election of its representatives in the Council, and for report and discussion of the welfare of the congregation, and may summon additional meetings as occasion requires.

3. If the meeting of Church members shall so determine, it may itself function as the Congregational Council.

XIII. *Diocesan Synod*

See VIII, 6

1. Every Diocesan Synod shall consist of the bishop, or bishops, of the diocese, all the presbyters of the diocese holding the bishop's authorization and regularly engaged in the work of the Church, and lay representatives, whether elected, nominated, or *ex officio*, at least equal in number to the congregations of the diocese.

2. Every Diocesan Synod shall determine in its own constitution the number, necessary qualifications, and method of election or nomination of the lay representatives in it, provided that these qualifications shall include communicant membership of the Church.

3. Every Diocesan Synod has power to make rules and take executive action for the general management and good government of the Church in the diocese, subject to the provisions of the constitution. In particular, it has the right to an effective voice in the appointment of its bishop, and the right to make regulations with

regard to the acceptance of candidates for ordination to the ministry, and with regard to the discipline of the officers and members of the Church, subject to the provisions of the constitution on these matters.

It has the duty of fostering the development of the evangelistic, pastoral, educational, and other work of the Church in the diocese, and, where it does not administer such work through its own committees, it should arrange for the co-ordination of the work of missionary and other administrative bodies within the diocese.

4. The Diocesan Synod shall be the ultimate financial authority of the Church in its diocese in all matters concerning its internal administration, subject to the rights of the Congregational Councils.

5. The normal duty of a Diocesan Synod is to deal with matters which concern only its own diocese, leaving it to the Assembly to deal with matters of common interest to the whole Church, but every Diocesan Synod shall advise the Assembly on all matters that may be referred to it by the Assembly, and has power to bring business before the Assembly.

6. Subject to the provisions of the constitution, a Diocesan Synod has power to frame, emend, or alter its own constitution, provided that no diocesan constitution or any alteration therein shall be of force if the Assembly shall rule that such constitution or alteration therein is at variance with anything contained in this constitution.

7. Every Diocesan Synod shall appoint an Executive Committee and may appoint other committees, and may delegate to them such of its functions and duties as it may think fit.

XIV. *The General Assembly*

See VIII, 1–5

Composition and Membership

1. All diocesan bishops and the officers of the Assembly shall be *ex officio* members of the Assembly.

2. Every diocese shall be represented in the Assembly by not fewer than two presbyters and two laymen.

3. Every Diocesan Synod shall hold a fresh election of the ministerial and lay representatives of the diocese in the Assembly at such intervals as shall be determined by the Assembly.

4. Every Diocesan Synod shall make rules for the election of the

ministerial and lay representatives of the diocese in the Assembly provided that every such representative shall be a communicant member of the Church not at the time under Church discipline, and shall be a member of a congregation within the diocese which he represents at the time of his election.

5. Every Diocesan Synod shall make rules providing for alternative ministerial and lay representatives to take the place of any representative who during his term of office may cease to possess the qualifications necessary for a representative, or be unable to attend the meeting of the Assembly, or resign, or die.

Officers of the Assembly

6. The officers of the Assembly shall be a president, a general secretary, and a treasurer.

(*Note.*—The advisability of the election of a permanent chairman (speaker) for the Assembly should be considered.)

7. In view of the history of the Church of Christ in this country, it will be appropriate that the Archbishop of Canterbury shall be *ex officio* president of the General Assembly.

8. The general secretary and the treasurer shall be elected by ballot of the Assembly, and for such period as the Assembly shall determine.

Powers of the Assembly. (*See also VIII, 4*)

9. The Assembly is the supreme governing and legislative body of the united Church of England, and the final authority in all matters pertaining to that Church.

10. It has power to make rules and to take executive action as may be necessary from time to time for the general management and good government of the Church and of the property and affairs thereof.

11. The Assembly shall deal with matters of common interest to the whole Church of England, and with those which affect the relation of the dioceses to one another and to the rest of the universal Church, and shall leave the Diocesan Synods to deal with the internal affairs of each diocese.

12. The Assembly has in particular power to determine the number and boundaries of the dioceses and to form new dioceses in the Church. It has also power to determine whether anything in the constitution of any Diocesan Synod is at variance with anything

contained in this constitution, and, if it find such variance, to rule that such part of such Diocesan constitution is of no force.

13. The Assembly has power to add to or otherwise alter the constitution of the Church. Any change in the constitution must be passed by a two-thirds majority of those present and voting at two successive annual Assemblies, subject to the provisions of VIII, 4. Provision should probably be made for reference to the Diocesan Synods before an alteration is adopted in any fundamental parts of the constitution.

14. The Assembly has final authority in all questions of the interpretation of the constitution and other official documents of the Church.

15. The Assembly has power to frame its own rules of debate and of procedure, subject to the provisions of the constitution.

16. An ordinary meeting of the Assembly shall be held once in every year at such time and place as the Executive Committee may determine. Special meetings of the Assembly may also be summoned by the Executive Committee.

17. The following persons or bodies have the right to bring business before the Assembly:

any officer of the Assembly;
any diocesan bishop;
any committee or board of the Assembly;
any Diocesan Synod of the Church;
and any ten members of the Assembly.

18. The Assembly shall appoint an Executive Committee, and may also appoint other standing committees as it may deem necessary, and special committees or boards.

19. The quorum for meetings of the Assembly shall be   members of each House.

The Executive Committee

20. The Executive Committee of the Assembly shall consist of the officers of the Assembly and   members of each House elected by the House. The Executive Committee shall have power to co-opt in addition   members.

21. The Executive Committee shall act as the *ad interim* committee of the Assembly and shall perform the other functions allotted to it in this constitution.

XV. *Discipline* (*Sketch, 10, 11*)

1. Where any occasion for the exercise of discipline arises the first step should be taken within the local fellowship, wherein brother pleads or remonstrates with brother; where this does not lead to desired reform and reconciliation, reference should be made to the presbyter-in-charge.

Cases of such gravity that they cannot be dealt with by the presbyter-in-charge and the elders must be referred to the diocesan authority, in which case the presbyter and the elders would have authority to suspend from Communion pending the decision.

2. When discipline in relation to a minister is needed, in connexion with doctrine or diligence or character, the case should be at once referred to the diocesan authority.

3. The bishop is the officer of the Church for the actual administration of spiritual discipline. He should always, where circumstances permit, seek to exercise pastoral influence before resorting to disciplinary action, but he is bound to discharge this responsibility in accordance with the law of the Church, and may be required to act in consultation with assessors chosen as may be determined by the constitution of the Church.

4. In all disciplinary cases, appeals would be permitted subject to regulations made by the General Assembly, from a decision of the bishop and the assessors to a Diocesan Synod, and from this to the General Assembly. If they so desire, any Diocesan Synod and the General Assembly may appoint special bodies to act for them in this matter. (This secures that the action of a subordinate council or court must, if it is to stand, be grounded not on personal or passing feeling, but on what can be stated and maintained before a subsequent impartial court of review.)

(*Note.* Provision should be made for the trial of a bishop. (*South India*, 68.))

XVI. *Matters not included in the Constitution*

For the avoidance of misunderstanding, it is here stated that when nothing is said in the constitution about any doctrine which has been taught, or any practice which has customarily been followed in any of the Churches from which the united Church has been formed, it must not be inferred either that that doctrine or practice is forbidden in the Church to be believed or followed, or that it is considered to be of no importance. Specific mention of a doctrine or practice has in some cases been regarded as unnecessary, since it was a matter of well-known common agreement among the uniting Churches; in other cases there has been disagreement among those Churches on matters which were of importance, yet not such that an agreement on them was regarded as a necessary condition of union in one Church, and it was believed that a united Church would in due time be able to come to agreement on them. (*South India*, 33–4.)

XVII. *Unity in Ministry and Life within the Church*

Every presbyter of the united Church may minister and celebrate the Holy Communion in any church thereof, and is eligible to be appointed to any charge therein, subject only to the subsequent provisions of this section.

The uniting Churches might severally bind themselves by a common pledge as follows—to come into force so soon as the union is effected; in order especially to ease the way during the period while the union is being fully consummated:

'The united Church recognises that the act of union has initiated a process of growing together into one life, and of advance towards complete spiritual unity. One essential condition of the attainment of such complete unity is that all the members of the Church should be willing and able to receive Communion equally in all churches of the united Church, and it is the resolve of the Church to do all in its power to that end.

'But it is convinced that such unity can only be attained on the basis of freedom of opinion on debatable matters and respect for even large differences of opinion and practice, and it believes that this freedom and mutual respect can be safeguarded not so much by the framing of detailed regulations, as by assurances given and received in a spirit of confidence and love.

'The Church, therefore, pledges itself that it will not in any of its administrative acts, knowingly transgress the long established traditions of any of the Churches from which it has been formed. Neither forms of worship or ritual, nor a ministry to which they have not been accustomed, or to which they conscientiously object, will be imposed upon any congregation; and no arrangements with regard to these matters will knowingly be made, either generally or in particular cases, which would either offend the conscientious convictions of persons directly concerned, or which would hinder the development of complete unity within the Church, or imperil its progress towards union with other Churches.' (*South India*, 28–9.)

XVIII. *Relations with Other Churches*

1. The Church desires to preserve for all its constituent groups and members such communion and fellowship with other Churches as they have enjoyed before the act of union. The united Church will at an early date determine its relation to other Churches, and will continually work towards the goal of the full union in one body of all parts of the Church of Christ.

Any communicant member of any Church with which the united Church of England has relations of fellowship shall be at liberty to partake of the Holy Communion in any church of the united Church of England. Any minister of such a Church shall be free as a visitor to minister or celebrate the Holy Communion in any Church of the united Church of England, if he is invited to do so by competent authority.

The Church will wish to accept invitations to send delegates as visitors to the assemblies or other representative bodies of such Churches, and will seek, by interchange of visiting delegates or such other means as may be available, to promote and maintain brotherly relations with other Churches.

None of the presbyters or members of the Church as an individual shall, because of the union, forgo any rights with regard to intercommunion and intercelebration which they possessed before the union.

Every presbyter of the Church shall be at liberty to exercise any ministry in a Church outside England which he was entitled to exercise before the union, provided that the latter Church permit him to do so.

In all these, as in other matters, the Church desires to avoid, on the one hand, any encouragement of licence, and on the other hand any unchristian rigidity in its regulations or in their application; and in all its actions it will seek the preservation of unity within, the attainment of wider union, and the avoidance of controversy on particular cases. (*South India*, 29–31.)

XIX. *Provisions for Inauguration*

1. *Initial Provisions of Ministry*. The bishops of the Church of England are accepted as bishops of the united Church, provided

that they assent to the basis of union and accept the constitution of the Church. In addition presbyters shall be chosen by each of the other uniting Churches for consecration as bishops. The number of these will be determined hereafter, probably in proportion to the communicant membership of the Church concerned. (See IX, 1, note, and *Bell*, ii. 88 [Document 122].)

All the other ministers of the uniting Churches in the area of the union who have been ordained as ministers of the Word and of the Sacraments are acknowledged as such and have the status of presbyters in the united Church, provided that they assent to the basis of union and accept the constitution of the Church. Every such presbyter of the Church is at liberty to minister and celebrate the Holy Communion in any church of the united Church, subject to the pledge given in section XVII above.

Similarly, subject to the same provision of assent to the basis of union and acceptance of the constitution, deacons and probationers retain in the united Church the status they had in their own Churches before the union. (*South India*, 34–5.)

2. *Consecration of Bishops.* It would seem to us appropriate that at the consecration to the episcopate of presbyters of non-episcopal uniting Churches (which would be the inauguration of union), ministers in those Churches who have hitherto administered ordination should join with the three consecrating bishops in the laying on of hands. This would symbolize the full concurrence of the uniting Churches and the coming together in the ministry of the united Church of the spiritual blessings previously enjoyed by the ministries of the several Churches in separation. (*Report of the Committee on the Unity of the Church received by the Lambeth Conference, 1930*, p. 129. *Sketch*, 16.)

3. As part of the inauguration there should be a solemn act of mutual recognition and welcome and of common offering for service in the united Church, to be shared in by all its bishops, both those who were formerly Anglicans and those who were formerly Free Churchmen. This would no doubt form part of the inauguration service.

It is suggested that one of the latter should be co-celebrant in the service of Holy Communion within which the rite of inauguration will take place.

Similar services might then follow in the cathedral church of each diocese for the presbyters.

APPENDIX

BELOW are set out some further provisions for the process of appointing a bishop, which seemed too detailed for inclusion in the text at this stage. They are added here as evidence that the scheme outlined in this paper has been thought through and is capable of elaboration into an actual and practicable constitution.

(*a*) The Diocesan Synod may, if it so desires, remit the whole election to a board of the Assembly composed as in IX. 10 either initially or after a failure to make an election of not less than two persons under the provision of rule 10.

(*b*) If a Diocesan Synod fails to fulfil the requirements of rule 10 within nine months from the date on which the bishopric became vacant, a bishop shall be appointed for the diocese by the electoral board of the Assembly.

(*c*) Every election or appointment of a bishop shall be subject to confirmation by the Executive Committee of the Assembly. Such confirmation may not be withheld except when the Executive Committee shall judge either the election or the appointment to have been invalid, or the person elected or appointed to be unfit in respect of character, conduct or teaching, to exercise the functions of a bishop.

(*d*) As soon as the General Secretary of the Assembly has been informed of the election or appointment of a person to the office of a bishop, and also of that person's willingness to accept the office, he shall inform every member of the Executive Committee by letter of the election or appointment, and ask him if he is willing to confirm it. He shall also take steps to secure that public notice of the election or appointment is immediately given in all the churches of the diocese for which it has been made.

(*e*) If within twenty-one days of this publication by the General Secretary any objection to the confirmation of the election or appointment be made in writing to the General Secretary, he shall summon a meeting of the Executive Committee to consider such objections. Provided that if an objection appear to him prima facie to be trivial and insufficient, he shall refer the matter to the other officers of the Assembly, and if the officers shall agree, he shall report to the members of the Executive Committee that the objection has been set aside on the grounds stated above. The Assembly may issue regulations to guard against the abuse of the right of making objections.

(*f*) If no objection reach the General Secretary within twenty-one days of his publication of notice, or any objection that has been made has been set aside as provided in the last rule, and he has received from a majority of the members of the Executive Committee letters expressing their willingness to confirm the election or appointment, he shall report this to the President, and if the President so think fit, he and the General Secretary shall in the name of the Executive Committee execute a certificate of confirmation in such form as shall be laid down by the Assembly, but if the President for any reason consider it desirable, he shall bring the question of confirmation before a meeting of the Executive Committee.

(*g*) When the confirmation of the election or appointment of a bishop is considered by the Executive Committee of the Assembly in session under the provisions of rule (*e*) or rule (*f*) above, the confirmation must be by the vote of at least two-thirds of the members present.

176. Resolutions of the Convocations of Canterbury and York

JANUARY 1938

CANTERBURY CONVOCATION. BOTH HOUSES

THAT this House commends to the careful attention of the Church the three documents prepared by the Joint Conference of Representatives of the Church of England and of the Evangelical Free Churches entitled *Outline of a Reunion Scheme*, *The Practice of Inter-Communion*, and *1662 and To-day*.

YORK CONVOCATION

The *Upper House* agreed

That this House commends to the careful attention of all Church people the three documents issued by the joint conference of Anglicans and Free Churchmen entitled *1662 and To-day*, *The Practice of Inter-Communion and the Doctrine of the Church*, and *Outline of a Reunion Scheme for the Church of England and the Evangelical Free Churches of England*.

It expresses the hope that these documents, and especially the *Outline*, may be studied at once sympathetically and critically by groups of clergy and laity, and by any associations or fellowships in which members of the Church of England and of the Free Churches meet together.

The *Lower House* endorsed the hope expressed in the resolution.

177. Reply of the Free Church Federal Council to the Joint Conference of Representatives of the Church of England and the Free Churches regarding the three documents presented to it by the Conference in 1938

1. *1662 and To-day.*
2. *The Practice of Inter-Communion and the Doctrine of the Church.*
3. *Outline of a Reunion Scheme for the Church of England and the Evangelical Free Churches of England.*

SEPTEMBER 1941

I

1. THE Federal Council of the Evangelical Free Churches of England, acting in the name and on behalf of the Free Churches at its special meeting in January 1938, received the three documents: and in accordance with the desire expressed in the Preface to the *Outline*—'We invite for it wide attention because we believe that it is calculated both to dispel prejudices and to point the way to fuller agreement and so at last to the union for which we pray'—passed the following resolution:

'That the Federal Council of the Evangelical Free Churches commends to the careful consideration of its constituent Denominations the three documents prepared by the Joint Conference of representatives of the Church of England and of the Evangelical Free Churches, entitled, *Outline of a Reunion Scheme*, *1662 and To-day*, and *The Practice of Inter-Communion*, and asks the Denominations after giving due consideration to the documents to report to the Federal Council.' The letter addressed to the Denominations in transmitting the Documents suggested that they should be remitted to the consideration of a Committee of its own by each Denomination before bringing them before its full Annual Assembly, was careful to state that in remitting the documents 'neither the Federal Council nor its sub-Committee is committed in any way to the contents of the documents', and asked for a considered report on the documents in sufficient time to allow the Federal Council to collate the replies from the various Denominations, and to report thereon in good time for the consideration of the next Lambeth Conference in 1940.

2. The Denominations gave the documents the consideration asked for, and reported in due course, confining themselves mainly to the *Outline*: and at the Annual Meeting of the Council, held on 30th January 1940, a report, indicating the contents and tenor of these denominational Reports, was after some discussion 'referred to the Continuation Committee to appoint a Special Committee of twelve from members of the Federal Council, with power to co-opt, to consider a reply to the Lambeth Joint Conference'.

3. Meanwhile two events have changed the situation, not as regards the attitude of the Churches, as shown in their Reports, but only regarding the consequent action of the Federal Council in preparing this Joint Reply. Owing to the War the Lambeth Conference has been indefinitely postponed, so that there was less urgency in dealing with the matter; and prior attention was claimed for the Amalgamation of the Federal Council and the National Free Church Council, the proposals for which were considered at the same Annual Meeting. This union was consummated on 16th September. The General Purposes Committee of the new organization, the *Free Church Federal Council* which is taking over all the functions of the two organizations, instructed the Representatives of the Council on the Joint Conference at Lambeth to take the necessary steps for the preparation of the Reply which is now made in its name, and on behalf of the Free Churches represented. All that this Reply attempts is to gather up agreements and differences in the Reports of the Churches represented.

II

1. We have received the documents with deep interest in the matters with which they deal, with a due appreciation of their crucial importance, especially of the *Outline*, for the future of the Christian Church in England, and with sincere gratitude for the valuable service to the cause of reunion rendered by those who with so marked ability, skill, and care, appreciation of, and impartiality to differences of conviction have prepared and submitted them to the consideration of the Churches; and we hope and pray that such

consideration has 'dispelled prejudices, and pointed the way to fuller agreement, and so at last to the union for which we pray'.

2. We record with satisfaction that as the Replies from the Churches show there is in them a general recognition of the essential unity of the Church as the community of believers in Christ, and a desire that this inward unity should be expressed more clearly in closer fellowship and co-operation in witness, worship, and service. Thus the world might be led to recognize that its mission and message are from God who is reconciling the world unto Himself in Christ. The Replies deplore the loss in authority and efficiency which these visible divisions involve, and welcome the world-wide movements towards reunion due to the guidance of the Holy Spirit promised by the Lord. They thank God for the growth of a new spirit of understanding between the sundered Christian communions in England, and in particular for the abatement of that ill will and bitterness which for long made more acute the division between the Church of England and the Evangelical Free Churches, as is shown in the document *1662 and To-day.* In placing on record these comments and criticisms of the *Outline*, they desire to promote a still clearer mutual understanding regarding the differing convictions, and to maintain in all practicable ways the more friendly contacts and the closer co-operation achieved since the Lambeth Conference of 1920. They do not abandon the aspiration for the United Church of England.

3. We are glad that all our Churches have agreed to the continuance of these conversations in the hope and prayer that by the guidance of the Spirit of Truth the dividing differences may be harmonized, or at least recognized as not essential enough to justify permanently the continuance of divisions. All of us are agreed that, as a means of promoting the desire for union in the membership as well as among the leaders, and as in itself desirable, every effort should be made to promote more intimate fellowship in faith and worship, and more constant co-operation in the tasks to which the world's need and the Spirit's call summon the Churches. Most widely spread is the desire, and most strongly held the conviction, that the unity in Christ already existing and the growing aspiration to show that unity in reunion will find its most satisfying token and most convincing proof in mutual inter-communion, a common table of the Lord, who died for men, and by His Spirit lives in all believers. The objections to Inter-Communion, presented in the

document on the subject, do not seem to us an adequate justification for refusal.

4. Union is not equally desired by all the members of our Churches. There are still many in them in whose judgement the divisions are not to be deplored, as they are rooted in conscientious convictions, and serve to exhibit to the world the manifoldness of the truth and grace of Christ, and the diversity of the operations of the Spirit of God. In their view, reunion is not *necessary* for the effective discharge of the functions of the Church; it is not *desirable* as imposing an outward uniformity which is not essential to exhibit the inward unity in the one Spirit which all believers now already experience; and it is not *practicable* as involving the loss of different traditions and customs that are not only still valued, but still have value. They support their contention by appeal to these documents, and the conversations which have led up to them, as disclosing differences so essential that any reunion would involve illegitimate compromise, a sacrifice of convictions, and would rest on too precarious a basis for the reality of unity. They believe that the cause of unity is not promoted so much by framing such schemes as by such close fellowship and co-operation as the differences will allow. They are not animated by any hostility to the Church of England; but do not feel any urgent call for present reunion.

5. We believe, however, that an increasing number in all our Churches do desire a union which will not enforce any uniformity, but will welcome variety-in-unity, will preserve all proved values, and will enhance the authority and the efficacy of the Church in preaching the Gospel and building up its members in their faith in Christ, and in the service of the Kingdom of God. But even among those who cherish this desire there are some who hold that there remain differences between the Church of England and the Evangelical Free Churches that have not yet been adequately reconciled, and that there is need for still further exploration of the ground before union can become a practicable proposal. Others hold that as the Free Churches are so much nearer to one another in doctrine and practice than to the Church of England, priority should be given to any proposals for reunion among them, and that the Federal Council should give its immediate attention to these.

III

The document, the *Outline*, does not profess to be an altogether fresh attempt to offer a solution of the problem of the structure of the United Church: as far as possible it brings together conclusions or proposals already reached in discussions of the subject here and elsewhere, indicating the sources on which it has drawn. Briefly to sketch its historical setting seems expedient.

1. The Joint Conferences began as a response of the Free Churches to an invitation of the Church of England to confer on 'An Appeal to all Christian People from the Bishops assembled in the Lambeth Conference of 1920'. 'We believe', said the Bishops in this Appeal, 'that the visible unity of the Church will be found to involve the wholehearted acceptance of:

'The Holy Scriptures as the record of God's revelation of Himself to man, and as being the rule and ultimate standard of faith: and the Creed commonly called Nicene as the sufficient statement of the Christian faith, and either it or the Apostles' Creed as the Baptismal confession of belief.

'The divinely instituted sacraments of Baptism and the Holy Communion, as expressing for all the corporate life of the whole fellowship in and with Christ.

'A ministry acknowledged by every part of the Church as possessing not only the inward call of the Spirit, but also the commission of Christ and the authority of the whole body.'

Regarding the last requirement, the bishops asked, 'May we not reasonably claim that the Episcopate is the one means of providing such a ministry?' They did not call in question 'the spiritual reality of non-episcopal ministries', but acknowledged that 'they have been manifestly blessed and owned by the Holy Spirit as effective means of grace' (Bell's *Documents on Christian Unity*, pp. 3–4 [Document 1]). While expressing their willingness to accept from the authorities of other communions a form of commission or recognition they stated their hope that ministers who had not received it 'would accept a commission through episcopal ordination' (p. 5). From the outset of the Conversations it was recognized that the insurmountable obstacle was not the acceptance of the episcopate as one element in the organization, a matter on which our Churches have not committed themselves, but have been willing to confer, but the requirement of episcopal ordination for non-episcopally ordained ministers.

2. We rejoice in the steps since taken in these Conversations to modify this requirement which for most of our ministers was one that their sense of vocation from Christ and recognition by the

Church as ministers of Christ's Church made it impossible for them to accept. In 1923 the representatives of the Church of England presented a Memorandum to the Joint Conference which opened a door of hope. The crucial passage may be quoted: 'It seems to us to be in accordance with the Lambeth Appeal to say, as we are prepared to say, that the ministries which we have in view in this memorandum [i.e. of the Free Churches represented], ministries which imply a sincere intention to preach Christ's Word and administer the Sacraments as Christ has ordained, and to which authority so to do has been solemnly given by the Church concerned, are real ministries of Christ's Word and Sacraments in the Universal Church.' (Op. cit., p. 159.) But this door was at once closed again, when these ministries, declared to be real, were regarded as so irregular that some form of episcopal ordination was needed to regularize them. Ordination *sub conditione* was proposed by the Anglican representatives, but declined as unacceptable by the Free Churchmen: as the Anglicans did not feel warranted in going any farther the Conversations were in 1925 brought to a *pause* (a word carefully chosen to indicate that they were not broken off, but held over until the *impasse* thus reached might be removed).

3. It was hoped that the door might again be opened at the *Lambeth Conference* of 1930; but that Conference, for reasons which need not now detain us, proved a disappointment. In the 44th Resolution satisfaction and gratitude are expressed at 'the great measure of agreement on matters of faith reached at the Conferences held from 1921 to 1925,' and the hope is also expressed that these Conferences may be resumed at an early date 'with a view to ascertaining whether the proposed scheme of Union prepared for the Churches in South India, or other proposals which have been put forward, suggest lines on which further advance towards agreement on questions of order can be made' (*Lambeth Conference* 1930, p. 53). The Conferences were resumed, and the three documents are an outcome of the conversations since held. As will be seen when we present the comments and criticisms of the Churches on the *Outline*, effect has been given to the recommendation that the South India proposals should be considered. Before we pass to that discussion, having sketched the historical background of the renewed conversations, it seems desirable that we should constructively describe our standpoint in an exposition of the title, 'Free Evangelical Churches'.

IV

1. The Appeal of 1920 is addressed to 'All Christian People', and the use of the term *Churches* is avoided, wittingly or unwittingly, and the term 'Christian Communions' (op. cit., p. 3) is used. The 'membership in the universal Church of Christ which is His body' is limited to 'those who believe in our Lord Jesus Christ and have been baptized into the name of the Holy Trinity' (op. cit., p. 1). On each of these points a brief comment seems necessary. (i) In the Reply of the Free Churches to the Appeal it was felt necessary to state how we regard our communions, and it seems to us still necessary to quote the words: 'We are Churches claiming to be in our corporate capacity parts of the one Holy Catholic Church of Jesus Christ. We claim this and cannot do less than claim it, because of our relation with Christ, who is the Head of His body, and who has recognized us and used us, not merely individually, but corporately for the ends of His Church' (p. 127). In this there is no boastful assertion of our merits, but humble gratitude for His grace to us and by us. We could not have any profitable consideration of differences with any who cannot so regard us. (ii) We gratefully recognize that in the *Report* accepted by the Joint Conference in May 1922, the definition of the membership of the one Church, the body of Christ has been so modified as to become fully inclusive of all believers, whether baptized or not, 'This one Church consists of all those who have been, or are being redeemed by and in Christ, whether in this world or in the world beyond our sight, but it has its expression in the world in a visible form. Yet the Church as invisible and visible is, by virtue of its one life in Christ, one' (p. 147). This definition is accepted in briefer form in the *Outline*, where the description of the visible Church on earth seems to be as inclusive. It 'was constituted by Christ as a fellowship of men and women united in Him with one another to be His witnesses and the servants of His Kingdom'. To some of us it appears a *non sequitur* when the *Outline* goes on to state that 'those only shall be members of the united Church of England who have by Baptism been admitted to Christ's Church visible on earth' (p. 10). Others of us would hold that it is quite proper for the Church to lay down rules for the admission of members without denying that in the eyes of God other people who do not conform to these rules may be within the Body of Christ. This issue is raised by the *Congregational Union Assembly* who desire that a place should

be found in the visible Churches for those 'who conscientiously refrain from the use of sacraments', e.g., the Society of Friends and the Salvation Army, and individual members of Churches where the use of the sacraments is the commonly acknowledged practice. That this difficulty is felt more widely than in one denomination is shown in the fact that it confronted the *Edinburgh Conference on Faith and Order* as well. (See *Report*, p. 20.) There are many in all the Free Churches who share this desire, but who would deeply regret any even apparent depreciation of the value of the sacraments. We hold that the issue cannot be dismissed without further consideration, and join in the trust expressed in Edinburgh that 'even here the Holy Spirit will show us His will'. The *Baptist Union Council* cannot accept the extension of the rite of Baptism to infants as 'these necessarily lack the cardinal requirements of repentance and faith'. While other churches cannot consent to abandon their practice, many of us hope that it will be found possible to maintain both forms in a united Church.

(iii) Although in the Appeal the nature of the Church is not explicitly discussed, yet all subsequent discussions have shown how crucial for all other matters is the conception held, and we, therefore, briefly state how the Church is conceived among us. Whether it be a merit or not, the Free Churches can claim to be as *comprehensive* in doctrine and practice as is the Church of England, and yet amid the diversity two tendencies may be discerned, each of which has points of contact with the New Testament. Jesus came as Messiah to the Jewish nation, and called it to repentance and faith that it might avert its doom and fulfil its destiny; but the response came from individuals, and He affirmed the infinite value of each man to the Father of all, and yet He at once formed the company of disciples to continue His Mission. In the Apostolic Church stress was laid on the personal relation of each believer to Christ as Saviour and Lord, and also on the *Koinonia*, the common privileges and obligations. The word Church is used, not in two senses, but in two applications, to the *whole Christian community*, and to *the local congregation*, but the local congregations are called *churches*, not in their distinctness and separation, but as the local presence and activity of the universal Church, which is not a whole as a sum of parts, but a whole in every part. Even as a living organism is affected by its environment, so has the thought and life of the Church been affected by the varied influences of the world around it. And each of the tendencies, the one laying the main stress on the individual believer and the other on the community of believers, have been affected by either the individualism, dominant in politics and economics during the last century, or by what we may call the *communalism* of the present time, which was already exerting an influence in the latter half of last century. In the one tendency the emphasis falls on the church, local or denominational, as in reponse to God's Call the voluntary association of believers for worship, witness and service resulting from their common convictions in religion and morals; here individual liberty and responsibility are claimed as primary conditions of the organization. In the other tendency the emphasis falls on membership in the community, not only local or denominational, but universal, on the unity and continuity of the one Church of God, which comes to view, partially and imperfectly, in the Church on earth; here the need of solidarity and authority is recognized. The tendencies are not merely antithetical; but there is need, desire, and effort for their synthesis. Whatever is of permanent value must be preserved for the progress of the Church to fullness and wholeness of life. While it is through the Church that Christ is presented to the individual as Saviour and Lord, yet faith must respond to grace before there is full fellowship in His body. Individualism is still a potent, if not dominant, influence in our Churches, but the movement generally is towards *communalism*. Whatever other differences there may be, we all hold with intense conviction the conception of the Church, as *one* in the *one* God and Father of all, the *one* Lord and Saviour of all, the *one* Spirit seeking and striving in all, as *holy*, because as consecrated to God by His call the children of God are called to be perfect, even as He the Father in heaven is, *catholic*, because destined for all mankind, and *apostolic*, as proclaiming the Apostolic Witness to Jesus as Christ and Lord, and continuing the Apostolic Mission to all mankind.[1]

2. As the term 'free' indicates, this communalism does not involve any abandonment of the freedom of the Christian man, as under law to Christ alone, still less of the freedom of the Christian Church, under His Lordship. (i) The primary reference in the use of the word 'free' is to the freedom of the Church from any control by the State, except in so far as it is a social institution the membership

[1] We appreciate the value of the discussion on *the Doctrine of the Church in relation to the Practice of Intercommunion* in one of the documents, but reserve any comment upon it, as it has not in our Churches received the same consideration as the *Outline*.

of which is subject to the common laws for the protection of persons and property and the promotion of the common good. In the Joint Reply of the Free Churches to the Appeal of the 1920 *Lambeth Conference* made in May 1921, it is clearly stated 'that Free Churchmen cannot be asked to consent that the civil power—which within its own sphere is called to be the Servant of God—has any authority over the spiritual affairs of the Church: or, further, to accept any position which would involve injustice or violate the rights of conscience' (p. 137). *A Short Memorandum on the Problems connected with the Union between Church and State* adopted by the Joint Conference in June 1925 claimed 'complete autonomy of the Church in the discharge of all its spiritual functions', and freedom 'to bring the highest and utmost possible influence to the service of the State in promoting the well-being of the people, and in bearing its witness to the authority of Christian principles in the affairs of the State'. On the Anglican side it was stated that 'if the union embraced a large majority of English Christians then the Church of England might be unwilling to press the continuance of the Establishment, if this proved to be a fatal obstacle to union', but the hope was expressed that 'in view of the prospect of a really national church' the 'relation to the State might assume a form which might be acceptable to the Free Churches' (Bell's *Documents on Christian Unity, Second Series* (pp. 95–7)). Since that Memorandum was prepared, the attitude of many in the Church of England has been modified in the direction of claiming more fully the autonomy of the Church. In the *Outline* there is a brief reference to the *Relation to the Secular Authority* (p. 18). We accept as satisfactory the assertion of the autonomy of the Church, that 'in respect to faith, worship, morals, discipline and government it must be free from the control of or reversal of any of its spiritual actions or decisions by any secular authority'. We should lay stress on freedom of preaching, the Church's witness to the Gospel. 'We agree that such freedom in spiritual matters from the control of the State does not necessarily exclude some form of State recognition of the Church as the expression for the nation of its religious allegiance,' e.g. religious instruction in the schools, the appointment of chaplains in the navy, army, and air force, and in public institutions, such as hospitals, the consecration of public functions by acts of worship in acknowledgement of the sole ultimate sovereignty of God over nations as well as individuals. We should welcome a thorough examination of the forms in which such State recognition of the Church may be accepted without impairing in any way the independence of the Church in the discharge of its proper functions. We recognize that the increasing complexity of the structure of modern society involves an expansion of the functions of the State to preserve and promote culture and morals; and that, in order to protect these higher values against secularization, a closer co-operation of the activities of the Church and of the State in these spheres is necessary, and should be encouraged, so long as the distinction between these two organs of the thought and life of the nation is preserved.[1]

(ii) The freedom of the Church, as we understand it, involves more than independence of the control of the State. The Church may be within itself 'entangled in a yoke of bondage' to its own traditions and customs, its past history, and its present constitution. 'We are Free Churches', says the Report of 1922 already quoted, 'claiming liberty in all spiritual affairs that we may be free to listen to and obey Him whom we all acknowledge as our only Head'. We do not hold a *static* view of the history of the Church, but a *dynamic*: in the *Reformation* and the Evangelical Revival we recognize a progressive movement in the Church of Christ. 'Jesus Christ is the same yesterday, to-day, yea, and for ever'; but the conditions and needs of to-day are not the same as those of yesterday, and the call of Christ comes to the Church to adapt its methods to those changes. As our age is so different from the Apostolic and the centuries that followed, when Greek thought ruled the minds, and Roman law the lives of men, we do not believe that an ecclesiastical organization adapted to, because largely adopted from, the existing environment can be regarded as valid, regular, or authoritative for all later centuries. We gratefully recognize the Providence of God and the guidance of His Spirit in the historical continuity of the Church in the Churches, overruling the sins and the crimes of men: yet we cannot accept the theory of Apostolic Succession, interpreted as 'the succession of bishops in the principal sees of Christendom handing down and preserving the Apostles' doctrine, and regarded, as in certain Churches it is regarded, as constituting the true and only guarantee of sacramental grace and right doctrine'. It is in our judgement unsupported by scholarship in the Anglican Church as well as in other Churches. It is not in accord with the spirit of

[1] The document *1662 and To-day* offers evidence regarding the division and antagonism in the life of the nation, which the dominance of a privileged Church as established by the State involved, and the improvement of the relations of that Church to the other Churches as the dominance decreases.

liberty in Christ, not bondage to the letter, which pervades the New Testament, as we read it. It is a reversion from the new covenant of grace, sealed by the blood of Christ, as we interpret it, to the old covenant of law: for God, revealed as Father in Christ, fulfils His purpose by the continuous inward guidance of the Spirit, 'putting His law in the inward parts, and writing it on the hearts', and not by an unchangeable outward law. This is not the place to offer an adequate demonstration of our convictions that the fetters of the dead past should not be imposed on the living Church. Should the Free Churches accept an episcopate, it would not be on account of this theory, but on the grounds stated in mutual agreement in the Report as accepted by the Conference in May 1922.

'In view of the fact that the Episcopate was from early times and for many centuries accepted, and by the greater part of Christendom is still accepted as the means whereby this authority of the whole body is given, we agree that it ought to be accepted as such for the United Church of the future. Similarly, in view of the place which the Council of Presbyters and the Congregation of the faithful had in the constitution of the early Church, and the preservation of these elements of presbyteral and congregational order in large sections of Christendom, we agree that they should be maintained with a representative and constitutional Episcopate as permanent elements in the order and life of the United Church. The Acceptance of Episcopal Ordination for the future would not imply the acceptance of any particular theory as to its origin or character, or the disowning of past ministries of Word and Sacrament otherwise received, which have, together with those received by Episcopal Ordination, been used and blessed by the Spirit of God.' (Op. cit., pp. 149–50.)

(iii) It is not only in relation to the Episcopate that we must maintain the principle of liberty, which we believe is necessary for the fullest and best development of Christian personality and community. The cause of most divisions in the past has been due to the insistence on uniformity, which we believe is not necessary for unity, and hinders such variety, as the differences of conviction, sentiment, and character in men, all one in their fellowship in Christ, demand and justify. We recall with sincere appreciation the vision of the Church in the Lambeth Appeal: 'Within this unity Christian Communions now separated from one another would retain much that has long been distinctive in their methods of worship and service.

It is through a rich diversity of life and devotion that the unity of the whole fellowship will be fulfilled' (op. cit., p. 3). The *Outline*, we are glad to find, consistently carries out this principle. Any reservations in this respect that we have to report will more fitly appear in other places. In the three respects we have discussed we are resolved to continue in the Apostolic Succession. 'With freedom did Christ set us free: stand fast therefore and be not entangled again in a yoke of bondage' (Gal. v. 1). Lest this assertion, however, should be misunderstood we add that we claim this freedom from human control only that we individually and corporately should be the bondslaves of Christ, whose we are, and whom we serve, and whose law we seek to obey in bearing one another's burdens. Love for our brethren in Christ is the limit and the motive of our liberty in the community of the Spirit, the body of Christ. Such freedom in Christ under grace we desire that all our fellow Christians should share.

3. We are Churches: we are Free; and we are *Evangelical*. 'We use the word in no party sense. But there is, we believe, a definite New Testament Gospel, and this, which carries with it its conception of the Church—we cannot and we dare not compromise for the sake even of union itself. This indeed is our supreme, and in a sense sole principle for it contains the others: the Church is an outcome of the Gospel—hence the importance which has always been attached by evangelical churches to the preaching of the Word—and the Church thus made by the Gospel must be free' (Op. cit., pp. 127–8. *Report on the Free Churches and the Lambeth Appeal*, May 1922). We are united in sharing the desire of the Methodist Conference that more emphasis should be laid on the Gospel and the duty of evangelization.

We, therefore, welcome the statement in the *Outline* [III. 2] regarding the Apostles' and the Creed commonly called the Nicene that 'this acceptance of the Creeds does not imply that they are regarded as a complete expression of the Christian Faith', since we desire that the Gospel in all its fullness should still be proclaimed in the Free Churches. We do not suggest the addition of any of the Protestant Confessions which reflect the divisions within Protestantism, but we wish as Protestants to maintain our inheritance from the Reformation, and our fellowship with other Protestant Churches.

In thus describing ourselves as *Evangelical Free Churches*, we have tried to offer a constructive contribution to mutual understanding:

we have not only provided the background necessary to appreciate some of the comments and criticisms by the Churches of the *Outline*, but also conveyed some of the contents of the Reports, even where no explicit reference is given: we now pass to deal with the remaining as yet unrecorded contents.

V

1. In regard to the acceptance of the ancient creeds as defining the *Faith of the Church* [III. 2], we should all be agreed that we should not place them in juxtaposition with the Scriptures, but insist on their subordinate and secondary character, and should, as the *Congregational Union Assembly* has expressly done in its Report, insist on the reservations on their acceptance mentioned in the *Outline*. While the other Churches have their authoritative standards and Congregationalists and Baptists alone maintain the objection to any subscription to a creed, although they are ready, when the occasion arises, to make their own Declaration of Faith, there is such liberty of interpretation conceded, that different as the standards, taken in the letter, may appear, there is among our Churches no such divergence of faith as would prevent our closer fellowship. The differences, to use a geometrical analogy, are not perpendicular as dividing one Church from another, but horizontal as differentiating sections in each Church. It may be added as a matter of importance as well as of interest for members of the Church of England that when the Federal Council of the Evangelical Free Churches was formed on March 26, 1917, a *Declaratory Statement of Common Faith and Practice* was adopted as 'desirable both as a basis of fellowship and co-operation, and as a means of making known to others the Truth for which these Churches stand'. When the Federal Council was united with the National Free Church Council on January 30, 1940, this Declaratory Statement was again accepted. Baptists and Congregationalists have found no inconsistency with their principles in sharing in that acceptance.

2. The *Baptist Union Council* and the *Congregational Union Assembly* take serious exception to the restriction [IV. 2] to the ordained ministry of the administration of the Sacrament of the Lord's Supper. While recognizing that such administration should be the normal practice, they insist that, as a recognition of the priesthood of all believers, a responsible lay person (man or woman) when there is good reason can be authorized by the Church (i.e. the local congregation) to administer the ordinance of the Lord's Supper.

In the *Methodist Church* the general usage is that the sacrament of the Supper is to be administered by fully acclaimed ministers, but dispensations are granted annually by the Conference where it can be shown that through lack of ministers any church is deprived of a reasonably frequent and regular administration. In the *Presbyterian Church of England* lay administration is permitted only to ordained elders, duly authorized by the presbytery, and only in cases where no ordained minister is available.

The *Lambeth Appeal* did not insist on *Confirmation*, and the *Outline* [IV. 3] recognizes alternative services of admission. All of us would agree that any such service should be of so solemn a character as to impress the candidate being admitted with the serious responsibility being assumed as well as the gracious privilege being accepted. Some of us would be prepared to adopt the rite of Confirmation, administered by the pastor as in more intimate relations with the candidate for admission and as in accord with the practice of the Protestant Churches on the Continent. In accordance with the autonomy of the Congregational Church the rite might be adopted in any one of them without let or hindrance, but the *Congregational Union Assembly* expresses its preference for the giving of the right hand of fellowship over the laying on of hands as the symbol of admission to communicant membership. In the *Baptist Churches* baptism is not in itself the rite of admission, but reception into the Church is by the giving of the right hand of fellowship at a Communion Service. As regards the doctrine of the Sacraments there is almost as great diversity among us as prevails in the Church of England, but it is probable that few of our ministers at least now adhere to the view that the rite means commemoration only, but most regard the symbol as so effective that in the observance of the rite in obedience to Christ's command and dependence on His promise, His grace is conveyed and sealed to faith as well as expressed: there is the Real Presence, and the real Communion with Him. In the Nonconformist Churches the influence of Calvin was more dominant than that of Zwingli in regard to sacramental doctrine, and that influence still largely remains.

3. In the historical sketch at the beginning of this statement, the steps have already been indicated that have led to the modification of the demand for episcopal ordination of non-episcopally ordained ministers [V. 4, 5], and these must be kept in view in considering the statement on the Ministry.

4. We all share with the *Methodist Conference* the welcome given to the freedom in worship contemplated [VI], and desire that such freedom should not be conceded only at the outset, but should remain a guiding principle in any later developments. The *Congregational Union Assembly* claims this freedom for each congregation, insists that in regard to any common prayer the pledge of respect of conscience shall be preserved, and that this principle shall be maintained in any ordering of the worship by a bishop, as is provided for on p. 22 of the *Outline*.

5. The Congregational Union Assembly makes three reservations as regards *Organization* [VIII]. (i) The United Church should not be committed to any of the arrangements existing in the Church of England. (ii) [VIII. 4] Some provision should be made for the adjustment of differences between bishops, clergy, and laity, when voting in separate houses. (iii) [VIII. 7] Having experienced the benefit to the life and work of the Church of the Church-meeting, open to all communicant members, and being convinced that, as in the use of the word *church* in the New Testament, the local church does represent locally the one Church, they urge that the Church-meeting not only may, but ought to, be the proposed Congregational Council.

In the judgement of the *Methodist Conference* the Scheme 'does not sufficiently allow for the free exercise of those differing forms of government and organization which have been granted to the various churches in their separated existence', and suggests that 'such of the uniting communions might at first be recognized as semi-autonomous within the united Church, each with its own discipline and form of government, but each submitting to and honouring the authority of the whole body (expressed in some way yet to be determined) as controlling the aims and developing life of every part'. We believe that this statement would find general support in all the Free Churches.

6. There is still among many Churches a strong aversion to episcopacy for which the history of the past offers some justification; and even if on other grounds an episcopate should be agreed to as one organ of the United Church the replies generally are very definite in rejecting the doctrine of Apostolic Succession as defined above. The *Methodist Conference* insists that there must not be any such application of the doctrine in practice as would exclude communion with non-episcopal churches, nor must episcopacy be

regarded as so essential to the existence of the Church that it would not be free to follow the guidance of the Spirit to a change of polity. The *Baptist Union Council* whilst prepared for a modification of polity does not consider that for the reasons given in the *Outline* [V and IX] 'episcopal ordination would provide a sure foundation for organic union: nor can they regard the Outline of a Reunion Scheme as affording a basis for organic reunion'. The *Congregational Union Assembly*, without committing the churches to the acceptance of episcopacy, is prepared to explore the possibilities of the combination of a constitutional and representative episcopate with the presbyteral and congregational order, as indicated in the *Outline*. The *Congregational Union Assembly* desires that the acceptance of candidates for the ministry should be guarded against the arbitrary action of any bishop by some right of appeal, and recommends the admission of women to the ministry on the same terms of equality as men, a practice already adopted in several of our Churches.

7. All our Churches are agreed on the great value of the lay ministry. In the witness and the worship of the Church, lay preaching has been found an indispensable agency; in the service and administration the Methodist stewards, the Presbyterian elders, and the Baptist and Congregational deacons have worthily discharged their functions; and some think that such a ministry might be provided for by modifying the order of Anglican deacons.

8. In the *General Assembly* [XIV] the *Congregational Union Assembly* desires the maintenance of such a proportion of bishops, presbyters, and laity as shall prevent the dominance of one section over the others, and deprecates any proposals as to the presidency as premature.

9. All our Churches welcome the principle of the *Unity of Ministry and Life* [XVII] within the Church and desire that by anticipation it should be made manifest even now in the practice of full intercommunion.

10. [XIX] In view of their deeply rooted objection to re-ordination as in their judgement a repudiation of their former ministry, all the Churches also welcome in the Provisions for Inauguration the recognition of the equal status of the ministers of the uniting Churches, and, as in their history they have stood for the rights of conscience, they cordially accept the pledge that the United

Church will not 'in any of its administrative acts knowingly transgress the long established traditions of any of the Churches from which it has been formed' (*Outline*, p. 33), as in appointing any minister to a church that takes any exception to him.

11. [XVIII] We all should deplore as a serious calamity if the union of our Churches in England were to involve separation from the Churches of kindred faith and order, with whom they have long enjoyed close communion and co-operation; as we desire, hope, and pray that if such a union were effected here, it would be an example and an encouragement of world-wide movement to make visibly manifest to the world the invisible unity of the one Church, the body of the one Saviour and Lord, the community of the one Spirit, the habitation of the one God and Father of all.

We have so fully and frankly expressed our own judgement, and reproduced the comments and criticisms of the governing bodies of our Churches in no factious spirit to put obstacles in the way of the consideration of reunion. While we have the authority of the Free Churches to offer this Joint Statement, it must be understood that none of them is necessarily committed to everything in this document, but only by their own official Replies. We desire in closing to express our cordial appreciation of the consideration and courtesy that our representatives on these Joint Conferences have received from the representatives of the Church of England, our sincere gratitude for the steadily growing friendliness of the Church of England to the Free Churches shown in many practical acts of helpfulness, and our steadfast resolve to pursue this God-given quest of the method by which all the spiritual treasures God has graciously bestowed on the Churches separately may be brought into one treasure-house of the United Church of England for the progress of the Gospel, the growing good of men, and the abiding glory of God. It is the Vision of what such a United Church of England might, with the blessing of God, be as the organ of His Kingdom, not only to this nation, but also through the world-wide extension of its influence, to all nations, which we rejoice to share with the Church of England, that alone can sustain our common aspirations and joint endeavours amid difficulties and disappointments, and can inspire our consecration to and perseverance in this task in which we pray that we may prove 'steadfast, immovable, always abounding in the work of the Lord, forasmuch as *we* know that our labour is not vain in the Lord'.

THE MORAVIAN CHURCH

178. Resolution of the British Provincial Synod of the Moravian Church (Unitas Fratrum), held at Fulneck, April 18–21, 1944

Church Union

THAT this Synod of the Moravian Church in Great Britain and Ireland, desiring both to foster the various movements by which the Christian Churches are endeavouring through joint action to present and apply the Gospel to the needs of the present day, and also to express its conviction of what constitutes a true basis for Christian unity, approve the following statement:

(*a*) The Moravian Church in Great Britain and Ireland is a part of an international Church which, largely through the mission work to which it was led, now includes among its members men and women in many parts of the world. It was the intention of Count Zinzendorf, who, at the beginning of the eighteenth century, was instrumental in restoring the old Brethren's Church of Bohemia, that it should be a Society in which Christians of all Churches and creeds could worship together as Brethren while remaining loyal to the traditions and continuing to participate in the communicant fellowship of their own Churches. By its history the Moravian Church has demonstrated its belief in the oneness of all believers, and to-day its conviction is no less intense. It therefore whole-heartedly welcomes every attempt to break down the barriers that separate the various Churches of Christendom, and in particular rejoices in every experience in which a unity of heart and spirit is manifested through their joint action.

(*b*) It is this experience of unity of heart and spirit that we would accept as a direction of the Holy Spirit to the different Churches to progress beyond co-operation towards mutual recognition. This would naturally include the practice of inter-communion. Nothing would be gained, and much would be lost, if the Christian experience were to be regimented or the riches of Christ spoiled of their variety. Rather should the Churches reach out towards a new appreciation of the manifold working of the spirit of Christ, who uses varying ways to bring Salvation to all men and inspire them to do God's will, even as peoples and individuals vary in type and differ in outward circumstances and historical background. When the individual members of our Churches are so filled with the spirit of Christ that they find it easy to recognize its workings outside themselves, and when they can join in mutual recognition, appreciation, and support, then true Christian unity will have been achieved.

(*c*) It may be taken for granted that with the disappearance of prejudices and misunderstandings there will be changes in the organization of the Christian Church, in order that it may manifest its unity to the world. But as our hearts and minds are enlarged in the freedom of Christ by mutual recognition and by discussion and co-operation, so, we believe, the spirit of Christ will shape its own body as it needs to express itself in its fuller freedom. Differences of practice and emphasis will then enrich, and not embarrass, our experience of Christ and our witness for His Gospel.

(*d*) In conclusion, the Moravian Church would pray and work for God's blessing on all efforts made for the union of Christendom. It would join in the declaration that Christ is the one hope of unity for the world in the face of the distraction and dissensions of this present time; and in the prayer 'that men may turn to Jesus Christ our Lord . . . and that the world may at last find peace and unity in Him'.

Note. As requested by Resolution 39 of the Lambeth Conference of 1930, the Archbishop of Canterbury, Dr. Lang, appointed a committee (under the chairmanship of the Bishop of Winchester, Dr. Garbett) to confer with representatives of the *Unitas Fratrum* on relationships with the Church of England. The result of the Conversations, as reported by the Archbishop of Canterbury to the Consultative Body in 1937, was a mutual agreement to take no further action at present.

VIII. THE CHURCH OF SCOTLAND

[In 1932 the Archbishop of Canterbury, Dr. Lang, presented the Lambeth Appeal, for the second time, to the General Assembly of the Church of Scotland, and as a result Conferences took place between representatives appointed by the Archbishop and the General Assembly respectively. Associated with them were representatives from the Episcopal Church in Scotland and the Presbyterian Church of England. In May 1933 the Scottish delegates made a provisional and prefatory report to the General Assembly. The Joint Report was presented in February 1934. The Deliverance of the General Assembly in May 1934, the Resolutions of the English Convocations, and the Observations of the Bishops of the Episcopal Church in Scotland, in the following year, are appended. In May 1936 the Committee of the General Assembly reported that no further action had been taken from the side of the Church of England. A similar report was made in May 1937. There at present the matter rests.]

179. General Assembly of the Church of Scotland. Deliverance, &c., on Provisional Report of Committee on Conferences held with representatives of the Church of England

MAY 1933

DELIVERANCE

THE General Assembly receive the Report and return thanks to the Committee, and especially to the Conveners and Secretary; learn with much interest of the harmonious spirit characterizing the conferences held, and of the steps taken towards reaching a better understanding between the conferring Churches; and reappoint the Committee, with instructions to continue conference and report to the next General Assembly.

ADDENDUM

The General Assembly, however, desire, with a view to prevent any possible misunderstanding, that the Committee should respectfully inform the representatives of the Church with which it confers that any agreement with regard to the Orders and Sacraments of the conferring Churches can only be based on the recognition of the equal validity of the Orders and Sacraments of both Churches, and of the equal standing of the accepted communicants and ordained ministers in each.

A vote was taken and there voted:

For the Addendum . . .	382
Against the Addendum . . .	369
Majority for Addendum . . .	13

The Deliverance with the above Addendum was then adopted.

180. Report of the Joint Committee appointed by the Archbishop of Canterbury and Representatives of the Church of Scotland

FEBRUARY 1934

JOINT REPORT

WE who submit the following Report were appointed by the Archbishop of Canterbury, in his capacity of Chairman of the Lambeth Conference, and by the General Assembly of the Church of Scotland of 1932 acting in response to the invitation which the Archbishop issued in accordance with Resolution 43 of the Lambeth Conference of 1930: associated with us are representatives appointed by the Episcopal Church in Scotland and the Presbyterian Church of England respectively.

The negotiation of possible terms of union being no part of the function of the Conference then authorized, the general procedure which commended itself to us at the outset was to deal in succession with the following four points:

1. That we should record the measure of agreement which already exists between the Churches;
2. That we should consider what degree of co-operation is possible and appropriate on the basis of such agreement;
3. That we should examine the points of difference between us with a view to mutual understanding;
4. That we should explore some part of the way towards a closer fellowship.

We have, in fact, given our attention to the first two of these, and the appended Joint Statement of Agreements as to things believed and things to be undertaken in common is the outcome of our deliberations.

A period of two years is not a long time for the exploration of the measure of agreement existing in our Churches after more than three centuries of separation. Nevertheless, it has been sufficient to reveal, beneath our differences, a remarkably wide area of common faith and common principle which should supply a strong foundation on which we and our successors may confidently build as we labour to promote the unity of our Churches and the furtherance of the cause of Christ at home and across the seas. Such a result calls for devout acknowledgement and thanksgiving to Almighty God.

At the same time, while profoundly thankful for what has been accomplished, we do not conceal from ourselves how much yet remains to be done. The goal which we have kept in view is that of 'an unrestricted intercommunion' among our members and an equally 'unrestricted fellowship' of our ministers, and it is only a first contribution towards the fulfilment of this ideal that the present Conference is able to offer to the Churches. The main obstacle preventing its fuller realization is familiar to all, and its effect and influence go deep. Both parties are agreed in holding that the Church, conceived as the fellowship of believers, is itself part of the gift of God to mankind in the Gospel, and that membership in it is a necessary element in full Christian discipleship. To both the Church is the Body of Christ informed by His Spirit; One, Holy, Catholic, Apostolic, and Evangelical; the living organism for the winning of the world and the establishment of His Kingdom. Differences arise in the sphere of order and polity, and in relation to the character and function of its ministry and sacraments as affected thereby. We believe that a fresh handling of these matters by representatives of our scholarship and churchmanship would issue in results affording grounds for further approach towards unity. Obviously, however, questions of grave historical and doctrinal importance are involved, the solution of which must necessarily require long and detailed discussion. Our own experience in conference has been such as to afford us great encouragement and hope, and we trust that at an early date further inquiry into those matters may be initiated.

Here, however, we must be content, without attempting to formulate more precisely the position of our respective Communions, to acknowledge the gravity of the differences referred to, the conscientious convictions by which these are supported, and the sufficiency of our underlying agreement to encourage a serious and prayerful effort to reconcile them at the bidding of God. Since closer outward relationship cannot precede but must be the outcome of inner unity, the immediate task of the Churches, in our judgement, must be to promote mutual understanding and appreciation from which full unity may come.

Accordingly we recommend to the authorities by whom we were appointed (*a*) that the Joint Statement of Agreements now submitted be commended to the consideration of the conferring Churches in order that the extent of the existing unity may be more adequately appreciated and understood; (*b*) that the action suggested as appropriate may, if approved by the respective authorities, be taken; and (*c*) that, on this approval being given, Committees be set up on both sides to consider and report on the methods to be adopted to carry into effect the practical proposals set forth in the Joint Statement.

Meanwhile we propose that these conferences should for the present be suspended—to be resumed, we trust, when in God's providence the time shall appear opportune.

We give thanks for the spirit of friendship and goodwill in which our discussions have been conducted, and we pray that God will so bless the fruit of our labours, overruling all that is due to our defects in vision or in faith, that they may promote His glory and the welfare, peace, and unity of His Church.

For the Church of England

W. EBOR: (*Chairman*)
[William Temple]
JAMES WAKEFIELD
[J. B. Seaton]
RICHARD SOUTHWARK
[R. G. Parsons]
E. G. SELWYN
J. W. HUNKIN
L. S. HUNTER
O. C. QUICK
A. E. J. RAWLINSON (*Secretary*)

For the Episcopal Church in Scotland

WALTER JOHN ROBBERDS
Bishop of Brechin, Primus
W. PERRY

For the Church of Scotland

ALEX MARTIN, JOHN WHITE } *Joint Chairmen*
D. S. CAIRNS
H. R. MACKINTOSH
J. CROMARTY SMITH
POLWARTH
(Alternate for the late Hon. Lord Sands)
R. L. ORR
JOHN HALL
W. A. CURTIS

For the Presbyterian Church of England

P. CARNEGIE SIMPSON
C. ANDERSON SCOTT

February 1934

APPENDIX

JOINT STATEMENT OF AGREEMENTS

INTRODUCTION

1. The *Lambeth Appeal to all Christian People in the interest of Unity* was laid in 1921 before the Assemblies of the Churches now constituting the Church of Scotland, and the considered replies returned the following year are evidence of the deeply serious and sympathetic spirit in which it was received. The Appeal was recognized as a conspicuous instance of what was reverently believed to be 'a working of the Spirit of God in the mind and life of His Church'; the evils of the present divided state of Christendom were 'acknowledged humbly' as 'tending to the impoverishment of the Body of Christ and the hindering of the faith of the world'; the Assemblies rejoiced in the 'vision' which had been brought before them of 'a Church genuinely Catholic, loyal to all truth, and gathering into its fellowship all who profess and call themselves Christians, within whose visible unity all the treasures of Faith and Order bequeathed as a heritage by the past to the present shall be possessed in common and made serviceable to the whole Body of Christ'; and they assured their Anglican brethren that they would 'on the first convenient occasion, welcome an unrestricted conference with representatives of the Church of England and of the Scottish Episcopal Church from whom the invitation had been received, with the view of arriving at a better understanding of each other's position, and of thoroughly exploring the possibilities of restoring the visible unity of the Church of Christ, on the lines that such a Conference, under the guidance of the promised Spirit of God, might direct'. Preoccupation with their own negotiations for Union precluded the Assemblies from taking practical steps in this direction at the time, but with the happy completion of these negotiations in 1929 the way was open for the acceptance of the renewed invitation to confer extended by the subsequent Lambeth Conference, and presented in person by the Archbishop of Canterbury to the Assembly of the reunited Church in May, 1932. What follows represents the outcome up to the present of the conferences then authorized. It should be added that, on the suggestion of the Church of Scotland, the Presbyterian Church of England cordially agreed to be associated with the Churches named for the purposes of this Joint Conference.

2. In the interval which has elapsed since 1920, the reasons which led to the issuing of the Appeal to all Christian People have certainly not lost in urgency, but have become more constraining than ever. The problems confronting human society call insistently for the aid of the Christian ideals and spirit in their solution. In these circumstances, it manifestly behoves all branches of the Church of Christ to address themselves with renewed earnestness to the cultivation of closer relations with one another, and to the discovery of means by which they may together become more effective in the promotion of the Gospel and Kingdom of our Lord Jesus Christ which are man's only hope.

3. The conferring Churches are the more sensible of this obligation in their own case because of the wide area of belief and duty which is already theirs in common. They are alike Reformed Branches of the Catholic Church. At home and abroad they work side by side. The Church of England and the Church of Scotland, in particular, as national Churches both acknowledge a peculiar responsibility for the maintenance of the faith of the British people and for ministering throughout the British Commonwealth of nations and in other lands to our countrymen overseas. It frequently happens that members of one Communion are resident in areas served only by the other. Their agents labour together not seldom under local arrangements of the happiest fellowship and co-operation. Each Church is linked in all parts of the world with associated Churches of the same order and family. Between them the Anglican and Presbyterian Communions represent a large and influential section of Evangelical Christendom.

I. *Things Believed in Common*

1. The conferring Churches find themselves agreed in their acceptance of the Scriptures of the Old and New Testaments as containing the Word of God, and furnishing the supreme standard of faith and morals; in the belief that these Scriptures ought to be placed within the reach of all men freely; and in the assurance that within a Catholic fellowship there is room for diversity of interpretation.

2. They are agreed that the faith and doctrine of the Church should be set forth in acknowledged standards; accordingly they reverence the Apostles' and Nicene Creeds as classical declarations of that faith and doctrine, which have served to unite the Church

Universal on a common basis of Scriptural truth and fact and to protect it from fundamental error; and they recognize as historic expressions of the Christian faith as they have severally received it later formulations (such as the Thirty-nine Articles and the Westminster Confession of Faith) which were evoked by later need.

3. Endorsing the agreed form of its presentation which was issued by the Lausanne Conference in 1927, they rejoice to declare as the Divine instrument of individual and social regeneration the same Gospel of God's grace:

> 'The Gospel is the joyful message of redemption, both here and hereafter, the gift of God to sinful man in Jesus Christ. Through His life and Teaching, His call to repentance, His proclamation of the coming of the Kingdom of God and of judgement, His suffering and Death, His resurrection and exaltation to the right hand of the Father, and by the mission of the Holy Spirit, He has brought to us forgiveness of sins, and has revealed the fulness of the living God and His boundless love toward us. Because He Himself is the Gospel, the Gospel is the message of the Church to the world. . . . It proclaims the only way by which humanity can escape from those class and race hatreds which devastate society at present into the enjoyment of national well-being and international friendship and peace. It is also a gracious invitation to the non-Christian world, East and West, to enter into the joy of the living Lord.'

4. The conferring Churches are at one in acknowledging that the Sacraments of Baptism and the Lord's Supper are divinely instituted as effectual signs and seals of the saving grace of God, and that through them members are admitted, renewed, and strengthened within the Body of Christ to form one fellowship in Him of life and service in believing and thankful dependence upon His Spirit.

5. They are agreed that the Ministry is the gift of the Lord Jesus Christ to the Church; that in accordance with His purpose it is a ministry not of any section of the Church but of the Church Universal; that He calls to this sacred service whom He wills; and that admission to it is through prayer and the laying on of hands by persons commissioned thereto, in the faith that God will bestow enabling grace on those whom He has called through His Son.

6. They are agreed in the faith that the Church is grounded not in the will of man but in the eternal will of God, who gathers men

into a fellowship rooted in Christ and sustained by the power of His Spirit; that the life of the Church is a life of worship towards God, of growth in grace and of service to mankind; and that the Church is charged with a Divine mission to bear witness to Christ and to proclaim to the whole world the Gospel of the redeeming grace of God through Him.

7. They are agreed in holding that the inward unity of believers in Christ, the one Head of the Church, ought to be made visible in a common Church life and fellowship; and they together acknowledge the obligation to seek and promote the visible unity of the Church wherever the pure Word of God is preached and the Sacraments are duly administered according to Christ's appointment.

8. They are agreed in holding that the Church manifests its continuity from age to age and throughout the world as one Body of which Christ is the Head; that it comprehends within the unity of its essential faith varying forms of devotion, service, and thought; and that it is called, within its own spiritual sphere, to own allegiance to its Lord alone.

9. They are agreed in recognizing the sovereign right of the Lord Jesus Christ to govern human life and conduct in every sphere, and they seek with united purpose the submission to His mind not only of the ecclesiastical order, but of the whole ordered life of mankind, domestic, public, national and international, and its direction by the light and power of the Holy Spirit.

II. *Things that might be Undertaken in Common*

In view of this large measure of agreement on vital matters, we, who have been called by the authorities of our respective Churches into conference, urge that it is desirable and indeed imperative that the measure of agreement and identity already existing should be publicly affirmed and be made more widely known, and that expression should be given to that unity and agreement between our Churches by the utmost mutual recognition and common action that their continuing differences permit.

Accordingly we recommend:

1. That inasmuch as the conferring Churches appeal to the same Scriptures and profess the same Creeds, appropriate measures be taken to secure, on a regular basis approved by the authorities concerned, the mutual admission to pulpits, as occasion

serves, of the ministers of either Communion, as persons duly ordained to the preaching of the Gospel according to the rule and practice of their own Church through prayer and the laying on of hands by those commissioned thereto:

2. That means be sought to recognize and place under a general rule the usage already common in Scotland, and existing in many places in England, by which communicant members of either Communion at home or abroad, when out of reach of their own accustomed ordinances, are welcomed in the other, as members of the Catholic Church of Christ, to the Table of the Lord:

3. That from time to time Delegations be invited to bring greetings and information from one Church to another, in formal Assembly, thus expressing fraternal recognition and conveying friendly encouragement in Christ:

4. That steps be taken to provide, if possible with the concurrence of other Churches, for the issue, as occasion demands, of joint pronouncements upon public, national, or international questions. Pronouncements on these subjects are already made, and they serve both to express and to educate the conscience of the Christian community, but they would be more effective if made in common:

5. That a Joint Advisory Council be set up for the preliminary consideration—without prejudice to any formal action which may later be found necessary on the part of Church Committees or other authoritative bodies responsibly concerned—of practical matters affecting the local relations of the conferring Churches at home and abroad. Experience in many parts of the world has shown how serviceable such a provision could be:

6. That in order to foster the spirit of mutual understanding and sympathy between the Churches, their clergy, candidates for the ministry, and laity be encouraged to seek opportunities of forming a better acquaintance with each other, of studying in either Communion the history and genius of the other, and of co-operating in public service.

CONCLUSION

The members of the Joint Conference are fully conscious that much still remains to be done in fulfilment of the task to which the conferring Churches have been called. Grave questions in doctrine and in history have to be discussed before those free and unhindered relations can be established between the Anglican and Presbyterian Communions to which the Appeal summons 'All Christian People'; and for their adequate discussion much time and thought will be needed when the suitable occasion is found. What has now been accomplished will then, it is hoped, by the blessing of God, be advanced yet further to His praise.

181. General Assembly of the Church of Scotland. Deliverance on Joint Report of Anglican and Scottish Representatives

MAY 1934

Deliverance

1. THE general Assembly receive the Joint Report and the Joint Statement of Agreements appended as the Response of the Church of Scotland to the *Lambeth Appeal on Christian Unity*, addressed to their respective Assemblies in 1921 and anew laid before the General Assembly of the reunited Church in May 1932.

2. The General Assembly commend the Joint Statement of Agreements to the consideration of the Church in order that the extent of the existing unity between the Conferring Churches may be more adequately appreciated and understood.

3. The General Assembly approve the recommendations contained in the Joint Statement of Agreements, viz. (i) That inasmuch as the conferring Churches appeal to the same Scriptures and profess the same Creeds, appropriate measures be taken to secure on a regular basis approved by the authorities concerned, the mutual admission to pulpits, as occasion serves, of the ministers of either communion, as persons duly ordained to the preaching of the gospel according to the rule and practice of their own church through prayer and the laying on of hands by those commissioned thereto. (ii) That means be sought to recognize and place under a general rule the usage already common in Scotland, and existing in many places in England, by which communicant members of either Communion at home or abroad, when out of reach of their own

accustomed ordinances, are welcomed in the other, as members of the Catholic Church of Christ, to the Table of the Lord. (iii) That from time to time delegations be invited to bring greetings and information from one Church to the other, in formal General Assembly, thus expressing fraternal recognition and conveying friendly encouragement in Christ. (iv) That steps be taken to provide, if possible with the concurrence of other Churches, for the issue as occasion demands of joint pronouncements upon public, national, and international questions. Pronouncements on these subjects are already made, and they serve both to express and to educate the conscience of the Christian Community, but they would be more effective if made in common. (v) That a Joint Advisory Council be set up for the preliminary consideration—without prejudice to any formal action which later may be found necessary on the part of Church Committees or other authoritative bodies responsibly concerned—of practical matters affecting the local relations of the conferring Churches at home and abroad. Experience in many parts of the world has shown how serviceable such a provision could be. (vi) That in order to foster the spirit of mutual understanding and sympathy between the Churches their clergy, candidates for the ministry, and laity be encouraged to seek opportunities of forming a better acquaintance with each other, of studying in either Communion the history and genius of the other, and of co-operating in public service.

4. The General Assembly hereby appoint a Committee, consisting of seven members, to consider jointly with a similar Committee appointed to represent the Church of England, and with the co-operation of such representatives as may be appointed by the Presbyterian Church of England and the Episcopal Church in Scotland, and to report to the General Assembly on the methods to be adopted to carry into effect the above recommendations.

5. The General Assembly rejoice to learn of the spirit of harmony and goodwill which has prevailed throughout the joint conferences; and they earnestly trust that the conferring Churches may increasingly be brought into such relations to one another, both of fellowship and of common service, as shall promote the cause of Christian Unity and further the interests of Christ's Kingdom at home and abroad. The General Assembly discharge the Committee.

182. Resolutions of Canterbury Convocation

JANUARY 1935

UPPER HOUSE

'THAT this House receives the Report of the Committee appointed to confer with representatives of the Church of Scotland, and commends it to the sympathetic and careful study of the Church.'

LOWER HOUSE

'That this House, having considered the Report of the Committee appointed to confer with representatives of the Church of Scotland, desires before passing any Resolution upon it that the Episcopal Church of Scotland, with which the Church of England is in actual Communion, may have an opportunity of expressing a corporate opinion upon the proposals contained in it.'

183. Resolutions of York Convocation

JANUARY 1935

UPPER HOUSE

'THAT this House receives the report of the committee appointed to confer with representatives of the Church of Scotland and commends it to the sympathetic attention and careful study of the Church.'

LOWER HOUSE

'That this Lower House receives the report of the committee appointed to confer with the representatives of the Church of Scotland and commends it to the respectful attention and careful study of the Church, and desires that the subject-matter of the report be brought before the House at the next group of sessions.'

JUNE 1935

LOWER HOUSE

'That this House, having considered the report of the committee appointed to confer with representatives of the Church of Scotland, welcomes the effort to promote mutual understanding and closer co-operation with the Church of Scotland, but is of opinion that no further steps should be taken in regard to the report without full consultation with the Episcopal Church in Scotland.'

184. The Episcopal Church in Scotland. Observations on the Joint Report of Conferences between Representatives of the Anglican Communion and of the Established Church of Scotland, drawn up by the Bishops in Conference

MAY 1935

THE Bishops of the Episcopal Church in Scotland have received from his Grace the Archbishop of Canterbury a copy of the Joint Report of the delegates appointed by him in his capacity as Chairman of the Lambeth Conference and of those appointed by the General Assembly of the Church of Scotland, and have given it their careful consideration. The Report was issued by the delegates in February 1934.

The Episcopal Church in Scotland lacks any machinery to secure the consideration of such a report by the Bishops, Presbyters, and Laity of the Church assembled together. The Bishops therefore set forth the following Statement for the consideration of their brethren and others:

1. Believing profoundly that it is in accordance with the mind of our Lord Jesus Christ that every opportunity should be taken to seek such constant and friendly intercourse between Christians as shall lead to mutual understanding, we welcome with thankfulness the record of the spirit of friendship and goodwill in which the discussions were conducted, and we join with the signatories in earnest prayer that God's blessing may rest on the fruit of their labours.

2. There are certain points in the report to which we feel constrained to draw attention, more particularly in Section 3 of the Introduction to the Appendix. There some points are assumed as agreed which in our opinion are still questions awaiting further discussion. Possibly these points would have been more fully discussed by the delegates but for the restricting resolution passed by the General Assembly in 1933. We cannot hide from ourselves the unhappy conviction that the result of that resolution was to impair the hopefulness with which the discussions began.

Further, we wish to point out that the value of the conversations lay not in the fact that the conferring Communions were 'National Churches' so much as in the fact that members of Christian Communions having different conceptions of the character of the holy Catholic Church and its ministry were seeking for points of agreement.

The aim held in view consistently by the Lambeth Conferences is the reunion of Christendom. That aim we desire to pursue whole-heartedly. While aware that in the process towards this end mutual understanding and large measures of co-operation between Episcopal and non-Episcopal Churches are to be encouraged, we submit that there is a real danger of substituting for Union merely a mutual recognition of Episcopal and non-Episcopal bodies as sister Churches enjoying equal validity and continuity of orders and authority.

We are sadly aware that in the past a certain reciprocal suspicion of arrogance has set up a barrier to any progress towards reunion. We recognize with much thankfulness that that spirit seems largely to be a thing of the past. For our own part we hope that it will be understood that we maintain the principle of Episcopacy as a matter of sacred trust which we hold for the good of the whole Church.

We proceed now to offer our comments on the section of the report headed 'Things that might be undertaken in common'. We are glad to welcome cordially the recommendations numbered 3, 4, 5, and 6, and especially the last, believing that 'opportunities of forming a better acquaintance with each other' offer the most useful and hopeful means of increased fellowship.

With regard to recommendations 1 and 2, dealing with 'mutual admission to pulpits' and admission of communicants of 'either Communion when out of reach of their own accustomed ordinances', it is important to bear in mind that these recommendations were not understood by the delegates representing the Episcopal Church in Scotland to suggest immediate interchange of pulpits or general intercommunion, but to recommend further counsel, deliberation, and conference on these questions.

Regarding recommendation 1 (Interchange of Pulpits). The Canons of our Church prohibit all but a very limited opportunity of this. The relevant clauses are these:

No Rector or Priest in charge shall permit any clergyman to officiate in his church until he shall have satisfied himself that the said clergyman has been episcopally ordained to the order to which he professes to belong, and will conform to the doctrine and discipline of this Church. (Canon XVI, 2.)

If at any time it shall seem desirable to the College of Bishops, in view of some project of Reunion, to invite representatives of other Communions to give addresses in some suitable church or churches of this Province, it shall be open to them to do so, provided that the Bishop of the diocese and the Rector or Priest in charge of the church consent. (Canon XVII, 1.)

We will gladly recognize the spirit of recommendation 1 by issuing invitations in accordance with Canon XVII, 1, to representative non-Episcopalian divines to give such addresses at certain centres, when a suitable occasion arises, provided that such addresses are not given in connexion with the canonical services of our Church.

Coming to recommendation 2, concerning occasional intercommunion, we observe that two questions are concerned both of which are, in our opinion, governed by words which occur in Resolution 42 of the Lambeth Conference of 1930: 'maintaining as a general principle that intercommunion should be the goal of, rather than a means to, the restoration of union'.

1. We have no power to give a general order to the clergy to admit unconfirmed persons who wish to communicate with us. No abrogation of the rubric concerning Confirmation would meet with our approval: but individuals who take the responsibility on themselves and in good faith present themselves for communion are never likely to be repelled at the altar.

2. As to members of our Church seeking communion in non-Episcopal Churches. We believe this not to be of common occurrence. When it does occur, each individual so acting must take personal responsibility for his action. Any laxity of practice in this respect merely tends to obscure the corporate aspect of Holy Communion, and to impair the personal loyalty of individual members to their own Church, while it may wound the consciences of their fellow churchmen. We could never take any action which seemed in any way to approve or authorize such a practice.

We would gladly welcome, when the time is ripe, truly unrestricted conversations about holy orders and any other matters of principle which still separate us from our brethren, but we are of opinion that the time is not yet ripe, while the resolution of the General Assembly of 1933 is still so fresh in the minds of the members of our Church. Mindful how the Lambeth Conference of 1920, in Resolution 11, 'recognizes that the task of effecting Union with other Christian Communions must be undertaken by the various national, regional or provincial authorities of the Churches within the Anglican Communion', we are ready to do what lies in our power to carry out this task when the opportunity appears favourable. Meanwhile we beg our fellow members of the Episcopal Church in Scotland to continue in prayer that we may all by God's grace be drawn together in mutual love and understanding.

ARTHUR, *Bishop of Moray, Ross, and Caithness, Primus.*
[A. J. Maclean.]
KENNETH, *Bishop of Argyll and the Isles.*
[K. Mackenzie.]
FREDERIC, *Bishop of Aberdeen and Orkney.*
[F. L. Deane.]
EDWARD, *Bishop of St. Andrews, Dunkeld, and Dunblane.*
[E. T. S. Reid.]
HARRY SEYMOUR, *Bishop of Edinburgh.*
[H. S. Reid.]
JOHN, *Bishop of Glasgow and Galloway.*
[J. R. Darbyshire.]
KENNETH, *Bishop of Brechin.*
[K. D. Mackenzie.]

10*th May* 1935.

IX. CHRISTIAN CO-OPERATION IN GREAT BRITAIN

185. *A Joint Letter to* The Times

DECEMBER 21, 1940

SIR,

The present evils in the world are due to the failure of nations and peoples to carry out the laws of God. No permanent peace is possible in Europe unless the principles of the Christian religion are made the foundation of national policy and of all social life. This involves regarding all nations as members of one family under the Fatherhood of God.

We accept the five points of Pope Pius XII as carrying out this principle (see *The Pope's Five Peace Points*, pp. 13–16):[1]

1. The assurance to all nations of their right to life and independence. The will of one nation to live must never mean the sentence of death passed upon another. When this equality of rights has been destroyed, attacked or threatened, order demands that reparation shall be made, and the measure and extent of that reparation is determined, not by the sword nor by the arbitrary decision of self-interest, but by the rules of justice and reciprocal equity.

2. This requires that the nations be delivered from the slavery imposed upon them by the race for armaments and from the danger that material force, instead of serving to protect the right, may become an overbearing and tyrannical master. The order thus established requires a mutually agreed organic progressive disarmament, spiritual as well as material, and security for the effective implementing of such an agreement.

3. Some juridical institution which shall guarantee the loyal and faithful fulfilment of conditions agreed upon and which shall in case of recognized need revise and correct them.

4. The real needs and just demands of nations and populations and racial minorities to be adjusted as occasion may require, even where no strictly legal right can be established, and a

[1] *Vide supra*, Document 153.

foundation of mutual confidence to be thus laid, whereby many incentives to violent action will be removed.

5. The development among peoples and their rulers of that sense of deep and keen responsibility which weighs human statutes according to the sacred and inviolable standards of the laws of God. They must hunger and thirst after justice and be guided by that universal love which is the compendium and most general expression of the Christian ideal.

With these basic principles for the ordering of international life we would associate five standards by which economic situations and proposals may be tested (see *The Churches Survey Their Task*, pp. 116, 117):

1. Extreme inequality in wealth and possessions should be abolished.

2. Every child, regardless of race or class, should have equal opportunities of education, suitable for the development of his peculiar capacities.

3. The family as a social unit must be safeguarded.

4. The sense of a Divine vocation must be restored to man's daily work.

5. The resources of the earth should be used as God's gifts to the whole human race, and used with due consideration for the needs of the present and future generations.

We are confident that the principles which we have enumerated would be accepted by rulers and statesmen throughout the British Commonwealth of Nations and would be regarded as the true basis on which a lasting peace could be established.

COSMO CANTUAR: [Cosmo Gordon Lang]
Archbishop of Canterbury.

A. CARDINAL HINSLEY,
Archbishop of Westminster.

WALTER H. ARMSTRONG,
Moderator, Free Church Federal Council.

WILLIAM EBOR: [William Temple]
Archbishop of York.

Note. The five peace points are taken from Pope Pius XII's Christmas Eve Allocution, 1939.

The five economic standards are taken from the Report of the Conference on Church, Community and State, held at Oxford in 1937, on the initiative of the

Universal Christian Council for Life and Work, and attended by delegates from the principal non-Roman Churches from all parts of the world. The Report was published by George Allen and Unwin as *The Churches Survey Their Task.*

186. Joint Standing Committee of 'Religion and Life' and the 'Sword of the Spirit'. Joint Statement on Co-operation

APRIL 1942

MEETINGS have recently been held between representatives of the Commission of the Churches for International Friendship and Social Responsibility, and representatives of the Roman Catholic organization entitled the Sword of the Spirit to explore the possibilities of co-operation between Christians in promoting the application of Christian principles to national and international life. The following Joint Statement was drawn up and agreed to by all the representatives on January 24th, 1942. On February 5th the Statement was approved by the Executive Committee of the Sword of the Spirit. On April 15th the Commission of the Churches (which has now set up the organization referred to in section 4 below, under the name 'Religion and Life') gave a general welcome to the Statement, approved the establishment of a Joint Standing Committee of Religion and Life and of the Sword of the Spirit, and agreed that the Statement should be issued on the authority of the Joint Committee. For information and guidance the Statement is now issued by the Joint Standing Committee.

1. We agree that a compelling obligation rests upon all Christian people in this country to maintain the Christian tradition and to act together to the utmost possible extent to secure the effective influence of Christian teaching and witness in the handling of social, economic, and civic problems, now and in the critical post-war period.

We are all profoundly impressed with the increasing danger that in our generation the Christian heritage, in which we all share, may be lost, and that our country may increasingly slip into accepting pagan standards and ideals. Believing, as we do, that the Christian Revelation has an intrinsic claim upon mankind, and that it is also the preserver of human society from excesses and errors, we feel that all Christians are bound in duty and charity alike towards their fellow countrymen to oppose the present tendencies to set Christianity aside and to treat it as a matter of private concern without relevance to the principles which should guide society.

2. We agree that there is a large area of common ground on which, without raising ultimate questions of Church order and doctrine which divide us, full co-operation is possible and is already taking place. The Church of England, the Church of Scotland, and the Evangelical Free Churches have already co-operated for some considerable time in the social and international field. There has also been, for more than twenty years, co-operation for limited social purposes with the Roman Catholic Church. But the first clear definition of a large common area is to be found in the Ten Points of *The Times* letter of December 21st, 1940, which was signed by the Archbishops of Canterbury and York, Cardinal Hinsley, and the Moderator of the Free Church Federal Council.

The Joint Declaration in *The Times* letter is a valuable point of departure. But there are many other pronouncements, such as that issued by the Malvern Conference, the document on Social Justice and Economic Reconstruction issued by the Commission of the Churches, the statement on A Christian Realm put out by the Church Union of the Church of England, the social Encyclicals of the Popes from Leo XIII onwards, and many others, all relevant to the common obligation we accept. Over this whole field, collaboration among Christians, already in progress, ought to be encouraged.

3. We agree that organized Christianity, to fulfil its proper function, must everywhere be secured in certain essential freedoms. Full freedom must mean freedom to worship according to conscience, freedom to preach, teach, educate, and persuade (all in the spirit of Christian charity), and freedom to bring up children in the faith of their parents. The Christian life is one lived in and through membership of a religious society, and its corporate nature and its constitutional freedom and independence must be recognized and guaranteed by the State.

4. Our purpose is to unite informed and convinced Christians all over the country in common action on broad lines of social and international policy. Already, in different localities, groups have come into being—groups of clergy and ministers, Christian Councils, study groups, and the like—including members of all Communions. Among Roman Catholics the work of organization is fulfilled by the Sword of the Spirit, a body with a recognized Constitution

and membership. The Commission of the Churches, as a result of the Religion and Life Weeks that it has promoted, is establishing an organization kindred in status, to do, within the Church of England, the Church of Scotland, and the Free Churches, what the Sword of the Spirit does inside the Roman Catholic Church, so that individuals or groups, moved by public meetings or otherwise, can be linked up.

The crisis of civilization, and the possibilities open to Christians in the period of reconstruction in the national and international field, make it essential that all this work of Christian co-operation should be greatly intensified and extended.

5. The striking thing about the Sword of the Spirit and similar movements is the spontaneity of support which they have received, and the great local enthusiasm which has accompanied public meetings arranged on this wide co-operative basis. Local spontaneity and freedom are of the highest value, and must not be overloaded by central organization. But, in our judgement, there must be a Joint Committee to give advice, direction, and encouragement to all who seek it, and to extend this joint movement to parts of the country it has not yet reached.

Linked by this Committee, the two Movements will work through parallel action in the religious, and joint action in the social and international field.

Note.—The Commission of the Churches in 1943 became part of the British Council of Churches. The Sword of the Spirit was founded by Cardinal Hinsley in August 1940 to deal with the issues raised by the war, the need for national unity, and the defence of the principle of human liberty and the Natural Law. Ordinary membership is open to all Roman Catholics who accept the aims of the movement. Associate membership is open to all others who accept the aims of the movement, in co-operation 'in the common cause of Truth and Justice'.

187. The British Council of Churches

INAUGURATED SEPTEMBER 23, 1943

[The counterpart in Great Britain of the World Council of Churches, combining in a single organization the chief agencies of British interdenominational co-operation since the Oxford and Edinburgh World Conferences 1937. The Archbishop of Canterbury (Dr. Geoffrey Fisher) was elected president in 1945, in succession to Archbishop William Temple.]

Articles of Amalgamation

I. The Council on the Christian Faith and the Common Life, the Commission of the Churches for International Friendship and

Social Responsibility, and the British Section of the World Conference on Faith and Order, shall be amalgamated in a single body to be called the *British Council of Churches*.

II. The basis of the British Council of Churches shall be that of the World Council of Churches, namely, 'a fellowship of churches which accept our Lord Jesus Christ as God and Saviour', with the understanding that any body which has hitherto been represented on the Commission shall continue in membership of the Council, if so willing, even though it does not itself accept the basis.

III. The functions of the British Council of Churches shall be:

1. To carry on the work of the Council on the Christian Faith and the Common Life, the Commission of the Churches for International Friendship and Social Responsibility and the British Section of the World Conference on Faith and Order.

2. To facilitate common action by the churches in evangelistic enterprise, in promotion of international friendship, in stimulating a sense of social responsibility, and in guiding the activities of the churches for the welfare of youth.

3. To facilitate such other common action as may later be determined.

4. To promote co-operation in study and to ensure adequate British participation in the studies promoted by the World Council of Churches.

5. To assist the growth of oecumenical consciousness in the members of all churches and generally to promote Christian unity.

IV. The British Council of Churches, as carrying on the work of the Council on the Christian Faith and the Common Life, shall collect from the churches of Great Britain their contributions to the budget of the World Council, and allocate among the British churches the places allotted to them on the Assembly and Council of the World Council.

V. The British Council of Churches shall be the connecting link between the Churches of Great Britain and the World Alliance for International Friendship through the Churches, its Department of International Friendship being recognized as the British Council of the World Alliance.

VI. The British Council of Churches shall consist of one hundred and twelve members, eighty-two to be elected by the Churches, ten by the interdenominational organizations and twenty co-opted; of those co-opted at least ten to be laymen and women.

Schedule of Representation

I. *Representative of the Churches*

A. The Churches in England:		
1. The Church of England	30	
2. The Free Churches:		
(*a*) The Baptist Union	5	
(*b*) The Congregational Union	5	
(*c*) The Methodist Church	10	
(*d*) The Presbyterian Church of England . .	3	
(*e*) The Churches of Christ	1	
(*f*) The Independent Methodist Church . .	1	
B. The Churches in Scotland:		
1. The Church of Scotland	7	
2. Other Churches in Scotland (nominated by the Scottish Churches' Council)	2	
3. Scottish Churches' Committee of the World Alliance	1	
C. The Churches in Wales	6	
D. The Churches in Ireland	5	
E. The Salvation Army	2	
F. The Society of Friends	2	
G. The Unitarian and Free Christian Churches . .	2	
	—	82
II. *Representative of Interdenominational Organizations*		
1. The Y.M.C.A.	2	
2. The Y.W.C.A.	2	
3. The Student Christian Movement	2	
4. The Christian Auxiliary Movement	1	
5. The Conference of British Missionary Societies .	3	
	—	10
III. *Co-opted Members*		20
		112

VII. The Council shall work mainly through Committees and Departments.

1. The Council shall appoint an Executive Committee to carry out between sessions of the Council any responsibilities which the Council may entrust to it.

2. The Council shall set up Departments of International Friendship, of Social Responsibility, and of Faith and Order. These Departments shall consist of (*a*) not less than ten and not more than twenty members of the Council; (*b*) not more than twenty co-opted members of whom not more than ten shall be selected from the membership of relevant church committees not already under (*a*) above. Membership of the Department of Faith and Order shall be confined to representatives of those churches which take part in the Faith and Order Movement, and its activities shall be conducted under the conditions which govern that Movement.

3. The Youth Committee of the Commission shall become the Council's Department of Youth.

4. The Council shall appoint a Committee on Evangelism (Religion and Life). This shall consist of not less than ten and not more than twenty members of the Council together with other persons co-opted by the Council for their special interest, sympathy, and ability in the work to a number not exceeding one-third of the total membership of the committee.

VIII. The Council as a whole shall meet at least twice a year for sessions lasting for at least a full day.

X. THE CHURCH OF FINLAND

[By Resolution 38 of the Lambeth Conference of 1930 the Archbishop of Canterbury was requested 'as soon as seems advisable, to appoint a committee to investigate the position of the Church of Finland and its relations to the Church of England'. In accordance with this Resolution, a Commission was appointed, which met representatives of the Church of Finland in 1934. A Joint Report was issued the same year. See *Report of the Committee Appointed to Confer with Representatives of the Church of Finland* (published by authority of the Archbishop of Canterbury), S.P.C.K., 1934.]

188. Report of the Joint Commission appointed by the Archbishop of Canterbury and the Archbishop of Turku

JULY 1934

TO THEIR GRACES THE ARCHBISHOP OF CANTERBURY AND THE ARCHBISHOP OF TURKU (ABȮ)

WE, the Commission appointed by you to consider the relations of the Church of England and the Church of Finland with one another, report as follows:

We have considered with great care the agreements and differences in the doctrine and customs of the two Churches, and have to report that on the most fundamental points of doctrine there is agreement. Such relations between the two Churches as we recommend do not require from either Communion the acceptance of all doctrinal opinion or of all sacramental or liturgical practice characteristic of the other, but imply that each believes the other to hold the most fundamental doctrines of the Christian faith. We are of opinion that both Churches hold the most fundamental doctrines of the Christian faith.

We recommend therefore:

1. That if the Archbishop of Turku (Abȯ) shall invite the Archbishop of Canterbury to appoint a bishop to take part in the consecration of a bishop in the Church of Finland, he shall commission a bishop for such a purpose; and in the same way, if the Archbishop of Canterbury shall ask the Archbishop of Turku (Abȯ) to appoint a bishop to take part in the consecration of a bishop in the Church of England, he shall commission a bishop for such a purpose.

2. The Anglican delegation recommends the admission of

communicants of the Church of Finland to Communion in the Church of England, and takes note of the fact that the Church of Finland is already accustomed to admit to Communion at its altars communicants not belonging to the Lutheran confession.

3. That if at the time of the Lambeth Conference or at any other time there shall be a conference between bishops of the Anglican Communion and bishops of other Churches in communion with it, bishops of the Church of Finland shall be asked to attend it, and that the Church of Finland shall invite Anglican bishops to similar conferences if they are held in the future.

ALEKSI LEHTONEN
(*Bishop of Tampere*).
ERKKI KAILA
(*Bishop of Wiipuri*).
MAX V. BONSDORFF
(*Bishop of Borgå*).
J. A. MANNERMAA
(*Dean of Oulu*).
U. PAUNU
(*Vicar of Valkeala*).
MATTI TARKKANEN
(*Mission Director Emer: of the Finnish Missionary Society*).
E. G. GULIN
(*Professor, Helsinki*).
Helsinki,
The 19th of July, 1934.

A. C. GLOUCESTR:
[A. C. Headlam.]
STAUNTON FULHAM.
[B. S. Batty.]
A. S. DUNCAN-JONES
(*Dean of Chichester*).
A. E. J. RAWLINSON
(*Archdeacon of Auckland*).
CHARLES E. RAVEN
(*Regius Professor of Divinity, Cambridge University*).
PHILIP USHER
(*Domestic Chaplain to the Bishop of Gloucester*).
CLAUDE BEAUFORT MOSS
(*Vice-Principal of St. Boniface College, Warminster*).

189. Convocation of York. Resolution on Relations with the Church of Finland

JANUARY 24, 1935

RESOLUTION passed by both Houses separately:

That this House receives and approves the report of the committee on the relations of the Church of England and the Church of Finland, and requests the President in conjunction with the President of the Convocation of Canterbury to take such steps as they may think fit to carry out the recommendations of the report.

190. *Convocation of Canterbury. Resolution on Relations with the Church of Finland*

JUNE 6, 1935

RESOLUTION passed by the Upper House.

Having learnt from the Archbishop of Turku (Abò) that he has authority, after consultation with the Conference of Bishops of the Church of Finland and with the agreement of its Church Assembly, to seek closer relations with the Church of England in response to the Archbishop of Canterbury's invitation (conveyed in pursuance of Resolution 38 of the Lambeth Conference, 1930), this House welcomes the approaches thus made, and expresses the hope that in due course complete intercommunion, based on a common episcopal ministry, may be achieved.

Further, and as a means towards such a complete unity, this House, noting that the Episcopal Ordination of Presbyters is the regular practice of the Church of Finland, and assuming that the Bishops of the Church will take steps to put the practice of the Church of Finland beyond doubt, approve the following recommendations:

That if the Archbishop of Canterbury be invited by the Archbishop of Turku (Abò) to appoint a Bishop to take part in the consecration of a Bishop in the Church of Finland, he may commission a Bishop for such a purpose; and in the same way, if the Archbishop of Canterbury shall invite the Archbishop of Turku (Abò) to take part in the consecration of a Bishop in the Church of England, it is hoped that he would be willing to commission a Bishop for such a purpose.

That members of the Church of Finland may be admitted to communion in the Church of England, provided that they are at that time admissible to communion in their own Church.

Note on Amendment by Lower House: The Lower House concurred in the first two paragraphs of the Resolution of the Upper House, as far as the words 'beyond doubt', following which it amended as follows:

is of opinion:

That if the Archbishop of Turku (Abò) shall invite the Archbishop of Canterbury to appoint a Bishop to take part in the consecration of a Bishop in the Church of Finland, he may commission a Bishop for such a purpose.

That members of the Church of Finland may be admitted to communion in the Church of England in accordance with the terms of Resolution 2(*a*) on the Unity of the Church communicated by the Upper House to this House on 4th June, 1931.[1]

191. Letter from the Archbishop of Turku to the Archbishop of Canterbury

MARCH 9, 1936

[In a letter of March 9, 1936, the Archbishop of Turku (Dr. Kaila) transmitted to the Archbishop of Canterbury the official reply of the Church of Finland to the Resolutions adopted by the Convocations of Canterbury and York (*Vide supra*, Documents 189 and 190). After saying 'We gladly acknowledge that in spite of the difference of emphasis observed during the conversations, there is a fundamental agreement in Christian doctrine', the letter continues as follows.]

THERE is another point, however, where greater differences appear. I mean the question of Church order. I agree with the Bishop of Gloucester that generally speaking 'the Church of Finland at the present time is, like the Church of England, the ancient Church of the country, reformed'. The old Church order has been preserved here in its essentials. For various reasons we also appreciate the laudable desire of the Church of England to emphasize the necessity for a valid ministry in the Church. Undoubtedly, this is a very important point. The Lutheran Church herself lays great stress on this according to Article XIV of *Confessio Augustana*: 'De ordine ecclesiastico docent, quod nemo debeat in ecclesia publice docere aut sacramenta administrare *nisi rite vocatus*.' Furthermore, during recent years it has been very clearly seen in different countries how necessary it is that the ministry of the Church is based on purely religious and ecclesiastical principles, if the danger is to be avoided of interference from circles which are alien to the real life of the Church. This danger can still arise in many Christian countries. It is certainly also very important that the proved and venerable historical methods of Church government are preserved. Interest for this matter is not lacking in the Church of Finland, nor in Northern Lutheranism in general. So as far as Finland is concerned this is made clear by the Report of the Joint Commission. Having said this, however, I must point out that we cannot in principle look upon the historical episcopacy, on which the Anglican Church lays such great stress, as a *conditio sine qua non* for a valid ministry,

[1] *Vide supra*, Document 171.

without abandoning our fundamental doctrinal basis. I might refer here to the Reply of the Lutheran Bishops of the Church of Sweden in the year 1923, where they say: 'No particular organisation of the Church and of its ministry is instituted *iure divino*'—'Our Church cannot recognize any essential difference, *de iure divino*, of aim and authority between the two or three Orders into which the ministry of grace may have been divided, *iure humano* for the benefit and convenience of the Church. The value of every organization of the *ministerium ecclesiasticum* and the Church in general, is only to be judged by its fitness and ability to become pure vessels for the supernatural contents, and a perfect channel for the way of Divine Revelation unto mankind.' We agree with this statement. The Church of Finland appreciates the historical episcopacy very highly as a singularly valuable form of Church supervision and as an outward sign of Church unity through the ages as is clearly seen also from her own history; but she differs from the standpoint represented by many Anglican churchmen and emphasized also during the conversations concerning closer union with the Church of Finland, according to which the historical episcopacy is necessary for an ordered ministry. We see in the historical episcopacy an order 'not divinely instituted, but divinely used and blessed', and the authority of it, strengthened by a long history from the early Church until the present age, full of God's merciful guidance, should not be shaken. Another thing must be made clear. The Church of Finland has invited bishops from neighbouring Churches in Sweden and Estonia to her Consecrations not in order to restore her broken outward succession, but as the late Bishop of Tampere, Dr. Gummerus, put it during the conversations in 1933, 'above all, as an act by which both churches witnessed to the unity of the Body of Christ'. We shall be happy to welcome an Anglican Bishop to a Finnish Consecration, when the time for such a step is suitable, on the understanding that reciprocity will follow, and that the Archbishops of Canterbury and of Turku (Abȯ) will agree on details. The Church of Finland gladly looks forward to such a widening of her relations with other Churches and to a fresh opportunity to promote the unity of the Universal Church.

As to the other question which has caused much discussion; I think that all that can be said at the present time concerning the canon of the Finnish Church Law (116), which permits ordination by a Dean or an older 'Assessor of the Chapter' has, as a matter of fact, already been said during the conversations. There is nothing essential to be added to the statements of the Finnish delegates published in the Report of the Joint Commission. It seems to me, that there should not be anything to prevent the suggested arrangements, if it be understood that we do not therewith imply any definite theory about episcopal ordination.

As to granting communicating members of the Church of Finland the right to communicate in the Church of England, our Church acknowledges with deep gratitude the decisions made by the Convocations of Canterbury and of York. These decisions include practically the same as is involved by the following canon in the Finnish Church Law (121): 'Upon a person of another confession the priest shall not press priestly duties, but if the priest is voluntarily asked to perform a priestly service for a person who confesses another faith, he shall not refuse to do this, in so far as such a performance is not an infringement of the general law, and this being the case, the priest shall perform the function according to the Manual of the Lutheran Church.' It has for a long time been tacitly understood in our Church that all Lutheran communicants may communicate in the Church of Finland. According to the canon quoted, however, our priests may administer to Christians of other confessions the holy rites of our Church in cases when they are voluntarily asked for them. The general law of Finland is to be specially observed, e.g. as to marriage. Yet, it is understood, that if a person who confesses another faith is permanently living in this country and wishes to be served by our priests, he should become a regular member of our Church in course of time, but there is, of course, no compulsion. Thus it appears that nothing at present hinders Anglican communicants from communicating in our churches, when they wish to do so. We welcome them most heartily to the Lord's table. With great gratitude we shall duly inform our parishes of the decisions of the Anglican Church regarding the right of our communicants to communicate in the Anglican Church. This will be a real privilege for our countrymen, who are living in the British Empire or travelling in other countries where there are no churches of their own, but where there is an Anglican church, as is the case, e.g. in many places in Switzerland. We also gladly see in this step an advance towards a time when the Holy Communion, instituted by our Lord as an instrument of *communio sanctorum*, will no longer be a sign of division.

192. Letter from the Archbishop of Canterbury to the Archbishop of Turku

APRIL 30, 1936

[The Archbishop of Canterbury (Dr. Lang) replied to the foregoing letter on April 30, 1936, as follows.]

I REJOICE to know that (to use your own words) 'in spite of the difference of emphasis observed during the conversations there is a fundamental agreement in Christian doctrine'. For indeed substantial unity of doctrine is a necessary foundation for the unity of the Church.

I fully realize that there may be a difference greater than one of mere emphasis in the standpoint of the Anglican Church with regard to the place and function of what you have called the historical Episcopacy. I note, indeed, that you regard the provision of a valid ministry in the Church as 'a very important point'; and that your Church 'appreciates the historical Episcopacy as an outward sign of Church unity through the ages'. The Church of England believes that it is through this historical Episcopacy and its succession both in office and consecration that a duly authorized ministry, a ministry which can be acknowledged by every part of the Church, can be at all times secured, and the continuity and unity of the Church can be maintained. To use the words of the Committee of the Lambeth Conference of 1930 on the Unity of the Church: 'We are persuaded that the historic continuity of the episcopal ministry provides evidence of the Divine intention in this respect such as to constitute a stewardship which we are bound to discharge.' It is for this reason that the Church of England requires for its own ministers and for the ministers of any Church with which it can be in full and formal union that they shall have received ordination through this historical Episcopate. I feel confident that in due course of time it will be shown that there is on this matter no fundamental difference between us. To quote the words of the resolution as passed in both Houses of the Convocation of Canterbury, I 'note that the Episcopal Ordination of Presbyters is the regular practice of the Church of Finland and assume that the Bishops will take steps to put the practice of the Church of Finland beyond doubt'. Accordingly I shall be most willing to receive and give effect to any desire which at any time you may express that, as a token of existing fellowship and as a step towards fuller union, I should commission a bishop of the

Church of England to take part in the consecration of a bishop of the Church of Finland. My hope is that similarly, if it were agreeable to you, I might be able to invite a bishop of the Church of Finland to take part in the consecration of a bishop of the Church of England.

Meanwhile we shall most gladly admit members of the Church of Finland to Holy Communion at our altars when they are deprived of the ministrations of their own Church. I shall take steps to inform the authorities of the various Anglican Churches throughout the world of the recommendations of the Report of our conversations and of the resolution of the Convocations of Canterbury and of York.

XI. THE CHURCHES OF LATVIA AND ESTONIA

[The Committee on the Unity of the Church of the Lambeth Conference 1930, in asking the Archbishop of Canterbury to appoint a Commission to consider the relations between the Anglican Church and the Church of Finland, suggested that such a Commission might then consider further other Scandinavian and allied Churches. The Committee noted specially that bishops had been consecrated for the Churches of Latvia and Estonia by the Archbishop of Upsala. In 1937, the Archbishop of Canterbury received a joint request from the Archbishop of Latvia and the Bishop of Estonia to arrange a Conference similar to the one earlier held with the Church of Finland. Accordingly, delegates were appointed from the three Churches, and they met under the chairmanship of the Bishop of Gloucester, the Archbishop of Latvia, and the Bishop of Estonia, at Lambeth in March 1936 and at Riga and Tallinn in 1938, a Joint Report being issued in this latter year. See *Conferences between Representatives appointed by the Archbishop of Canterbury on behalf of the Church of England and Representatives of the Evangelical Lutheran Churches of Latvia and Estonia*, S.P.C.K., 1938.]

193. Joint Report of the Commission appointed by the Archbishop of Canterbury, the Archbishop of Latvia, and the Bishop of Estonia

JUNE 1938

TO THEIR GRACES THE ARCHBISHOP OF CANTERBURY, THE ARCHBISHOP OF LATVIA, AND HIS LORDSHIP THE BISHOP OF ESTONIA

WE, the Commission appointed by you to consider the relations of the Church of England, and the Churches of Latvia and Estonia, with one another, report as follows:

We have considered with great care the agreements and differences in the doctrine and customs of the three Churches, and have to report that on the most fundamental points of doctrine there is agreement. Such relations between the three Churches as we recommend do not require from any of the three Communions the acceptance of all doctrinal opinion or of all sacramental or liturgical practice characteristic of either of the others, but imply that each believes the others to hold the most fundamental doctrines of the Christian faith. We are of opinion that all three Churches hold the most fundamental doctrines of the Christian faith.

We recommend therefore:

1. That if the Archbishop of Latvia or the Bishop of Estonia shall invite the Archbishop of Canterbury to appoint a bishop to take part in the consecration of a bishop in either of the Churches

of Latvia or Estonia, he shall commission a bishop for such a purpose; and, in the same way, if the Archbishop of Canterbury shall ask the Archbishop of Latvia and the Bishop of Estonia to appoint a bishop to take part in the consecration of a bishop in the Church of England, they shall commission a bishop for such a purpose.

2. The Anglican delegation recommends the admission of communicants of the Churches of Latvia and Estonia to communion in the Church of England, and takes note of the fact that, as it is stated, the Churches of Latvia and Estonia would be ready to admit to communion at their altars communicant members of the Church of England.

The Conference further recommends:

3. That if at the time of the Lambeth Conference or at any other time there shall be a conference between bishops of the Anglican Communion and bishops of other Churches in communion with it, bishops of the Churches of Latvia and Estonia shall be asked to attend it, and that the Churches of Latvia and Estonia shall invite Anglican bishops to similar conferences if they are held in the future.

4. That the Anglican clergy should be ready to baptize and marry members of the Latvian and Estonian Evangelical Churches in England or in any British colony, and that the clergy of Latvia and Estonia should perform like functions for members of the Anglican Church who have not access to an Anglican clergyman. It is to be desired also that they provide certificates of Baptism and Marriage.

A. C. GLOUCESTR:
[A. C. Headlam.]

JOHN DERBY.
[A. E. J. Rawlinson.]

A. S. DUNCAN-JONES
(*Dean of Chichester*).

A. J. MACDONALD
(*Rector of St. Dunstan's-in-the-West*).

HERBERT M. WADDAMS
(*Chaplain of Liddon House*).

H. B. RAHAMÄGI
(*Bishop of Estonia*).

F. JÜRGENSON (*Provost*).

H. KUBU (*Provost*).

J. AUNVER (*Provost*).

J. TAUL (*Lecturer, Tartu*).

A. ROOMEES
(*General Secretary of the Consistory*).

T. GRÜNBERGS
(*Archbishop of Latvia*).

EDG. RUMBA (*Lecturer, Riga*).

Tallinn.
The 24th of June 1938.

194. Convocation of Canterbury. Upper House. Resolutions on the preceding Report

JANUARY 19, 1939

1. THAT the Report of the Commission appointed to consider the relations of the Church of England and the Churches of Latvia and Estonia with one another be received.

2. That the following recommendations receive the authority of the Convocation of Canterbury:

(1) That if the Archbishop of Latvia or the Bishop of Estonia shall invite the Archbishop of Canterbury to appoint a bishop to take part in the consecration of a bishop in either of the Churches of Latvia or Estonia, he shall commission a bishop for such a purpose; and, in the same way, if the Archbishop shall ask the Archbishop of Latvia and the Bishop of Estonia to appoint a bishop to take part in the consecration of a bishop in the Church of England, they shall commission a bishop for such a purpose;

(2) the Anglican delegation recommends the admission of communicants of the Churches of Latvia and Estonia to communion in the Church of England, and takes note of the fact that the Churches of Latvia and Estonia are ready to admit to Communion at their altars communicant members of the Church of England;

(3) that if at the time of the Lambeth Conference or at any other time there shall be a conference between bishops of the Anglican Communion and bishops of other Churches in communion with it, bishops of the Churches of Latvia and Estonia shall be asked to attend it, and that the Churches of Latvia and Estonia shall invite Anglican bishops to similar conferences if they are held in the future;

(4) that the Anglican clergy should be ready to baptize and marry members of the Latvian and Estonian Evangelical Churches in England and in any British Colony, and that the clergy of Latvia and Estonia should perform like functions for members of the Anglican Church who have not access to an Anglican clergyman. It is to be desired also that they provide certificates of Baptism and Marriage.

195. Convocation of Canterbury. Lower House. Resolutions on the preceding Report

MAY 23, 1939

(A) THAT the Resolutions appended to this Report be now considered.

(B) 1. That this House welcomes the approaches made by the Archbishop of Latvia and the Bishop of Estonia to the Archbishop of Canterbury, and expresses the hope that in due course complete intercommunion, based on a common faith and a common episcopal ministry, may be achieved.

2. The House is of opinion that in the meanwhile:

(*a*) if the Archbishop of Latvia or the Bishop of Estonia shall invite the Archbishop of Canterbury to take part in the consecration of a bishop in either one of their Churches, he may commission a bishop for the purpose;

(*b*) members of the Churches of Latvia and Estonia may be admitted to Communion in the Church of England in accordance with the terms of Resolution 2(a) on the Unity of the Church communicated by the Upper House to this House on the 4th June, 1931.[1]

3. That this House expresses the hope that if, at the time of the Lambeth Conference in 1940, any conference of Anglican Bishops with representatives of other Churches in friendly relations with the Church of England be held, the Archbishop of Latvia and the Bishop of Estonia be invited to take part in such a conference.

4. That this House is of the opinion that the clergy of the Church of England should be ready to solemnize the marriages of members of the Latvian and Estonian Churches in England or in any British colony and to baptize their children. When this is done, or when like offices are performed for members of the Church of England by ministers of the Latvian or Estonian Churches, care should be taken to inform the competent authority of each Church concerning what has taken place.

Note on action of York Convocation: The Upper House of the Convocation of York on January 18, 1939, approved similar Recommendations to those carried in the Upper House of the Convocation of Canterbury, except that Recommendation No. 4 was adopted as follows:

[1] *Vide supra*, Document 171.

4. That this House would welcome the institution of a regular system by which a Latvian or Estonian coming to live in England should bring a letter of introduction to the Bishop, who would arrange for his pastoral supervision, for his marriage if desired, and for the baptism of his children.

XII. THE UNITED STATES OF AMERICA

THE PROTESTANT EPISCOPAL CHURCH AND THE PRESBYTERIAN CHURCH IN U.S.A. APPROACHES TO UNITY (1937–47)

[Official negotiations between these Churches on a definite basis began as a result of an invitation issued by the General Convention of the Protestant Episcopal Church to the authorities of the Presbyterian Church in U.S.A. in September 1937, and accepted by the General Assembly of the Presbyterian Church in U.S.A. in May 1938. The Declaration of Purpose, in which both Churches have joined, is the basis of the negotiations and is given below (Document 196). Reports have been presented to the General Convention and the General Assembly every three years. In 1940 the General Convention reaffirmed its adherence to the Declaration of Purpose and, without committing itself to any particular project, urged further study. In 1943 a Majority and a Minority Report were presented to the General Convention by the Commission on Approaches to Unity; and both Reports were referred to the Church for study. It was also decided to ask the counsel of the Lambeth Conference before any commitments were made. In 1946 the Commission on Approaches to Unity presented the Document printed as No. 197. The views of the two Churches are expressed in the Resolutions and Report which follow.]

196. Invitation and Declaration of Purpose. Resolutions adopted by the General Convention of the Protestant Episcopal Church

SEPTEMBER 1937

RESOLVED, That the General Convention of the Protestant Episcopal Church in the United States of America, acting with full realization of the significance of its proposal, hereby invites the Presbyterian Church in the United States of America to join with it in accepting the following declaration:

The two Churches one in the faith of the Lord Jesus Christ, the Incarnate Word of God, recognizing the Holy Scriptures as the supreme rule of faith, accepting the two Sacraments ordained by Christ, and believing that the visible unity of Christian churches is the will of God, hereby formally declare their purpose to achieve organic union between their respective Churches.

Upon the basis of these agreements the two Churches agree to take immediate steps toward the framing of plans whereby this end may be achieved, and be it further

RESOLVED, That the Presiding Bishop be and hereby is requested to convey this invitation to the authorities of the Presbyterian Church in the United States of America, and be it further

RESOLVED, That the Commission on Approaches to Unity be instructed to enter upon the negotiations contemplated in the invitation and report a plan to the next Convention.

Note. This invitation was accepted and the Declaration of Purpose adopted by the General Assembly of the Presbyterian Church in U.S.A., May 1938.

197. Report of Joint Commission on Approaches to Unity submitted to the General Convention of the Protestant Episcopal Church

SEPTEMBER 1946

THE Joint Commission on Approaches to Unity begs leave to submit its report to the General Convention of 1946.

The membership of the Commission is as follows: The Rt. Rev. R. E. L. Strider, D.D. (Chairman), The Rt. Rev. G. R. Fenner, S.T.D., The Rt. Rev. S. E. Keeler, D.D., The Rt. Rev. G. A. Oldham, D.D., The Rt. Rev. Harwood Sturtevant, D.D., The Rt. Rev. B. M. Washburn, D.D., The Rev. C. R. Barnes, D.D., The Rev. S. E. Johnson, Ph.D., The Rev. L. C. Lewis, S.T.D., The Very Rev. C. W. Sprouse, S.T.D., The Rev. T. O. Wedel, Ph.D., The Very Rev. A. C. Zabriskie, D.D. (Secretary), Mr. W. L. Balthis, Mr. H. T. Foulkes, Dr. Alexander Guerry, Mr. J. G. Mitchell, Mr. J. C. Spaulding, and Professor G. F. Thomas.

PART I

Since the General Convention of 1943 the Commission has had regular and well-attended meetings at which the various matters referred to it by General Convention have been fully and frankly discussed. Three times a special committee of the Commission has met with a like committee of the Presbyterian Department of Church Co-operation and Union, and once the entire Episcopal Commission has met in joint session with the Presbyterian Department.

Informal contacts have been maintained with representatives of the Methodist Church but there have been no meetings with them.

In all discussions and negotiations relative to union with the Presbyterian Church in the United States of America the effort has been made to give due consideration to two great underlying principles. First, the subject under discussion is not the co-operation or federation of the two Churches but organic union, and organic union means ultimately, to quote the language of a formal resolution adopted by the Commission at one of its meetings, 'one Church, with one standard of faith, one communicant list, one ministry, one system of government'. This conception of the final goal before us, therefore, has directed all the discussions of the Commission and underlies the plan herewith submitted.

Secondly, the members of the Commission have sought to bear in mind that the enterprise now being carried on by the Episcopal and Presbyterian Churches is but one phase of that oecumenical movement in progress throughout Christendom. We have tried therefore to envisage not only the union of two particular communions, but also the ultimate reunion of all disciples of our Lord.

The Commission, in accordance with the instructions of the General Convention of 1943, has studied both the majority and the minority reports as submitted by the Joint Commission to that Convention. It has also continued negotiations with the representatives of the Presbyterian Church in the United States of America looking towards the organic union of the two bodies. Out of these studies and negotiations has come a plan entitled 'A Proposed Basis of Union' which follows as a part of this report. This document still leaves a number of important issues for further negotiations—for example, the organization of the General Assembly or Convention, and property and contractual rights. The latter problem has received careful preliminary study from a committee of this Commission.

The Commission has been assured by the Department of Church Co-operation and Union of the Presbyterian Church in the United States of America that, in the event this General Convention shall refer the Proposed Basis of Union to the Dioceses for study and report, the Department will propose similar action to the General Assembly of its Church in 1947.

Some of the members of this Commission are signing this report because they approve the plan in substance and are convinced that it is the proper basis for union and for the drafting of a Constitution. Others are signing the report because they wish the clergy and laity to be given opportunity to face the issues it presents and to register judgement thereon, and not because they endorse or agree with the plan in all its details. All reserve the right to support or oppose the proposals in the light of further study, and when they are submitted for further action.

PART II

THE PROPOSED BASIS OF UNION BETWEEN THE PROTESTANT EPISCOPAL CHURCH IN THE UNITED STATES OF AMERICA AND THE PRESBYTERIAN CHURCH IN THE UNITED STATES OF AMERICA

Preamble

Through the events of our time as well as through His revelation of His will in Jesus Christ, God is imperatively calling upon all who believe in Him to become one flock under one Shepherd, so that the world may believe in its Creator, Redeemer, and Sanctifier. All the Churches stand at the bar of God's judgement. The unity of Christians is not merely a pious aspiration, it is essential if the Church is to live and to fulfil its mission both at home and abroad. It is not remote from the need of our age. Upon us the end of a world has come, and the events of the last decades have shown that unless the Church becomes increasingly effective in human affairs, as a united community of faith which transcends nationality, race, and class, and therefore can hold divided groups in co-operation, further and more destructive ideological wars are inevitable.

The aim of the negotiations between the Presbyterian Church in the United States of America and the Protestant Episcopal Church in the United States of America is to achieve such a basis of union that other Churches can adhere to it so that, if it be God's will, the union of the two Churches can be the nucleus of a more inclusive union. The united Church will seek to maintain fellowship with the Churches with which either of the uniting Churches is in communion, especially with the Churches of the two families, Anglican and Reformed, from which the uniting Churches have sprung.

The avowed goal of the negotiations is organic union. That term implies that when the unifying process is complete there will be one Church, with one standard of faith, one communicant list, one ministry, one system of government. The essential purpose is to find a means whereby each uniting Church may contribute its heritage of faith, order, and practice to the united body and each may recognize and be assured that those things which are precious to its people are preserved in the united Church.

The following articles are proposed by the representatives of the two Churches for study, and if adopted will become the basis for further negotiations looking toward the drafting of a constitution.

I
Doctrine

1. *General Statement*

Both Churches accept the Scriptures of the Old and New Testaments as the Word of God. The Apostles' Creed and the Nicene Creed set forth and further defined by the first four General Councils of the undivided Church are to be received as the statement of the Church's belief. The Confession of Faith and the Catechisms, and the Book of Common Prayer with the Articles of Religion, are recognized as containing the system of doctrine taught in Holy Scripture as the uniting Churches have respectively received it.

The Basis of Union permits any teacher of the united Church to use for the instruction of the faithful any teaching in the formularies authorized in either of the uniting Churches before the union, provided that such teaching is consistent with the Basis of Union and such doctrinal standards as may be officially set forth by the united Church, and provided also that whenever definite conflicts are disclosed between the formularies of the two uniting Churches, such conflicting teachings shall not be taught as necessary to salvation or so as to break fellowship in the united Church.

2. *Specific Statements*

(*a*) The Triune God. God, the Lord of the universe and of history, has revealed Himself as one God in three Persons, the Father, the Son, and the Holy Ghost.

(*b*) The Incarnate Word. Jesus Christ, truly God and perfect man, is the Founder and living Head of the Church.

(*c*) The Bible. The Holy Scriptures are the record of God's revelation of Himself for the redemption of man, and are the supreme sources for our knowledge of Him and of His will. The truth of such knowledge is attested by the Holy Spirit in the corporate witness of the Church and in the hearts of Christians, who by Him are led to understand and obey the Word of God.

(*d*) The Church. The visible Church is the fellowship of all those, together with their children, who, being baptized, profess faith in Jesus Christ as their Saviour and Lord; which fellowship is responsible to Him for the proclamation of the Gospel, for the perpetuation of the ministry which He gave it, for the use of the

Sacraments instituted by Him, for the maintenance of its unity as His Body in the Spirit of love, and for the promotion of God's righteousness in the world. It was constituted by Christ as a fellowship of disciples united with Him, and in Him with one another, to be His witnesses and the servants of His kingdom on earth.

(*e*) The Sacraments. The two Sacraments ordained by Christ, Baptism and the Supper of the Lord, are sure witnesses to the mighty acts of God and are means of grace appropriated by faith. Baptism is a sign and seal of God's covenant in Christ, of ingrafting into Him, of remission of sins by His death, of regeneration by His Spirit, and of incorporation into His Church. In the Lord's Supper, or Holy Communion, Christ communicates Himself to His people for their spiritual nourishment and growth in grace, and maintains the bond of fellowship whereby Christian people are joined to one another and to their Lord. The Lord's Supper shows forth the Lord's death till He come. It is offered as the memorial of His sacrifice which He commanded us to make, in which the faithful also offer themselves as a living sacrifice to God through Him.

(*f*) The Ministry. Christ supplies the Church, of which He is the living Head, with a ministry continuous through the centuries and empowered by the Holy Spirit to proclaim the Word and minister the Sacraments. The Church thankfully receives this ministry and through it exercises the prophetic, priestly, and pastoral functions committed to the Church by its Lord.

II

Government

1. *General Statement*

There shall be in the united Church a series of graduated councils (or judicatories). Such councils shall be established within the parish, within the diocese or presbytery, and within the province or synod; and there shall be a supreme judicatory, the General Assembly or Convention.

2. *Specific Statements*

(*a*) Councils. (Judicatories)

1. Within the Parish. The Parish Council shall consist of the minister or ministers of the parish, and the ruling elders elected by the congregation. The minister shall have oversight of the worship of the parish, with the advice of the Council. The Council shall be responsible for the spiritual upbuilding of the congregation. The

Council shall have oversight of the religious education and of the various societies, agencies, and other activities of the parish. It may recommend candidates for confirmation, examine and receive persons into the life of the parish, and commend them, upon removal, to other congregations. A congregation, either directly or through its Parish Council, may elect one or more wardens and delegate to the wardens such powers and duties as may be deemed desirable.

2. Within the Diocese or Presbytery. The Presbytery (Convention) shall consist of the Bishop or Bishops, all the presbyters (priests) within the diocese, and ruling elders delegated by the Parish Councils to represent the congregations; provided that congregations which have not previously had ruling elders shall, during a period of time to be specified in the Constitution, have the right to send other representatives; and such representatives also shall be eligible for election to the higher councils of the Church. The Bishop of the diocese, or, in his absence, the assistant Bishop, if there be one, shall be its presiding officer or moderator. The Presbytery shall elect its bishop or bishops. It shall have power to receive and examine candidates for the ministry. At ordinations, clerical representatives of the Presbytery shall participate with the Bishop in the laying on of hands. It shall have power to install pastors in their charges, and to dissolve the pastoral relationship. The Presbytery shall have power to receive complaints against ministers and to arrange for their trial. It shall enact a constitution and canons binding within its jurisdiction, provided that they are consistent with the laws of the united Church; and it shall provide for judicial procedures to deal with questions of discipline arising therefrom. In general, it shall take orders for whatever pertains to the spiritual welfare of the churches under its care and for the spread of the Gospel. It may appoint standing committees and prescribe their functions and powers.

3. Within the Province or Synod. The Province shall consist of six or more dioceses. Its council, the Synod, shall consist of representatives (bishops, presbyters [priests], and ruling elders) from all the Presbyteries within the Province. It is the intermediate council (judicatory) between the Presbytery and the General Assembly; and its forms of organization, powers, and responsibilities shall be as provided in the Constitution of the united Church.

4. The General Assembly (Convention). The supreme council (judicatory) of the united Church shall be a General Assembly (Convention) which shall be composed of bishops, presbyters (priests),

and ruling elders, and shall exercise appropriate powers and functions according to a plan to be set forth in the Constitution of the united Church.

III

Ministry and Lay Leadership

1. *General Statement.* In accordance with the following general principles, the Constitution will make provision so that all men ordained after the effective date of the union will bear the authority of both traditions. It will also provide that ministers who have been ordained in either Church prior to the effective date of the union will receive the authority of the other.

2. *The Clergy*

(*a*) The Episcopate. Bishops shall have the powers and duties traditionally theirs, and these shall be set forth in the Constitution. These powers and duties, exercised in concurrence with the Presbytery, shall include supervision of public worship, discipline, and leadership in the spread of the Gospel. As Chief Pastor, the Bishop shall exercise oversight of the Churches and their teaching, shall administer Confirmation, and, with clerical members of the Presbytery, shall officiate at ordinations of presbyters (priests) and deacons on behalf of the whole Church. He shall preside at or take order for meetings of the Presbytery (Diocesan Convention), and at inductions and installations and similar offices, and shall counsel with pastors and with candidates for the ministry.

The office of a bishop is also a teaching office, and he should do all in his power for the edification of the presbyters (priests) and congregations of whom he has oversight by instructing them or providing for their instruction concerning the truths of the Christian faith. Also on each bishop in his diocese, and on the Bishops of the Church as a body, is laid the responsibility of publicly witnessing to the doctrine of the Church and of urging its application to the conditions of the age.

There are within the uniting Churches differing views and beliefs regarding episcopacy, which have been recognized throughout the negotiations. Episcopacy is a form of Church government which has persisted through the centuries; and while differing views and beliefs have been held regarding it, and will be permitted in the united Church, it is agreed that the continuity of the episcopate which has come down from the undivided Church shall be effectively maintained, both at the inauguration of the union and thereafter.

(*b*) The Presbyterate. In the ministry of the Word and the Sacraments of the Gospel presbyters (priests) share equally with bishops. Their responsibilities are preaching and teaching the Word of God, officiating at the Sacraments and in the services of public worship, the ministry of reconciliation and the cure of souls, the leadership of parishes, and the fulfilment of other ministries, to which they have been duly called. As members of the presbytery, they shall participate with the Bishop in the government of the Church. They shall serve in the higher councils of the Church when elected thereto.

At such time as the union is effected, in every diocese and presbytery there shall be formal services of mutual recognition and extension of authority to minister in the united Church. The Moderator of the presbytery and his attending presbyters will lay their hands upon the Episcopal bishops and priests to be commissioned; likewise the Bishop and his attending presbyters will lay their hands upon the Presbyterian ministers to be commissioned. The Moderator or Bishop shall use the form following:

Here the Moderator or Bishop shall say to the minister to be commissioned:

> The ministry of the Word and Sacraments which thou hast already received is hereby recognized; and the grace and authority of Holy Orders as conferred by this Church are now added.

Then the Moderator or Bishop with attending presbyters shall lay hands on the minister to be commissioned and say:

> Take thou authority to execute thy ministry and to dispense the Word of God and His holy Sacraments in this united Church; in the Name of the Father, and of the Son, and of the Holy Ghost, Amen.

(*c*) The Diaconate. Candidates for the ministry shall first be ordained to the diaconate, and shall generally be continued in this status for one year. Before such ordination the candidate shall have a probationary period, the length of which shall be within the discretion of the Presbytery of jurisdiction, and shall meet such spiritual, intellectual, and other requirements as the Constitution of the united Church shall prescribe.

Deacons shall have the right to preach and teach under the licence and supervision of the bishop and presbytery, and to distribute the elements at an administration of the Holy Communion when requested by a presbyter (priest).

3. *The Laity*

To the whole Church of God and to every member of it belongs the duty and privilege of spreading the good news of the Kingdom of God and the message of salvation through Jesus Christ and of interceding for the brethren. All, according to their measure, share in the priesthood which the Church derives from Him.

(*a*) Congregations. The uniting Churches recognize the right of congregations to select their pastor or pastors, either directly or through officers chosen by themselves as each congregation may determine, subject to such discretion as the Constitution may vest in the bishop and presbytery. The laity shall also take their appropriate part in the election of other officers and in the general government of the Church. Administration of the property and temporal affairs of parishes may be vested in the parish councils; or these duties may be committed to wardens and vestrymen, or to trustees, in accordance with applicable ecclesiastical or civil law.

(*b*) Ruling Elders. Ruling elders are the lay representatives of the people, chosen by them for the purpose of exercising government and discipline in conjunction with presbyters (priests) or pastors. They shall be communicants of faith, wisdom, and character. They shall serve with presbyters (priests) in the superior councils of the Church when elected thereto. They shall take vows of loyalty to the doctrine and government of the Church, and shall be set apart by prayer and the laying on of hands by a presbyter (priest). A ruling elder, duly examined and qualified for such service, may be commissioned by the bishop and presbytery to have pastoral charge of a congregation having no minister. The Constitution may authorize the setting apart of laymen as ruling elders for membership in the higher councils of the Church or for performance of special duties without first serving in the Council of the Parish.

(*c*) Lay Deacons. Congregations which so desire may elect lay deacons and deaconesses. These may be set apart to serve the church, under appropriate vows, in its ministry of teaching, social service, and charity.

IV

Other Basic Provisions

1. *Baptism.* Baptism by water in the name of the Father, and of the Son, and of the Holy Ghost is the method by which candidates are incorporated into the Church.

A profession of faith in Jesus Christ, the Son of the Living God, as Lord and Saviour shall be required of adult candidates for baptism, and of parents or sponsors of young children presented for this Sacrament; and parents or sponsors shall also promise to do their utmost, with God's help, to rear baptized children in the Christian faith and life.

2. *Confirmation.* Confirmation is a rite through which increase of grace is bestowed by the Holy Spirit and by which baptized persons publicly renew their baptismal vows, assume for themselves the full responsibilities of Church membership, and are admitted to the Holy Communion. Candidates for adult baptism and for confirmation shall be carefully instructed in the Christian faith and in the obligations of Church membership, and shall be examined and approved by the minister and parish council as to their knowledge and faith.

The rite shall be administered by the laying on of hands, with prayer, by the bishop, or by a presbyter (priest) duly authorized by the bishop and presbytery.

3. *The Lord's Supper.* In the celebration of the Sacrament of the Lord's Supper, bread and wine shall be used, and every rite in the united Church shall contain at least the following:

(*a*) A confession of sin and a declaration of God's forgiveness.

(*b*) A commemoration of the Lord's death and passion, and the recital of His words and acts in the institution of the Sacrament, in or with

A prayer of thanksgiving and consecration;

A presentation of the elements to God and a self-offering of the communicants;

An invocation of the Holy Spirit upon the elements and the congregation;

The Lord's Prayer.

(*c*) The Apostles' Creed or the Nicene Creed on appropriate occasions.

4. *Ordination.* In all ordinations and consecrations the true ordainer is God, Who, in response to the prayers of His Church, and through the words and acts of its representatives, commissions and empowers for the office and work to which they are called the persons whom the Church has selected.

In every ordination service there shall be the imposition of hands, with prayer, an authorization to minister, and a designation of the office to which the candidate is being ordained.

All ordinations of presbyters (priests) and deacons shall be by the bishop and the presbyters (priests) of the presbytery of jurisdiction, who shall join in the laying on of hands.

In the service of consecration of bishops in the united Church there shall be: (1) the solemn presentation of the person (or persons) to be consecrated to the bishops who are taking part in the consecration by two presbyters (priests) of the diocese to which the candidate is elected, (or, if a missionary bishop, the presbytery of which he is a member); (2) a prayer of consecration, asking that the person to be consecrated may receive the gift of God's Holy Spirit for the office and work of a bishop in His Church; and (3) the laying on of hands by the bishops (who shall be at least three in number) and presbyters (priests) representing the presbytery of jurisdiction.

In every ordination and consecration, vows shall be taken to maintain the Holy Scriptures as the Word of God and as containing all things necessary to salvation, and to minister the doctrine, Sacraments, and discipline of the Church in accordance with its constitution.

When a congregation shall so request, the bishop and presbytery shall require of the pastor elect a promise to minister the doctrine and worship in accordance with the forms to which the parish is accustomed. In all such cases the bishop and presbytery shall insure that such conditions are fulfilled.

V

Worship

1. *General Statement.* It is anticipated that in due time the united Church will have a common service book which will express the unity and breadth of its faith and life, and which will result naturally from fellowship in the united Church. This will include a variety of forms, liturgical and non-liturgical, to meet the needs of various parishes and groups in the Church, and to preserve the distinctive values in the two traditions of worship. There are sacramental rites, Confirmation, Marriage, Absolution, Ordination, and the Anointing of the Sick, which minister God's grace to those who receive them in faith, and they will continue to be available in the united Church. No attempt will be made to abolish diversity of worship, but forms of public worship and usages connected with them which have been authorized or permitted in either of the

uniting Churches under the Book of Common Prayer or the Directory for the Public Worship of God and the Book of Common Worship, may be continued. No change shall be made in the worship of any parish without the agreement of the pastor and congregation, and the approval of the bishop and presbytery.

2. *The Liturgical Commission*

(*a*) The Constitution shall provide for a standing Liturgical Commission.

For a period of twenty-five years after the adoption of the Constitution, and thereafter until otherwise provided by amendment to the Constitution, this Commission shall be composed of twenty members, divided into two sections of ten members each, herein to be designated as Sections A and B. Section A shall consist of ministers (presbyters [priests] and bishops) and ruling elders (in proportions to be determined later) chosen from among those who customarily use the Directory for Public Worship of God and the Book of Common Worship. Section B shall consist of three bishops, three presbyters (priests), and four laymen, chosen from among those who customarily use the Book of Common Prayer.

(*b*) The two sections of the Commission, sitting together, shall prepare a book to be offered to the General Assembly (Convention) for adoption as the common service book of the united Church. This book shall contain liturgical services, directions for worship, orders of service with provision for the use of extempore prayers, services for special occasions, and forms for the administration of the Sacraments and for other rites and ceremonies.

(*c*) Until such time as this book may be adopted and promulgated, for the fostering of unity and other special purposes the Liturgical Commission may set forth forms of worship which any presbytery may authorize for use in the diocese.

(*d*) In order to safeguard the existing forms of worship until a common service book shall be adopted, the two sections of the Liturgical Commission shall from time to time sit separately. Section A shall have sole power to recommend to the General Assembly (Convention) amendments to the Book of Common Worship and the Directory. Section B shall have sole power to recommend to the General Assembly (Convention) amendments to the Book of Common Prayer. It may also make recommendations for the enforcement of the Prayer Book's provisions.

(*e*) Nothing in this article shall be construed as giving authority to the Liturgical Commission to abridge the freedom in forms of worship assured in Section 1.

VI

Property and Contract Rights

(Qualified committees of both Churches should give further careful study to matters relating to property and contract rights as they would be affected by the union of the two Churches.)

* * * *

PART III

The Commission recommends the adoption of the following resolutions:

1. *Resolved*, The House of   concurring, that the Joint Commission on Approaches to Unity be continued, and that it be directed to continue negotiations with the Presbyterian Church in the United States of America, and to further or initiate such conversations with representatives of other Christian bodies as in its judgement may lead to our closer fellowship with them.

2. *Resolved*, The House of   concurring, that the accompanying document 'The Proposed Basis of Union between the Protestant Episcopal Church in the United States of America and the Presbyterian Church in the United States of America' is hereby received and submitted as worthy of the serious study of the Bishops, Clergy, and Laity of our Church; and that looking forward to decisive action by the General Convention of 1949, the Secretary of the House of Bishops and the Secretary of the House of Deputies shall transmit to the Bishop of each Diocese and Missionary District, and to the Secretaries of the Conventions of the several Dioceses and Missionary Districts respectively, 'The Proposed Basis of Union' for study and report.

3. *Resolved*, The House of   concurring, that it shall be the duty of each Diocese and Missionary District to formulate and to execute such plans as in its judgement will best promote thorough and systematic study of 'The Proposed Basis of Union' by its Clergy and Laity.

4. *Resolved*, The House of   concurring, that it shall be the duty of the Ecclesiastical Authority of each Diocese and

Missionary District to forward the results of the study undertaken therein to the Presiding Bishop ten months before the General Convention of 1949, and that the Presiding Bishop be requested to transmit these reports to the Joint Commission on Approaches to Unity.

5. *Resolved,* The House of concurring, that the Presiding Bishop be requested to present the Proposed Basis of Union to the meeting of the Lambeth Conference in 1948 for its consideration and advice.

6. *Resolved,* The House of concurring, that in its report to General Convention of 1949, the Joint Commission on Approaches to Unity shall include a statement of the results of the studies undertaken in the several Dioceses and Missionary Districts.

7. *Resolved,* The House of concurring, that the Treasurer of General Convention be directed to provide the sum of $6,000.00 for the expenses of the Commission on Approaches to Unity during the coming triennium.

(*Signed*) R. E. L. STRIDER (*Chairman*)
STEPHEN E. KEELER
BENJAMIN M. WASHBURN
SHERMAN E. JOHNSON
THEODORE O. WEDEL
ALEXANDER C. ZABRISKIE (*Secretary*)
WILLIAM L. BALTHIS
ALEXANDER GUERRY
JOHN C. SPAULDING
GEORGE F. THOMAS

MINORITY REPORT

We, the undersigned members of the Commission on Approaches to Unity cannot sign the majority report nor recommend the Proposed Basis of Union to the Church for study because we judge that the Proposals radically distort the religion of our Lord. We see no point in asking the Church to study for a period of years what we are certain would, if adopted, cause only disunity among ourselves and superficial unification with others.

I. We do not admit that the Commission was appointed, as has been asserted in some quarters, merely to be a negotiating committee to accomplish union with the Presbyterians immediately and at any price. The Resolution of 1937 in regard to unity with the Presbyterians was passed unanimously and without debate. It is unthinkable that our Church could have voted to destroy its General Convention and to liquidate itself, all in the space of a few years, without at least some debate upon the subject and some opposition. The fact that there was no debate and no opposition is clear evidence that the Resolution was not understood by the Church then as it has been interpreted by some recently.

Secondly, it would be a distinct act of apostasy for our Church or any Church, to pledge itself to an act of unity blindfolded, by giving a blank cheque in regard to Christian faith and practice. That would be tantamount to saying that our religion is not concerned with belief and practice, and thus debase it to the plane of sentiment. We feel sure that our Church, by the Resolution of 1937, did not intend to degrade itself in this fashion and therefore we vigorously repudiate any 'compulsion' under this resolution to accept without question whatever the Presbyterians may insist upon.

II. It has been said that the Presbyterians have accepted the episcopate. This we deny to be the case save in the most Pickwickian sense. The role of a bishop has indeed varied through the centuries and we have no desire to restrict the variety of its manifestations, but one fact has remained constant and unchanged. That fact is that only a bishop can validly ordain. From the years during which St. John was presumably still alive at Ephesus, there is the unbroken testimony through the centuries that the peculiar and necessary function of a bishop is to ordain. This the Presbyterians flatly deny by asserting that their ministry is on precisely the same foundation as an episcopally ordained ministry, and refusing even to accept a supplemental ordination of any kind. Some have urged that the Proposed Formula for the Interim Period is really a supplemental ordination. We do not deny that by theological agility it might be so interpreted, but we are confident that it would be dishonest so to interpret it, when the Presbyterians have explicitly declared to our Commission that it is just with this interpretation that they will *not* accept it.

Further, they strenuously assert the parity of Orders. This phrase is not altogether familiar in our Church, but its meaning is that all ministers of the Church have absolutely the same spiritual power, and that no one has any more spiritual authority than any other. In other words, bishops, priests, and deacons are all on the same level of authority, and a bishop has no more spiritual power than a priest or a deacon. This principle has indeed been an historic Presbyterian principle and the Presbyterian Department frequently and strongly asserted it when we met. We were informed that parity of Orders is a fundamental Presbyterian conviction and that 'we will never give it up.' Further, in their desire for a unicameral assembly, they urge that such organization should be set up 'because it expresses governmentally the parity of the clergy.' Such doctrine has never been the doctrine of the Anglican Communion and was one of the great points of conflict in the English Civil War between the Church and the Presbyterians.

Even beyond this, the Presbyterian view of the ministry utterly rejects the Prayer Book idea of the priesthood. In their official publication 'Why a Presbyterian Church' it is definitely asserted that a minister 'is in no sense a "priest" beyond any other sincere Christian believer' (p. 17). It would be hard to find any doctrine of the Ministry more contradictory of what we have learned from our Prayer Book than this.

III. The Proposals suggested would, if carried out, ultimately do away with our Prayer Book. It is true that for a certain period of years they allow the Presbyterians to continue their accustomed forms of worship and us to continue to use our Prayer Book. This, however, is only for a limited time. After that time, the new Church, with the Presbyterian element vastly outnumbering ours, will issue its own book of worship which will supersede all others. It is absurd to suppose that this large Presbyterian majority will continue to favour our historic Prayer Book against which they have fought so bitterly through the centuries. Hence, however this Proposal may be camouflaged, it still remains that a vote for it is a vote ultimately to destroy our Prayer Book.

IV. The present Proposals would automatically remove the Episcopal Church from the Anglican orbit of Churches and make it a member of the Presbyterian orbit of Churches. According to the announcements made in regard to the South India plan, which is a far less radical scheme than these present Proposals, the Anglican Church which accepts it is to be cut off from communion with Canterbury. Hence, were our Proposals to go through, our Church would be out of communion with Canterbury and our bishops would not be invited to Lambeth. Even more, by these Proposals, the new Church would be in communion with the Presbyterian Church of Scotland and so in communion with all the Presbyterian Churches throughout the world. In other words, these Proposals would swing our Church definitely and unequivocally out of the Anglican Communion and make it a part of the Presbyterian Communion. We cannot feel that this is desirable.

Summary

We regret that we cannot acquiesce in presenting the present Proposals to the Church for study. We recognize that the majority report explicitly does not approve the Proposals in any way, but merely presents them to the Church for study for three years. We know that several members of the majority group do not themselves approve of the Proposals, but only agree to their presentation to the Church for study. Nevertheless, we cannot believe that it is right in the sight of God and in loyalty to His Church to ask the Church to study, with at least the possibility of accepting, what we are profoundly convinced is repugnant to the mind of Christ.

We still feel that the two points which led many of us at an earlier stage to hope for some achievement in unity are entirely disregarded by these proposals. The first of these points is that anything considered in regard to the Presbyterians should be judged in the light of further possibilities of union with other Communions. It is a patent fact that the present Proposals would move us farther and farther from any of the great historic Catholic Communions and that in fact we should become rather a laughing-stock before the eyes of Christendom in any claim to be a 'Bridge Church'. We should have become merely one of several hundred other Protestant sects.

The second point upon which much has been spoken and written and of which we had hoped much was that union was to be achieved by all Communions giving to the new Church what they themselves possessed and had found valuable. No Communion was to give up, but every Communion was to give. This is not the purport of the present Proposals. The historic ministry of the Church as understood by the majority of Christians throughout the world, and the sacramental system authorized by our Church and binding us to that larger fellowship of Christians, these have not been given by us because they have not been accepted by the Presbyterians. The bishop has been transmuted into merely a permanent Moderator. Any student of ecclesiastical institutions reading the present Proposals impartially would come to only one conclusion, namely, that our Church had ceased to preserve its historic identity and had become a new kind of Presbyterian Church. Since we do not wish to participate in this change, we find ourselves unable to approve these Proposals.

GOODRICH R. FENNER
HARWOOD STURTEVANT
C. RANKIN BARNES
LEICESTER C. LEWIS
CLAUDE W. SPROUSE
HOWARD T. FOULKES
JAMES G. MITCHELL[1]

198. General Convention of the Protestant Episcopal Church in U.S.A. Resolutions on Approaches to Unity

SEPTEMBER 1946

RESOLVED, That the Joint Commission on Approaches to Unity be continued, and that it be directed to continue negotiations with the Presbyterian Church in the United States of America, and to further or initiate such conversations with representatives of other Christian bodies as in its judgement may lead to our closer fellowship with them, and be it further

RESOLVED, That we receive both the majority and minority reports of the Joint Commission on Approaches to Unity with appreciation of the great service rendered the Church in presenting the results of negotiations with the Presbyterian Church in the U.S.A., and be it further

RESOLVED, That since the results of these negotiations have reached a point at which it becomes necessary to set forth an authoritative statement of the basis upon which the Protestant Episcopal Church in the U.S.A. will act, the Joint Commission on the Approaches to Unity be continued, and be requested to prepare a statement of faith and order, in harmony with the Lambeth Quadrilateral, upon which the Protestant Episcopal Church in the U.S.A. is prepared to enter into intercommunion and to proceed toward organic federation with the Presbyterian Church in the U.S.A. or with any other interested Christian body, the Commission to report to the next session of the General Convention; and be it further

RESOLVED, That the Protestant Episcopal Church in the U.S.A.

[1] Mr. Mitchell agrees with this report, but desires to supplement its findings.

extend to the Presbyterian Church in the U.S.A. its cordial greetings and gratitude for the brotherly courtesy manifested in the discussions which have been held, and request that the Department of Church Co-operation and Unity of the Presbyterian Church in the U.S.A. prepare a similar formulation, taking into account the points of the Lambeth Quadrilateral, and

WHEREAS, the subject of Unity is of the utmost concern to the entire Anglican Communion, and

WHEREAS, for one part of the Anglican Communion to consider union with any Christian body necessarily involves the life and unity of our whole Communion, therefore be it

RESOLVED, That the Presiding Bishop be requested to refer to the 1948 Lambeth Conference such proposals for Church Unity as are being considered by our Church, and which are related to the Anglican Communion, including the statement to be prepared by the Joint Commission on Approaches to Unity based upon the Lambeth Quadrilateral, as provided herein above, and be it further

RESOLVED, That the Treasurer of the General Convention be directed to provide the sum of $6,000.00 for the expenses of the Commission on Approaches to Unity during the coming triennium.

199. General Assembly of the Presbyterian Church in U.S.A. Report of Department of Church Co-operation and Union

MAY 1947

[The following is section IV of the Report.]

The Protestant Episcopal Church

THE members of the Department of Church Co-operation and Union of the Presbyterian Church in the United States of America deeply regret that the Protestant Episcopal Church at its General Convention last September, did not see fit to submit to the dioceses of the Church for consideration, the proposed basis of union which had been formulated by a Joint Drafting Committee representing its Commission on Approaches to Unity and this Department. It instead adopted resolutions directing its Commission 'to prepare a statement of faith and order in harmony with the Lambeth Quadrilateral upon which the Protestant Episcopal Church in the United

States of America is prepared to enter into intercommunion and to proceed toward organic federation with the Presbyterian Church in the United States of America, or with any other interested Christian body', and requesting this Department to 'prepare a similar formulation, taking into account the points of the Lambeth Quadrilateral'. This action was at once officially reported to our Church through the Stated Clerk of the General Assembly, Dr. Pugh. Later, Bishop R. E. L. Strider, Chairman of the Commission on Approaches to Unity, wrote Dr. Pugh transmitting the resolutions of the Protestant Episcopal General Convention, which are appended.

It was clear to the Department at its meeting last November that this action would probably retard considerably the efforts toward union then in progress between the two Churches. But the Department thought that before making any comment upon the resolutions, it should seek a clarification of their practical effect from the Commission on Approaches to Unity which had not then met. Hence it decided to defer any statement until there was opportunity for discussion with the Commission.

It was then hoped and expected that before this meeting, the Drafting Committee of the Department could meet with a like committee of the Episcopal Commission and explore the situation. Unfortunately this has not been possible. The organization of the Episcopal Commission was delayed and the Commission will not be meeting until April.

Under the circumstances, the Department is still not in a position to make any definite expression upon the possibility of union with the Protestant Episcopal Church. Whether or not the action of that Church at its Convention nullifies or alters the previous basis of negotiations necessarily depends on clarification of the position of the Episcopal Church which is now awaited by this Department.

In this situation, the Department would recommend that judgement continue to be suspended, and that our Church refrain from action. At the same time we believe that we should be receptive to any suggestions looking toward union that may come from our Episcopal brethren, and be willing to consider them. This is the attitude we have consistently maintained since overtures were received from the Episcopal Church in 1937.

Admittedly the action of the Episcopal General Convention appears to be a reverse to the movement for union with that body. But the union of all Christ's followers is of such supreme importance that we must not allow ourselves to be halted or discouraged by this seeming setback. In his letter to Dr. Pugh, Bishop Strider wrote:

> 'I earnestly appeal to you and to other leaders in the Presbyterian Church to be willing to continue the negotiations with us. To break them off would give an enormous setback to the cause so dear to the hearts of almost the whole of Christendom.'

We feel deeply that it is our part as Christians to meet Bishop Strider and his associates in this spirit, and to try again under God's guidance to go forward.

XIII. CANADA

THE CHURCH OF ENGLAND IN CANADA AND THE UNITED CHURCH OF CANADA

[At the Jubilee Session of the General Synod of the Church of England in Canada, held in Toronto in September 1943, a Resolution presented by the Committee on Reunion was adopted in both Houses. This Resolution stated that 'the Synod now expresses its hearty desire and readiness to meet, through its own representatives, in conference and prayer, with representatives of any Christian Communion which shares its hopes and aspirations for a reunited Christendom, and it extends a cordial invitation to the Christian communions of Canada thus to initiate "conversations" '. Replies were received to this invitation from the United Church of Canada, the Baptist Churches in Canada, and the Presbyterian Church in Canada, and conversations began with each of these. The 'Conversations' with the two latter Churches have not yet proceeded far enough to produce any definite recommendations, but in 1946 a Report was issued by the Committees which, since February 1944, had been carrying on 'Conversations' between the Church of England in Canada and the United Church of Canada. Attached to the Report, but not forming part of it, were two 'Papers Bearing on Particular Points of the Common Problem'. This Report was considered by the General Synod of the Church of England in Canada on September 10 and 11, 1946, when a statement was issued by the House of Bishops, with the Lower House concurring.]

200. *Report of Committees Provided for by the Church of England in Canada and the United Church of Canada on the Procedure whereby our two Ministries can be Conferred Each upon the Other*

SEPTEMBER 1946

INTRODUCTION

1. In presenting this report, we desire first to make clear the reasons which have led us to confine our attention to the study of the practical steps, which, in our judgement, are required to secure a ministry of the Word and Sacraments which will be mutually acceptable to both the Communions engaged in these conversations.

2. The ultimate motive behind all the approach of the two Communions to each other is doubtless that, some day, our Lord's prayer for His Church may be visibly realized: 'That they all may be one.' But the immediate and pressing motive is to be found in

the manifest needs of Canada for the unifying of the Christian forces of our land, especially in its outlying regions. Our knowledge of the present situation, in which some 1,500,000 persons, who claim to belong to us, are lapsed from any visible connexion with us, while at the same time we are squandering our resources of men and material in what is little better than competition with each other, is a knowledge which distresses our consciences. Moreover, we are aware that our unco-operative divisions are a source of an indifference to, and irritation with, the Church, which, if it continues to grow, bodes ill for the true welfare of our country.

3. We rejoice to know of all the steps that are being taken to correct the evil of separation, in the formation of the Canadian Council of Churches and by means of the conversations which the Church of England in Canada and the United Church of Canada are holding, separately, with other Christian Bodies.

4. But we also think that a special responsibility for leadership in co-operative unity falls upon our two Communions. Between us we include at least two-thirds of reformed Christendom in Canada; and, still more important, between us we do by far the largest part of the work in those frontier regions on which our eyes are particularly fixed.

5. At the same time we fear that any large proposals for unifying the two Communions in polity would be in advance of the present opinion of our people, and to standardize them in Worship would be undesirable in itself. Much active co-operation and experience of each other are required before we can satisfactorily blend the Episcopal and Conciliar systems, so as to secure the benefits of each. As far as Worship is concerned, it is obvious that simple and spontaneous expressions appeal to large numbers of Canadian Christians, and that any tendency to impose specific forms upon them would re-create the divisions we are anxious to see obliterated. On the other hand, there are also large numbers to whom liturgical forms of worship are rich with spiritual meaning and for whom these must always be preserved. We have before us, therefore, as a first step, the fashioning of a relation in which our two Communions, while retaining their separate identities and freedoms in Worship, can engage, easily and fully, in combined operations for the Kingdom of God.

6. We find ourselves not only agreed concerning the essentials of the Faith but also united in the possession of a common sacramental

life in the great primal Sacrament of Holy Baptism. Since we are one in Faith and one in Baptism we believe that we have already the promised presence of the One Lord Jesus Christ in our assemblies where two or three are gathered together in His Name, and that through Him a multitude of souls in both communions has been brought into union with the One God and Father of us all. But we still lack sacramental unity at the Lord's Table and unity in the Ministry, without which we cannot work together effectively. We suggest, therefore, that the next steps be towards a Ministry recognized by both Communions and towards unity at the Lord's Table. To the problems involved therein we have addressed ourselves, and now present to you, for your considerations, our recommendations and findings.

7. We have divided our findings under four heads: A. A Mutually Acceptable Ministry: B. Recommendations relating thereto: C. Access of communicants to the Lord's Table in both Communions: D. General Conclusions.

A

A Mutually Acceptable Ministry

1. We have considered the subject of the Ministry in both Communions and are of the opinion that these two Ministries are best considered as parallel to one another rather than identical. The Church of England has the threefold Ministry of Holy Orders: the United Church has the Holy Order of Presbyterial Ministry in which there is no distinction of orders, and has its Church Courts. The Church of England distributes the functions of the Ministry among the three Orders of Bishops, Priests, and Deacons: The United Church distributes the functions of the Ministry between the Ministers and the Church Courts. It is, therefore, impossible to say at any point that there is an exact identity. For instance, the functions of the second Order of the Ministry in the Church of England are not identical with the functions of the Ministry of the United Church. For United Church Ministers are not only equal one with another but, in virtue of their membership in Church Courts, are responsible along with their brethren for actions which in the Church of England are reserved for the Bishops. On the other hand the parish priest in the Church of England has disciplinary authority which, in the United Church, is reserved for the Session. We point to this dissimilarity as a fundamental consideration in our approach to the problem with which we are faced.

2. The Church of England members of the Committee gladly acknowledge the reality of the United Church ministry as having been used by God for the conversion and growth in grace of multitudes of people, not only since Union, but in the time when it functioned in the Congregational, Methodist, and Presbyterian Churches. They recognize that had it not been for the Ministry of these Churches many people in Canada would have gone without the blessings of the Christian Religion, and that many saintly persons owe their religion to the help received through this Ministry. They recognize also that this United Church Ministry possesses a quality and tradition of its own. They recognize among other things that it is of a specially constitutional character because, through the operation of the Church Courts, the faithful people and the presbyters have an effective voice in the outward call of a man to the Ministry and in the recognition of his inward call. There is also the special quality of this Ministry which is harder to define but which manifests itself in the pulpit Ministry, in the conduct of public worship, and in the sharing of pastoral care with the members of the local Church Session. The Church of England members of the Committee, therefore, consider their United Church brethren to be Ministers of Christ, and to have in their Ministry a real contribution to make in any future union. They are of the opinion that there have been from time to time Ministries parallel to the threefold Orders, and that these Ministries have been used by God for the edification of His Church. Therefore, they gladly recognize their United Church brethren as Ministers of Christ in the Church universal, and would be most unwilling that they should be asked in any way to deny the reality of their call, or of the Ministry they have already received and exercised for the edification of God's people. Consequently, they suggest that all such words as 'valid' or 'invalid', 'regular' or 'irregular', be not used, inasmuch as they are technical terms whose proper application is solely to the threefold Ministry of Holy Orders.

3. The United Church members of the Committee, on their part, gladly acknowledge the reality of the Ministry of the Church of England in its threefold Holy Orders of Bishops, Priests, and Deacons. They recognize that this ancient Ministry possesses an historic continuity with the Ministry of the Church from very early days, and also a special quality of its own in its emphasis on the sacramental life, in liturgical worship, in its manner of pastoral care,

and in that ordering of the Church's life which culminates in the oversight exercised by the Bishop as a Father in God.

4. The whole Committee considers it desirable, therefore, that in any future union each Communion should contribute the *whole* of its Ministry each to the other. As a step towards this end, we suggest that once each Communion is satisfied that the formularies of the other teach sufficiently the true Christian Faith, and after sufficient instruction of the Ministers in the practical exercise of the other Ministry, any Minister of the United Church could receive Holy Orders according to the form and manner of the Church of England in Canada, and any clergyman of the Church of England in Canada could be admitted to the Ministry of the United Church by the appropriate Court of that Church, and according to the form used in the United Church Book of Common Order. We recommend that in both cases it should be made clear, by a preface to be read before the Service, that in neither case is any man denying the reality of the Ministry he has already received and exercised, but that he is seeking a commission for a further Ministry, and the necessary grace from God to perform the same.

5. The object of this mutual reception of our respective Ministries is to make it possible for the Ministers of each Communion to minister in the other Communion, under the licence and direction of the Bishop of the Diocese in the one case, and of the proper Church Courts in the other case. The further object of this mutual reception of the Ministry is the removal of an obstacle to unity by the provision of a Ministry in each Communion which is acceptable in the other Communion.

B

Recommendations

1. We recommend that in the conferring upon Ministers of each Communion of the Ministry of the other, the following declaration shall first be read by the Presiding Officer:

> 'In the name of the Father and of the Son and of the Holy Ghost, Amen. Beloved in the Lord, it has been agreed by the Church of England in Canada and the United Church of Canada that in dependence upon Almighty God, in faith in the Lord Jesus Christ and seeking the aid of the Holy Spirit, we come to these solemn acts wherein we convey each to the other the graces of our several ministries, neither denying to the other its heritage

in the Holy Catholic Church, nor the reality of its ministry, as a ministry of Christ, but both desiring to increase our gifts and enlarge our opportunities for the extension of Christ's Kingdom.'

2. The above declaration shall also be read immediately before the service of ordination to the priesthood and to the full ministry respectively.

3. In the following orders of services:

(*a*) A priest of the Church of England in Canada is first received into full communion in the United Church of Canada, then is licensed to preach and then ordained to the full ministry of the United Church.

(*b*) A minister of the United Church of Canada is first confirmed, then ordained to the diaconate, and then advanced to the priesthood of the Church of England in Canada.

4. In the case of a Priest of the Church of England in Canada, upon whom the Ministry of the United Church is to be conferred, the following steps shall be taken:

(*a*) He shall produce to the appropriate Church Courts evidence of his Baptism and Ordination, and of his having familiarized himself with the doctrine, discipline, and worship of the United Church. He shall promise that in ministering in congregations of the United Church of Canada he shall conform thereto.

Reception to Full Communion

(*b*) He shall stand before the presiding Minister and make profession of faith in Jesus Christ and of obedience to him, reciting the Apostles' Creed and answering the following questions:

The Apostles' Creed and Questions

I believe in God the Father Almighty, Maker of heaven and earth;

And in Jesus Christ His only Son our Lord, Who was conceived by the Holy Ghost, Born of the Virgin Mary, Suffered under Pontius Pilate, Was crucified, dead, and buried; He descended into hell; The third day He rose again from the dead; He ascended into heaven, And sitteth on the right hand of God the Father Almighty; From thence He shall come to judge the quick and the dead.

I believe in the Holy Ghost; The Holy Catholic Church; The

Communion of Saints; The forgiveness of sins; The Resurrection of the body; And the Life everlasting. Amen.

Will you then endeavour to keep God's holy will and commandments, and to walk in the same all the days of your life?

Answer. I will.

Do you promise to make diligent use of the means of grace, and in all things to seek earnestly the peace and welfare of the Church of God?

Answer. I do so promise, God being my helper.

Then shall the Minister say:

Let us pray.

Almighty and everlasting God, strengthen, we pray thee, these thy servants with the Holy Spirit the Comforter, and daily increase in them thy manifold gifts of grace; the spirit of wisdom and understanding; the spirit of counsel and might; the spirit of knowledge and true godliness; fill them, O God, with the spirit of thy holy fear; and keep them in thy mercy unto life eternal; through Jesus Christ our Lord, Amen.

Then the Minister, offering to him the right hand of fellowship shall say:

The God of all grace, who hath called you unto his eternal glory by Jesus Christ, confirm you to the end, that ye may be blameless in the day of our Lord Jesus Christ. Amen.

The Licensing to Preach

(*c*) He shall then be licensed to preach as follows:

The Presiding Minister shall say:

Beloved in the Lord, God has given commandment unto his Church, not only to pray for the increase of the Ministry, but also to prove those who seek the sacred office, that no man be ordained suddenly, but that men of pure heart and right conduct, able to speak edification, be found for his holy service. This Presbytery (Conference), therefore, having inquired concerning you, and also examined you, and having found you to be of good report, of sound faith, and of sufficient learning, does now commend you to the Conference as qualified to preach the Gospel of the grace of God. And we follow you with our prayers.

Then shall the Presiding Minister say:

Let us pray.

Almighty God, who hast given unto thy Son, Jesus Christ, to be head over all things to thy Church; we beseech thee to bestow upon these thy servants the grace of thy Holy Spirit, that they may be endued with power to preach thy Gospel, and may prove their fitness to serve thee in the Ministry of the Word. Replenish them with the truth of thy doctrine and adorn them with innocency of life, that they may faithfully serve thee both by word and example. Give them grace to preach the unsearchable riches of Christ, to instruct with meekness those that oppose themselves to the truth, and to gather into the fold of Christ many that are wandering in the ways of error and sin. Grant that, going forth and labouring in dependence upon thee, they may have abundant fruit of their labours, and obtain the reward of faithful servants in thy heavenly kingdom; through Jesus Christ our Lord. Amen.

Our Father who art in heaven, Hallowed be thy name; Thy Kingdom come; Thy will be done; in earth as it is in heaven. Give us this day our daily bread. And forgive us our trespasses as we forgive them that trespass against us. And lead us not into temptation; But deliver us from evil; For thine is the kingdom, the power and the glory, for ever and ever. Amen.

And he may bless them, saying:

The Word of the Lord be nigh you, even in your mouth, and in your heart.

The blessing of God Almighty, the Father, the Son, and the Holy Spirit be with you. Amen.

The Ordination to the Full Ministry

(*d*) On the same or some subsequent day he shall come before the appropriate Court of the United Church to be admitted into the Ministry of the United Church of Canada.

The Presiding Minister shall read the following declaration:

In the name of the Father and of the Son and of the Holy Ghost. Amen. Beloved in the Lord, it has been agreed by the Church of England in Canada and the United Church of Canada that in dependence upon Almighty God, in faith in the Lord Jesus Christ and seeking the aid of the Holy Spirit, we come to these solemn acts wherein we convey each to the other the graces of our several ministries, neither denying to the other its heritage in the Holy Catholic Church, nor the reality of its ministry as a ministry of Christ, but both desiring to increase our gifts and enlarge our opportunities for the extension of Christ's Kingdom.

The Minister appointed thereto shall then read the following declaration which shall take the place of the Presentation of the Candidates in the Form of Ordination and also be inscribed on the letters of Orders:

A.B. who has already been ordained Priest in the Church of God according to the use of the Church of England in Canada desires to exercise the Ministry in the United Church of Canada. We recognize the Ministry which he has already received and acting under the authority of the Church are about to admit him to the Sacred Ministry as the United Church of Canada has received the same, calling down upon him the blessing of the Holy Spirit, that he may have all necessary grace and power faithfully to fulfil the same, and granting him authority to minister among us.

Here shall silence be kept for a space, that prayer may be made for them that are to be ordained.

(*e*) Then shall the Presiding Minister proceed with the service, in which the Prayer for Grace, Epistle, and Gospel shall be as followeth:

The Prayer for Grace

Almighty God, Giver of all good things, who by the Holy Spirit hast appointed the Ministry of the word and Sacraments: Mercifully behold these thy servants now called to this holy office, and replenish them so with the truth of thy doctrine, and adorn them with innocency of life, that, both by word and good example, they may faithfully serve thee in this Office; to the glory of thy name, and the edification of thy Church; through the merits of our Saviour Jesus Christ, who liveth and reigneth with thee and the Holy Spirit, world without end. Amen.

The *Epistle*. Eph. iv. 4–8, 11–13 shall be read.

The *Gospel*. John xxi. 15–17 or John x. 1–11 or Matt. xxviii. 18–20, shall be read.

(*f*) Then shall follow a Sermon, declaring the duty and office of such as come to be admitted Ministers of the Word and Sacraments, how necessary that Order is in the Church of Christ, and also how the people ought to esteem them in their Office.

(*g*) Then shall follow a Prayer for the whole state of Christ's Church.

(*h*) After this, the Presiding Minister shall say unto them that are to be ordained:

You have heard, Brethren, as well in your private examination, as in the exhortation which was made to you, and in the holy Lessons taken out of the Gospel, and the writings of the Apostles, of what dignity, and of how great importance this Office is, whereunto you are called. And now again we exhort you, in the name of our Lord Jesus Christ that you have in remembrance into how high a dignity, and to how weighty an office and charge you are called; that is to say, to be Messengers, Watchmen, and Stewards of the Lord; to teach and to admonish, to feed and provide for the Lord's family; to seek for Christ's sheep that are dispersed abroad, and for his children who are in the midst of this evil world, that they may be saved through Christ for ever.

Have always, therefore, in remembrance how great a treasure is committed to your charge. For the Church and Congregation whom you must serve is the Spouse and the Body of Christ. And if it shall happen that his Church, or any Member thereof, do take any hurt or hindrance by reason of your negligence, you know the greatness of the fault. See, therefore, that you never cease your labour, your care and diligence, until you have done all that lieth in you to bring such as are committed to your charge to the faith and knowledge of God, and to perfectness of life in Christ.

We have good hope that you have well weighed and pondered these things with yourselves long before this time; and that you have clearly determined, by God's grace, to give yourselves wholly to this Office whereunto it has pleased God to call you; so that, as much as lieth in you, you will apply yourselves to this one thing, and draw all your cares and studies this way; and that you will continually pray to God for the fullness of his grace, that by daily reading and weighing of the Scriptures, you may grow riper and stronger in your Ministry; and that you will strive to fashion the lives of you and yours after the rule and teaching of Christ, that you may be wholesome and godly examples and patterns for the people to follow.

And now that this Congregation of Christ here assembled may also understand your mind and will in these things, and that this your promise may the more move you to do your duties, you shall answer plainly to these things which we, in the name of God, and of his Church, shall ask of you touching the same.

Do you believe yourself to be a child of God, through faith in our Lord Jesus Christ?

Answer. I do so believe.

The Presiding Minister:

Do you believe yourself to be called of God to the Office of the Christian Ministry, and your chief motives to be zeal for the glory of God, love for the Lord Jesus Christ, and desire for the salvation of men?

Answer. I do so believe.

The Presiding Minister:

Are you persuaded that the holy Scriptures contain sufficiently all doctrines required for eternal salvation in our Lord Jesus Christ? And are you resolved out of the said Scriptures to instruct the people committed to your charge, and to teach nothing which is not agreeable thereto?

Answer. I am so persuaded, and am resolved, by God's grace.

Then shall the Presiding Minister say:

Almighty God, who hath given you the will to do all these things; grant also unto you strength and power to perform the same; that he may accomplish his work which he hath begun in you; through Jesus Christ our Lord. Amen.

After this, the Presiding Minister shall say to the people:

Let us pray, dear brethren, that God in his loving kindness may bestow a plentiful grace upon these his servants; that what things they now undertake through his gracious call they may, by his help, be enabled to fulfil.

Then shall the Congregation make their humble supplications to God; for the which Prayers silence shall be kept for a space.

(*i*) After which shall be sung or said Veni Creator Spiritus (the persons to be ordained all kneeling).

Come Holy Ghost, our souls inspire, &c.

(*j*) That done, the Presiding Minister shall pray in this wise, and say:

Lift up your hearts.

Answer. We lift them up unto the Lord.

Minister. Let us give thanks unto our Lord God.

Answer. It is meet and right so to do.

Then shall the presiding Minister continue:

It is very meet, right and our bounden duty, that we should at all times and in all places, give thanks unto thee, O Holy Lord, Father Almighty, Everlasting God: Who, of thine infinite love and goodness towards us, hast given to us thy only and most dearly beloved Son, Jesus Christ, to be our Redeemer, and the Author of everlasting life; who, after he had made perfect our redemption by his death, and was ascended into heaven, sent abroad into the world his Apostles, Prophets, Evangelists, Pastors and Teachers, by whose labour and ministry he gathered together a great flock in all the parts of the world, to set forth the eternal praise of thy holy name; for these so great benefits of thy eternal goodness, and for that thou hast vouchsafed to call these thy servants here present to the same Office and Ministry appointed for the salvation of mankind, we render unto thee most hearty thanks, we praise and worship thy holy name; through Jesus Christ our Lord. Amen.

O God, the Source of all authority and of all holiness, of whom are true consecration and the fullness of blessing; send down, we pray thee, thy Holy Spirit upon these thy servants, whom we, in thy name, do now Ordain and Set Apart to be Ministers in thy Church, committing unto them authority to minister thy Word and Sacraments. Grant unto them such fullness of thy grace that they may be faithful and wise stewards whom thou settest over thy household to give to thy family their portion in due season. May constant faith, pure love, true peace, abound in them. Grant them, O Lord, the ministry of reconciliation, in word and in deed, and in thy power. Bestow on them the keys of the kingdom of heaven, that they may meekly use the power thou givest them to save and not destroy. May they be in care unwearying, in spirit fervent, hating pride, lovers of humility and truth, yielding neither to flattery nor menace. Be thou unto them authority, power, and steadfastness. Multiply upon them thy blessing and thy grace that in all things they may be found faithful, and at last be received, by thy mercy, into glory and immortality in thine eternal kingdom; through our Lord Jesus Christ, who liveth and reigneth with thee and the Holy Ghost, ever one God, world without end. Amen.

(*k*) When this prayer is done, the Presiding Minister, with two or more of the Ministers present, shall lay their hands upon the head of every one that receiveth Ordination, the Receivers humbly kneeling upon their knees, and the Presiding Minister saying:

The Lord pour upon thee the Holy Spirit for the Office and Work of a Minister in the Church of God, now committed unto thee by the authority of the Church through the Imposition of our hands. And be thou a faithful Dispenser of the Word of God, and of his holy Sacraments; in the name of the Father, and of the Son, and of the Holy Spirit. Amen.

(*l*) Then the Presiding Minister shall deliver to every one of them, kneeling, the Bible into his hand, saying:

Take thou Authority to preach the Word of God, and to minister the Holy Sacraments in the Congregation.

(*m*) When this is done, the Presiding Minister shall give a solemn Charge to them that have been ordained.

5. In the case of a Minister of the United Church who is to receive Holy Orders according to the use of the Church of England the following steps shall be taken:

(*a*) He shall produce to the Bishop evidence of Baptism and Ordination, and of his having familiarized himself with the doctrine, discipline, and worship of the Church of England in Canada. He shall promise that in ministering in congregations of the Church of England in Canada he shall conform thereto.

The Confirmation

(*b*) The Bishop shall then administer Confirmation beginning with the following prayer for the strengthening in him of the gifts of the Holy Spirit:

'Almighty and everlasting God, who hast vouchsafed to regenerate these thy servants by Water and the Holy Ghost, and hast given unto them forgiveness of all their sins; strengthen them, we beseech thee, O Lord, with the Holy Ghost the

Comforter, and daily increase in them thy manifold gifts of grace: the spirit of wisdom and understanding; the spirit of counsel and ghostly strength; the spirit of knowledge and true godliness; and fill them, O Lord, with the spirit of thy holy fear, now and for ever. Amen.'

The Bishop shall then lay his hand upon his head and say:

'Defend O Lord this thy servant with thy heavenly grace that he may continue thine for ever and daily increase in thy Holy Spirit more and more until he come unto thine everlasting kingdom.'

Ordination to the Diaconate

6. This having been done the Bishop shall admit him to the Diaconate, using at least the following parts of the Order for the making of Deacons. (Book of Common Prayer, page 618.)

The Collect:

'Almighty God, who by thy divine providence hast appointed divers Orders of Ministers in thy Church, and didst inspire thine Apostles to choose into the Order of Deacons the first Martyr Saint Stephen, with others: Mercifully behold these thy servants now called to the like office and administration; replenish them so with the truth of thy doctrine, and adorn them with innocency of life, that, both by word and good example, they may faithfully serve thee in this office, to the glory of thy Name, and the edification of thy Church; through the merits of our Saviour Jesus Christ, who liveth and reigneth with thee and the Holy Ghost, now and for ever. Amen.'

The *Epistle.* 1 Tim. iii. 8, or Acts viii. 2, shall be read.

(*d*) Then the Bishop shall say: 'Do you trust that you are inwardly called by the Holy Ghost to take upon you this office and ministry to serve God for the promoting of his glory and the edifying of his Church?'

Answer. 'I trust so.'

(*e*) Then shall the Bishop lay his hands upon the head of the candidate and say: 'Take thou authority to execute the office of a deacon in the Church of God, committed unto thee; in the name of the Father, and of the Son, and of the Holy Ghost. Amen.'

(*f*) Then he shall deliver to him the New Testament saying:

'Take thou authority to read the Gospel in the Church of God and to preach the same if thou be thereto licensed by the Bishop himself.'

(*g*) Then shall be read the *Gospel*, Luke xii. 35.

(*h*) The Nicene Creed shall be recited.

(*i*) The Holy Communion may follow or the Bishop may let them depart with the blessing.

Ordination to the Priesthood

(*j*) On the same or some subsequent day the Minister shall come before the Bishop, other clergy, and people, and be admitted to the Order of Priesthood according to the form prescribed in the Book of Common Prayer, of which the essential parts would be as follows:

(*k*) Before the service the Bishop should read the declaration as found on page 4 of this report as follows:

> 'In the name of the Father and of the Son and of the Holy Ghost, Amen. Beloved in the Lord, it has been agreed by the Church of England in Canada and the United Church of Canada that in dependence upon Almighty God, in faith in the Lord Jesus Christ and seeking the aid of the Holy Spirit, we come to these solemn acts wherein we convey each to the other the graces of our several ministries, neither denying to the other its heritage in the Holy Catholic Church, nor the reality of its ministry as a ministry of Christ, but both desiring to increase our gifts and enlarge our opportunities for the extension of Christ's Kingdom.'

(*l*) The Bishop shall then read the following declaration which shall take the place of the Presentation of the Candidate in the Form of Ordination and also be inscribed on the letters of Orders:

> 'A.B. who has already been ordained a minister of Christ according to the usage of the United Church of Canada desires to exercise the Ministry in the Church of England in Canada. We, recognizing the ministry which he has already received, and acting under Canon . . . of the General Synod, are about to admit him to the holy Order of Priesthood as required for the exercise of the Ministry in the Church of England in Canada, calling down upon him the blessing of the Holy Spirit that he may have all necessary grace and power faithfully to fulfil the same, and granting him authority to minister among us.'

(*m*) The Bishop immediately after the reading of the Declaration shall begin with the Communion Office. He shall use the Collect:

'Almighty God, giver of all good things, who by thy Holy Spirit hast appointed divers Orders of Ministers in thy Church; mercifully behold these thy servants now called to the office of Priesthood; and replenish them so with the truth of thy doctrine, and adorn them with innocency of life, that both by word and good example they may faithfully serve thee in this office, to the glory of thy Name, and edification of thy Church, through the merits of our Saviour Jesus Christ, who liveth and reigneth with thee and the Holy Ghost, world without end. Amen.'

(*n*) The *Epistle*, Eph. iv. 7 and the *Gospel*, Matt. viii. 36, shall be read.

(*o*) Then the Bishop shall call for the secret prayers of the congregation, and after a space of silent prayer, the Veni Creator shall be sung over the candidates.

(*p*) Then the Bishop shall say the prayer:

'Almighty God and heavenly Father, who of thine infinite love and goodness towards us hast given to us thy only and most dearly beloved Son, Jesus Christ, to be our Redeemer and the Author of everlasting life; who, after he had made perfect our redemption by his death, and was ascended into heaven, sent abroad into the world his Apostles, Prophets, Evangelists, Doctors, and Pastors, by whose labour and ministry he gathered together a great flock in all the parts of the world, to set forth the eternal praise of thy holy Name; for these so great benefits of thy eternal goodness, and for that thou hast vouchsafed to call these thy servants here present to the same office and ministry, appointed for the salvation of mankind; we render unto thee most hearty thanks, we praise and worship thee, and we humbly beseech thee, by the same thy blessed Son, to grant unto all, which either here or elsewhere call upon thy holy Name, that we may continue to show ourselves thankful unto thee for these and all other thy benefits; and that we may daily increase and go forward in the knowledge and faith of thee and thy Son by the Holy Spirit. So that as well by these thy Ministers, as by them over whom they shall be appointed thy Ministers, thy holy Name may be for ever glorified, and thy blessed kingdom enlarged; through the same thy Son Jesus Christ our Lord, who liveth and reigneth with thee in the unity of the same Holy Spirit, world without end. Amen.'

(*q*) When this prayer is done, the Bishop with the Priests present shall lay their hands severally upon every one that receiveth the Order of Priesthood, the receivers humbly kneeling upon their knees, and the Bishop saying:

> 'Receive the Holy Ghost for the office and work of a Priest in the Church of God, now committed unto thee by the imposition of our hands. Whose sins thou dost forgive, they are forgiven; and whose sins thou dost retain, they are retained. And be thou a faithful dispenser of the Word of God, and of his holy Sacraments; in the Name of the Father, &c.'

(*r*) Then the Bishop shall deliver the Bible to each of them saying:

> 'Take thou authority to preach the Word of God and to minister the holy Sacraments in the congregation, where thou shalt be lawfully appointed thereunto.'

(*s*) Then shall the Nicene Creed be said.

(*t*) When this is done the Bishop shall go on in the service of the Communion, which all they that receive orders shall take together, &c. (Book of Common Prayer.)

C

The Access of Communicants to the Lord's Table in Both Communions

After careful consideration, your Committee are unanimously of opinion that the problem of mutual access to Holy Communion should be given further and prayerful study before any solution is submitted to the Commissions and that to this end the same Committee be continued.

D

Conclusions

1. It will be observed that the essential proposition, on which all the rest of this report depends, is that the two types of ministry are different. If that is conceded, then the grace of each may be conveyed to the other, without reservation.

2. It is at least plain that both our ministries are incomplete in practical affairs. While the Church of England is denied the assistance of a ministry which it acknowledges to be manifestly used of God, and while the United Church is denied the co-operation of

a ministry whose reality it fully recognizes, both ministries are obviously less than they might be in the range of their operations. But if we realize that our ministries have been developed separately for historical reasons, and that they differ both in function and in the source of their temporal authority, it becomes possible to unify them fully and without irrelevant and invidious comparison.

3. However, it may be asked whether the gains of any such unifying would be commensurate with the upset to our ecclesiastical habits, which the process would necessarily involve. We are unanimously of the opinion that they would. Each Church has treasures that would be of benefit to the other, and as we work together we shall mutually become aware of them, and so be drawn into closer unity. Some of these 'treasures' are indicated in Annex I and II. Meantime, we are convinced that there are practical gains obtainable in a nearer future. We think that wherever a unified ministry existed and was utilized with wisdom and good feeling, a better distribution of man-power would be quickly felt on the frontiers, where at present there is so great a need. Moreover, we believe that, with experience, some of the problems of city ministries might become less severe. It is probably true that a large part of the 1,500,000 lapsed members of our two Communions are to be found in our large centres of population; and there, with a mutual ministry, 'colleges of churches' could be formed working the needy districts together, especially in pastoral evangelism. A supreme necessity for the cities is the re-creation of the parish as a living and effective reality; and that might be accomplished where a group of churches was mutually responsible for its well-being, all working loyally in the interests of each other, shepherding the people into the fold to which they prefer to belong. In the course of time, it might be possible to create parish centres, in which the social work could be carried on, while the separate churches would be responsible for worship and direct religious work within their own walls, yet aiding one another in their ministry in times of stress and sickness. Moreover, the Churches together could communicate to each other new types of ministry, such as are found in Brotherhoods and Communities. The Church of England has its Society of St. John the Evangelist; The United Church may be an inheritor of the Iona Community, whence so much new life is springing in the Church of Scotland, and it already has its Church of All Nations, where people of many tongues and traditions worship according to the tradition

of their fathers and yet work together in a common religious home. The advantages of closely knit theological colleges on the Campus of every University, with a strong, diversified staff and a large body of students, keeping the vision of the Unseen before the University as a whole, and exhibiting unity in diversity, are too obvious to elaborate.

4. Beyond all this, and much more that we can dream of, we shall convince those who are now returning to us from the strange brotherhood of war that the Christian Church is facing the unknown future, forgetting the unhappy things that are behind and pressing to the future, determined to use its power solely against evil and for good, and that it, too, having learned the lesson of unity, cares first for the Christian good of Canada.

5. Far off stands the splendid goal of the Reunion of Christendom. But it will only be reached by those who are willing to take one step at a time. We venture to suggest such a step, in the confidence that those whom we represent will consider the matter, with an intention to achieve, and in the belief that in seeking unity, we are within the Will of God.

PAPERS BEARING ON PARTICULAR POINTS OF THE COMMON PROBLEM

ANNEX I

Mutual Benefits from an Anglican Point of View

There are many examples of more than one Rite functioning in a single area. Even in the Roman Church, with all her rigid uniformity, there may be in a single city Churches which are each worshipping and celebrating the Sacraments with different rites and ceremonies. Each rite has its own organization (Uniat, Dominican, &c.). No pressure should be brought to bear upon either the Church of England in Canada or the United Church to conform exactly one to the other. They would go on as two rites and two organizations until it was clear to each that one organization would suffice.

Each rite, however, has treasures that would be of benefit to the other. We think that these are some of the treasures that the United Church has to offer.

The Church Session, in which the members of the Session help the Pastor with his pastoral work.

The great *Corporate Communion* of the whole communicant body, before which the members of Session call upon the communicants and invite them to the service of preparation.

The Presbytery, in which Ministers and lay representatives of an area corresponding to an Archdeaconry meet to care for the congregations of their area, to supervise Ordination candidates, and to induct Ministers.

The system of careful superintendence of Ordinands, and the effective voice of people and Presbytery in recommending them to the ordaining authority.

The public Confession of Faith in Christ and obedience to Him, by those seeking to become communicants.

The freer type of Public Worship.

We think that the Church of England has these treasures to offer:

The Sacramental Life expressed in frequent Communions and other rites.

Confirmation by the Bishop as bringing the candidates that special blessing of the Holy Spirit, and contact with the life of the great Church beyond the parish limits signified by the Bishop's ministration of that rite.

The ancient *Threefold Orders* that have so continuous a history in the Church, and are still the type of Ministry of the greater part of Christendom.

The Bishop's Office as Pastor of the pastors, and as the link with the general Church.

The Liturgical way of Worship closely associated with the Church Year in setting forth in regular order the mighty acts of God whereby we are saved, and as the means whereby we render to God the sacrifices of prayer and praise.

The consciousness of the *Priestly nature of the Church* as the Body of Christ, the great High Priest, who has appointed his Church to offer up spiritual sacrifices acceptable to God by Jesus Christ, showing forth the praises of Him who has called us out of darkness into His own marvellous light.

ANNEX II

Mutual Benefits From a United Church Point of View

The present proposals are directed to the single aim of common action in a time of spiritual crisis for our country and for the world.

We are concerned, not so much with what we can get one from another, as with what, together, we can give and do for our fellow-men. Nevertheless, in closer co-operation we are bound to communicate, each to each, the particular graces and excellencies with which, separately, we have been endowed. We of the United Church recognize gladly how much that is peculiarly Anglican, both in kind and in degree, we ought righteously to covet; and we desire to set down our conception of some of these benefits, realizing that experience of each other will enlarge our mutual understanding and appreciation.

1. The Church of England has, uniquely amongst the Reformed Communions, kept alive the sense of God as the Uncreated Loveliness. In Presbyterianism, witness has been borne to the Ancient Truth; in Methodism, to the Outpoured Energy; but Anglicanism, while not forgetting these, has emphasized the Beauty of the Lord; and the soul of man cannot rest and be satisfied until, in its worship, it gives back beauty for beauty, the reverence which is the Lord's due.

2. In its Episcopal Order the Church of England possesses an outward and visible sign of the historic continuity of the Church. We claim, and passionately claim, our true spiritual continuity in the Church Catholic; and we hold that we possess a genuine historic continuity despite the reformings. Nevertheless, we acknowledge the value of an expression of that continuity which all men may see, and thus be enabled to understand that, while Crowns and Thrones may perish, the Church of Christ constant will remain.

3. We also perceive the gain that may accrue from the possession of a Pastor Pastorum. We perceive that Episcopal and Conciliar systems, on their governmental side, may well be unified; but that the former, on the pastoral side, possesses a source of help, which is needed for the strengthening of the ministry in a far-flung land and in a Church which is largely missionary.

4. We also note the emphasis which the Anglican Church places on the Sacrament of Holy Communion, and we believe that the spiritual life of our people would be enriched if frequent opportunities were given for individual reception. We think that in our conception of corporate Communion we have something of supreme value to contribute; but we realize that the single soul should always find the Table spread in order, at any time of need, to make covenant and receive grace.

5. We, further, covet the links with other Communions in the

Church, which the Anglican Church possesses. In particular, we are agreed on the vital importance of relation with the Eastern Orthodox Churches; and, while we hold that we also have links with other branches, those that are provided by the Anglican Church must be retained and developed.

6. We remember, with thankfulness, the roll of saints and scholars, which is the heritage of the Anglican Communion, and we would rejoice to be able to claim them as our own. Among these scholars we especially remember those to whom we owe the King James Version of the Bible.

7. Finally, we perceive thankfully the comprehensiveness of the Church of our Anglican brethren. Within their fold they exhibit that diversity in unity, which we likewise hold to be essential. We believe that together we shall gain in true Christian liberality of mind, while building faithfully on the one foundation, which is Jesus Christ.

201. *The General Synod of the Church of England in Canada. Message from the Upper House*

SEPTEMBER 1946

THE Upper House of General Synod records its gratitude to the Committee on the Reunion of Christendom for the report presented and notes with satisfaction the progress which has been made in the conversations with the United Church but regrets that no report is yet possible concerning conversations with other communions. It is their earnest hope that these conversations will continue and that others will be initiated.

In the report before the house the Committee submits to the governing bodies of both communions a proposal that there should be sent to their members for study a plan for providing a mutually acceptable ministry. It is the result of several conversations in which the difficulties and advantages were discussed frankly with mutual understanding. This house is of the opinion that the plan is well worthy of study and recommends its acceptance as such. It is, however, to be observed that the question of corporate Church Union is not before either communion. Early in the conversations the question of union was canvassed but it was agreed that it was premature.

Before General Synod meets again there will be held a meeting of the Lambeth Conference at which will gather over 300 Bishops from all parts of the world and that will afford an opportunity of discovering the mind of the whole Anglican Communion on this question. We are concerned that the cause of the 'Reunion of Christendom' throughout the world may not be hindered by any independent action on our part.

The importance of the report demands careful examination in the course of which changes and amendments will no doubt be made. This examination should be carried out with the aid of scholars whose work may be made available to every member of the Church for study. For no plan could be accepted or action taken until general approval has been won for it throughout the Church.

We are much moved by the evident spirit of good-will which has characterized the conversations and we pray that this same spirit will be spread abroad throughout both our communions in all our future study and work together.

[The Lower House unanimously concurred.]

XIV. AUSTRALIA

202. *A Summary of the Discussions and Proposals of an Australian Group*

1937–43

[The group consisted of ten Anglicans, including the Archbishop of Brisbane (J. W. C. Wand), and the Bishops of Riverina, Armidale, and Newcastle, six Congregationalists, including the Rev. A. P. Campbell, five Methodists, including the Rev. L. E. Bennett, and six Presbyterians, including the Rev. J. W. Burton.]

INTERCOMMUNION

Ut omnes unum sint

1. *A Brief History*

In April, 1937, there was held in Sydney a National Missionary Conference, composed of representatives of nearly all the Non-Roman communions, which discussed missionary problems, especially those of the South Pacific. There came a vision of a United Church in the Pacific, for it was felt that, whatever reasons might be advanced for denominational separateness at the Home Base, none could consistently be given for such a lack of unity among the infant Churches of the South Seas.

For the most part the Non-Roman Missionary bodies work in clearly defined areas and there is very little 'over-lapping'. This is a wise arrangement and illustrative of the comity of Missions; but it creates some problems, one of which arises when native Christians change their residence from one missionary area to another. The Conference felt that it should be possible for any Christians so transferred to have the privilege of full fellowship in the Church established in the area in which they find themselves.

On examination it was found that the obstacle to this course is that there is no one view of the Christian ministry so generally acceptable as to make intercommunion possible, and that, though there is much happy friendliness and helpful co-operation among the missionaries of the several Churches, fellowship fails at the very point where it should find fullest expression—at the Table of our Lord.

A Committee was set up to investigate this question of a United Church in the Pacific.

A few days after the close of the Conference, the Bishop of Newcastle wrote to the Chairman of the National Missionary Council, the Rev. J. W. Burton, stating that this question of intercommunion on the Mission Field had been laid increasingly upon his conscience, and expressing the hope that some attempt might be made immediately to explore the possibility of finding some basis for intercommunion. After some correspondence Bishop Batty suggested that three members of each of the three non-Roman denominations engaged in Mission work in Papua—Anglican, Methodist, and Congregationalist—should meet for informal conference on the subject. It was agreed that such conference should be entirely unofficial, and should not be regarded otherwise than as a meeting of friends to discuss a subject of common interest to them all. To avoid possible misunderstanding it must be clearly stated that none of the members of the original group regarded himself as in any way officially representative of his denomination, or of any denominational society.

On this understanding there met the Bishop of Newcastle, Canon J. S. Needham, Revs. Dr. P. A. Micklem, A. P. Campbell, H. L. Hurst, Dr. G. H. Wright, L. E. Bennett, W. E. Bennett, and J. W. Burton to discuss informally the situation in Papua where these three Churches are at work and where the difficulties regarding intercommunion had been cited. Thus commenced our Intercommunion Group which has since been considerably enlarged.

As time went on we discovered that we could not limit our inquiries and discussions to any particular mission field, for there were practical difficulties in the way while the Churches at home remained apart. Hence it was borne in upon us that we must face the whole question of intercommunion as it presents itself both at home and abroad. At this stage, therefore, we invited our Presbyterian brethren to join us, so that the four largest non-Roman Communions—Communions which had in the past been considering a closer unity—might together study the situation.

The Group, however, does not restrict its membership to these four denominations, for it has expressly stated by resolution that it will welcome the members of any other Communion to this fellowship and will make suitable provision for the ministers of any Church who may wish to participate in this extension of ministerial privilege.

2. *The Spirit of the Group*

Whether or not the Group has had revealed to it any basis of intercommunion that will be acceptable over a wide area, the fact is indisputable that we, its members, have experienced a remarkable, we may even say, a unique, fellowship and have been deeply and humbly conscious of the presence and guidance of the Holy Spirit. We have come to know one another in a sacred intimacy and with an ever-increasing mutual confidence.

From the outset we determined to be utterly frank with one another, and things were said plainly and even bluntly which in a different atmosphere might have been deeply resented; but never once was there said an unkind word, never once a shadowed hint of friction or of impatience. While we treated each other's cherished convictions with the reverence due to holy things, we were absolutely loyal to our own conscience. Over and over again it seemed as if we had reached an impasse and it appeared, for the while, that we could go no farther and still keep company with honesty and sincerity; yet we dared not say farewell one to another, but quietly waited in confident faith for guidance and direction. 'Necessity was laid upon us.' By the good Spirit of God we were held together in earnest prayer and rich fellowship until at last, without strain or laboured effort, we came to a unanimity which, considering the divergent elements composing the Group, must be considered remarkable. It is because we feel so strongly that this working is of the Spirit of God, and not of us, that we humbly offer our proposals for the prayerful consideration of the Churches represented in the Group.

We would add that we do not look upon anything we have done as complete or final, but are content if our work should prove to be a finger-post suggesting the direction which we, as members of the Church Universal, are required to take.

3. *The Chief Point at Issue*

We felt from the first that any variation in our theological views was entirely secondary. We all accepted the great facts of Sin and Redemption through the free grace of God manifested in our Lord and Saviour Jesus Christ, as generally expressed in the historic creeds of Christendom. In the matter of doctrine there was possibly much greater difference of interpretation between individual members of each communion than between the communions themselves.

Nor did the problems of Church government greatly exercise our minds, for we felt that these could all be solved by intelligent and reasonable men.

The great obstacle to our meeting together at the Holy Table was found to be our differing conceptions of the authority and function of the Christian ministry, and it was to that particular difficulty that we addressed ourselves. Our task was to find some way to ensure a ministry acceptable to and recognized by all concerned, without doubt or scruple to any.

The non-episcopal members of the Group urged that all that was necessary was a common recognition of the Ministry of their respective Churches. With this recognition, only a formal commission to preach and administer the sacraments in each branch of the Church would be required, the ministers of the Congregational, Methodist, and Presbyterian Churches holding that their ordination is a sufficient qualification.

The Anglican representatives urged that in view of the essential importance attached by very large numbers of Anglicans to episcopal ordination, such a proposal could not form a basis for intercommunion with the Church of England as a whole.

These two divergent views were examined with great care over a long period. In the end it was seen that we were faced with the question whether to wait until one or other of these views was acceptable to the majority in each of the Communions concerned (and, consequently, until one side or the other acknowledged its error, and surrendered convictions, deeply and sincerely held), or whether to explore some other path. This latter course was determined on.

It must be clearly understood that the discussions of the Group have not been related to the problems of Church Union *per se*, though we are not without hope that the removal of barriers to intercommunion may eventually result in a closer co-operation and unity in the great and common task committed to us by our Lord. All that we are, at this present, concerned about is to remove every obstacle, real or imaginary, which prevents members of our several communions from visibly expressing their unity at the Table of their one Saviour and Lord.

4. *The Draft Proposal*

At a certain stage we reported that the results so far achieved could be expressed in the following proposals:

(*a*) The Churches concerned recognize the Nicene Creed as a general statement of Christian belief, and shall agree to minister the sacrament of Holy Communion with the elements ordained by Christ, and with the use of His words of Institution.

(*b*) There shall be a general interchange of ministerial commissions.

(*c*) Each Church shall give its commission in and by the form used at the ordination of its own ministers.

(*d*) It is understood that the acceptance of a wider ministerial commission does not in any sense imply re-ordination, but represents, in the view of those who have taken part in these conferences, the only practical method of securing such an extension of ministerial authority as will accomplish the desired end.

In reaching these conclusions we were greatly helped by the Archbishop of Brisbane, Dr. J. W. C. Wand; though he was not able to meet with us as frequently as we could have wished, we have had the advantage of his wide scholarship and sympathetic understanding which have enabled us, at times, to clarify our own thinking.

As we continued our discussions we came to realize that section (*c*) was ambiguous and might in the minds of some be interpreted as a belittling of previous ministerial commissions and experience. Helped largely by the suggestions of the Bishop of Riverina, we came to feel that we should have a Common and Mutual Formula for the interchange of ministerial commissions; and that we should not attempt to define in any way the meaning and scope of the commissions so exchanged, but should leave each member to avow, by a solemn declaration, that he believed himself called and fully ordained to the Ministry of the Christian Church.

For some time, as we have already pointed out, we kept our Intercommunion Group purely informal and unofficial; but authoritative bodies of the Anglican, Congregational, Methodist, and Presbyterian Churches have now, without accepting any particular conclusions, appointed representatives to the Group so that the fullest exploration of the situation might be made.

Appended hereto is the revised draft of the instrument we have prepared and we present it first to God, as a humble offering of our mind and heart, and then to the Church for its prayerful thought and careful consideration.

Signed on behalf of the Group,
JOHN W. BURTON,
Secretary.

139 CASTLEREAGH ST., SYDNEY.
20th Feb., 1940.

DECLARATION AND MUTUAL FORMULA

(Final Revision–29th October, 1943)

PREFACE

1. Seeing that the witness of the Church is lamentably weakened by division and misunderstanding among Christians, and that responsibility for such human frailty must be shared by all Christian communions, we are led to believe that divergent conceptions of the Ministry have, at least in part, been caused by undue or inadequate emphasis on some functions of the Ministry.

2. Accordingly, we believe that all who have exercised their ministry within the limitations of a divided Church should be enabled to extend and fulfil their ministry in a reunited Fellowship.

3. It is our conviction that such a reunited Fellowship is the Will of God and that it should be initiated by the mutual laying on of hands with prayer, and with the use of such a formula as shall leave no room for scruple or doubtfulness.

4. It is understood that the acceptance of a wider ministerial commission does not in any sense imply re-ordination, but represents, in the view of those who have taken part in these conferences, the only practical method of securing such an extension of ministerial authority as will accomplish the desired end.

5. To effect this purpose, we individually make the following declaration, as a general expression of our convictions, and as a basis of action through which God's will may be accomplished.

THE DECLARATION

(*a*) I, believing myself to have been duly called and ordained to the ministry of the Word and Sacraments in the Church of God, am yet conscious of a desire for a wider exercise of the office in a reunited Fellowship.

(*b*) I, also believing that God wills one Communion and Fellowship for the building of His Kingdom, and that there should therefore be an interchange of Commissions between all who have been regularly called and lawfully set apart for the Ministry of His Holy Word and Sacraments, am humbly prepared by the mutual laying on of hands with prayer, freely and willingly, to give and to receive, to bestow and to share, so far as lies within my power, such further authority as shall seem 'good to the Holy Ghost and to us'.

THE MUTUAL FORMULA

Prayer

Almighty God, Who hast bestowed upon Thy servants diverse gifts of the Holy Spirit and hast called them to minister on Thy behalf to the souls of men; Empower by Thy Holy Spirit this laying on of hands with prayer that it may be used of Thee to the enrichment of our ministries in the service of Thy Holy Church through Jesus Christ our Lord. *Amen.*

The Formula

Receive the Holy Ghost for the wider exercise of thy ministry in the Church, take thou authority to preach the Word of God and to minister Christ's Sacraments, in fulfilment of the ministry of reconciliation in the congregations whereunto thou shalt be further called or regularly appointed; and see that thou stir up the grace bestowed upon thee in the Call of God and by the laying on of hands.

RUBRICS

The procedure in the Declaration and the Mutual Formula, together with subsequent ministerial status, are to be governed by the following rubrics:

1. In any area where it is desired to put these proposals into effect the Formula of Prayer for the laying on of hands is to be said by a group consisting of at least two duly chosen and appointed ministers of each Christian Communion committed in this way to intercommunion and fellowship.

2. All such duly chosen and appointed ministers shall individually receive the mutual laying on of hands with Prayer on the occasion of their first participating in this mutual rite, but no

minister shall receive such laying on of hands more than once from any one Communion.

3. This having been fulfilled the same formula shall be used by such duly chosen and appointed ministers when laying their hands with Prayer on the head of each minister presenting himself for participating in this mutual rite.

4. All, who have received the mutual laying on of hands with Prayer may be 'further called' to officiate temporarily in any other participating Communion, if invited to do so, by the lawful authority of that Communion or may be 'regularly appointed', without further laying on of hands with Prayer, to a pastoral charge in that Communion, provided that the customary tests and regulations have been observed.

NOTES

(*a*) It is understood that the procedure in the Declaration and Formula is governed by the Rubrics which follow them.

(*b*) It is understood that this mutual laying on of hands with Prayer does not supersede the normal rite of ordination in each participating communion; nor does it commit anyone so participating to a particular theory of the Ministry.

(*c*) 'Further called' shall mean lawful invitation to officiate temporarily in any other participating Communion.

'Regularly appointed' shall mean appointment in accordance with the tests and regulations which are customary prior to ordination by the participating Communions concerned.

XV. NORTH INDIA

203. *Round Table Conference on Church Union Proposed Basis of Negotiation*

JULY 1947

[In April 1929 a Round Table Conference on Church Union was held at Lucknow between representatives of the Baptist and Methodist Churches and the United Church of North India. A second Conference was held at Delhi in November 1930, in which representatives of the Church of India, Burma, and Ceylon joined, a third at Lucknow in November 1939 and a fourth at Allahabad in 1941. The Proposed Basis of Negotiation then adopted was revised by a further meeting of the Round Table Conference held at Allahabad on July 23 and 24, 1947. This last conference was attended by the Bishop of Delhi, and four other representatives of the Church of India, Burma, and Ceylon; five representatives of the Methodist Church (British and Australian Conferences), including the Rev. W. Machin, Hon. Secretary; five representatives of the Methodist Church in Southern Asia, and six representatives of the United Church of North India. It unanimously approved the following revised 'Basis of Negotiation'.]

Doctrines

(i) THE uniting Churches in Northern India hold the faith which the Church has ever held in Jesus Christ, the Redeemer of the World, in whom men are saved by grace through faith, and in accordance with the revelation of God which He made, being Himself God incarnate, they worship one God, Father, Son, and Holy Spirit.

(ii) They accept the Holy Scriptures of the Old Testament and the New Testament as containing all things necessary to salvation and as the ultimate standard of faith.

(iii) They acknowledge the witness of the Apostles' Creed and the Creed commonly called the Nicene Creed to that faith, which is continuously confirmed in the spiritual experience of the Church of Christ.

The Sacraments

(i) The uniting Churches believe that the Sacraments of Baptism and the Holy Communion are means of grace through which God works in us.

(ii) The uniting Churches believe also that, while God's mercy is extended to all men, Christ plainly teaches that, in following His appointed way of salvation, there should be a definite act of reception into the family of God and continued acts of fellowship with Him in that family. The Sacraments of Baptism and the Holy Communion are means instituted by Him for this purpose.

(iii) The Sacrament of Baptism shall be administered with water in the name of the Father, the Son, and the Holy Spirit, and the Sacrament of the Holy Communion with unfailing use of Christ's words of institution and of the elements ordained by Him.

(iv) Provided they conform to the above essentials, any forms of service which were in use in any of the uniting Churches before union may be continued in the united Church. The united Church may also develop new forms of service adapted to the needs and experience of the country; but, without seeking any rigid uniformity, it would be desirable to secure some measure of agreement on the important elements to be included in the service of Holy Communion, as suggested in the *South India Scheme*.

Membership

(i) At the time of union all full communicant members, members on probation or under instruction, members under discipline, catechumens and other persons in connexion with the uniting Churches shall be accepted by the united Church with the corresponding status.

(ii) The full privileges and obligations of membership in the united Church should belong to those persons who, having attained years of discretion, having gained some measure of experience in the Christian life, and having received due instruction in Christian truth and in the duties of their Christian calling, make public profession of their faith and of their purpose, with God's help, to serve and follow Christ as members of His Church. They shall make this confession at a public service, which should include prayer for them that they may be strengthened by the Holy Spirit and may receive His manifold gifts of grace for their life and work (*vide S. I. Scheme*, chap. iii, para. 2, 1935).

(iii) Those only shall be members of the united Church who have by baptism been admitted to Christ's Church visible on earth. Baptism may be administered in infancy or upon profession of faith.

The Ministry

(i) The Church is a 'royal priesthood' of believers (1 Pet. ii. 5 and 9), and all its members have direct access to God. This signifies that, 'all the members have their share in the commission and authority of the whole Church. Confirmed by the Holy Spirit, they all have the rights and duties of a priesthood of believers, offering to God in and with His Son the sacrifice of themselves and all their powers. To the whole Church and to every member of it belong the duty and the privilege of spreading the good news of the Kingdom of God, and the message of salvation through Jesus Christ.' (Constitution, Church of India, Burma, and Ceylon, 1930, Declaration 3, p. 14.)

(ii) The uniting Churches are all linked with the Church of apostolic times by an essential continuity of doctrine, of experience, and of allegiance to the Lord Jesus Christ, and by a fellowship in the continued proclaiming of the message of salvation through Him. In different ways also they have all sought to maintain continuity with the primitive Church in matters of order.

(iii) Thus the Ministry is a Ministry representative of the risen and ascended Christ and of the Holy Catholic Church, which is His body (Eph. i. 23). This ordained Ministry is descended from Christ and His apostles, and under the guidance of the Holy Spirit continues to derive its authority from Christ through the Church.

The uniting Churches 'believe that in ordination God, in answer to the prayers of His Church, bestows on and assures to those whom He has called, and His Church has accepted, for any particular form of the Ministry a commission for it and the grace appropriate to it'. (*S. I. Scheme*, 1936.)

'The Ministry of the Church, alike in its priestly, pastoral and prophetic aspects, derives from the heavenly pattern of the risen and ascended Christ, who is at once the great High Priest, the Chief Shepherd of souls, and the Eternal Word of God. It is committed to us as a function of the whole body of Christ, and cannot therefore be claimed exclusively by individuals or by one order within the Church.' (International Missionary Conference, 1938. See Eph. iv. 11–13, and 1 Cor. xii.)

The Minister is in his own pastorate the representative of the Church as a whole, and also represents his own pastorate to the Church as a whole.

(iv) The Churches desiring to unite mutually acknowledge each others' Ministries as Ministries of Christ in His Word and Sacraments, although in our present state of division they cannot be regarded as fully representative of the Church as a whole. These

Churches acknowledge that all their Ministries have been in God's providence manifestly used by the Holy Spirit in His work of enlightening the world, converting sinners, and perfecting saints.

(v) It is the intention of the uniting Churches that after union full communion and fellowship shall be maintained with each of the various communions from which they derive.

(vi) After the inauguration of union all new Presbyters shall be ordained and all new Bishops elected and consecrated according to the rule of the united Church.[1]

(vii) It is the intention of the uniting Churches to initiate a process of growing together into complete unity in the spiritual life. It is essential therefore that as quickly as possible the unification of the Ministry and complete freedom of communion throughout the united Church should be realized.

(viii) This Conference accepts the principle of the Unification of the Ministry by the mutual laying on of hands in an act of supplemental ordination to the Ministry of the United Church. This involves the acknowledgement of a common lack in all our Ministries due to our divisions, in that they are limited in authority and have not the seal of the whole Church.

We propose that at the inauguration of Union, the existing presbyters and bishops of each of the uniting Churches should accept through the laying on of hands of the duly authorized persons of the other Churches uniting with them the additional authority and grace that they lack in separation. This should take place at a solemn service, an essential part of which should be prayer for the additional gifts that God alone can bestow.

We are of opinion that it would be necessary after the consecration of the bishops of the united Church for services to be held in each area for supplemental ordination, in which the authorities of

[1] [The text given above is the official text. But a separate loose slip was inserted in the leaflet containing the text marked *Addendum.* This repeats certain words included in earlier editions of the *Basis*, and is as follows:

'*Addendum*: The uniting Churches should seek union on the basis of accepting an *ad interim* period of adjustment during which the uniting Churches may, if they so determine, continue to function as separate jurisdictions, provided that all the uniting Churches shall be represented in the Synod, which shall provide the general legislation for the united Church as a whole, but during the interim period no legislation shall be binding on any jurisdiction until accepted by it.

(N.B. Some members of the Conference are of opinion that these words were intended to stand until the report of the Continuation Committee should be dealt with.)' See *Note* on p. 222.]

all the uniting Churches would take part. (See section on Episcopate, para. (v).)

We suggest that at the laying on of hands the following words or words closely similar should be used: Receive the Holy Ghost for the fuller exercise of Christ's ministry and priesthood in the Church of God; and for a wider and more effectual service therein take thou authority to preach the Word of God, to fulfil the ministry of reconciliation, and to minister Christ's sacraments in the congregations whereunto thou shalt be further called or regularly appointed. And see that thou do all these things in brotherly partnership with God's fellow workers whom in this union of Churches He has made thine.

(*See Appendix for the resolution of the General Council of the Church of India, Burma, and Ceylon passed in February 1944.*)

Selection, Training and Discipline of Ministers

1. In the selection of candidates for the Ministry the following principles should be observed:

(*a*) a consciousness of inward call on the part of the candidate and a period of service as a layman in the Church;

(*b*) the approval of the local Church of which the candidate is a member; and

(*c*) the acceptance for training by the Diocesan Council, or some representative body appointed by it, after such examination as may be considered necessary. (In the acceptance of a candidate regard shall be paid to the likelihood of his future regular employment as a Minister.)

2. The training of candidates for the Ministry should normally include a period of not less than three years at a recognized Theological Institution. Such training should be closely linked with the work of the Church, and should include practice in pastoral work, preaching, and the conduct of worship. The recommendation of the Theological Institution on the general progress and fitness of the candidate, as well as the results of any examinations taken by him, should be considered in finally approving the candidate for ordination.

After such a period of training there should ordinarily be a period of not less than a year in service as a probationer under the supervision of an experienced Presbyter, before ordination to the Presbyterate.

3. The appointment and stationing of Ministers shall be carried out by the Bishop of the diocese after consultation with the Diocesan Council or any other body prescribed by the rules of the diocese. While wherever possible due regard should be given to the wishes of the pastorate concerned, Ministers shall be stationed as may be deemed best in the interests of the Church as a whole, and it shall be the responsibility of the Bishop and his Diocesan Council to see that every efficient Minister shall be given an appointment and every pastorate provided with adequate ministration of the Word and Sacraments.

4. The ends of Church discipline are the good of the offender and the purity of the Church.

Charges against a Minister shall in the first instance be submitted to the Bishop of the diocese, who shall, if possible, settle the matter by personal inquiry and advice and, if necessary, admonition, or in grave cases temporary suspension of the authorization of the Minister concerned. But if the Bishop shall direct, or the accused Minister demand, that the case shall be referred to the Court of the Diocesan Council, it shall be so referred. A Bishop may not withdraw his authorization permanently from a Presbyter except by way of carrying out a sentence duly passed by the Court of the Diocesan Council, or in cases where the Presbyter voluntarily submits himself to the decision of the Bishop. (*S. I. Scheme*, chap. xi, Rule 7.)

The Diocesan Court should include Presbyters and laymen chosen from a panel appointed by the Diocesan Council; provided that in cases concerning doctrine the decision of the Court shall be framed and the sentence passed by the ministerial members of the Court, the lay members acting as assessors. (*S. I. Scheme*, chap. xi, Rule 8.)

The Ministry of the Laity

1. To the whole Church and to every member of it belong the duty and privilege of spreading the good news of the Kingdom of God and the message of salvation through Jesus Christ. The united Church therefore welcomes, and will provide for, the exercise by lay persons, both men and women, of such gifts of prophecy, evangelization, teaching, healing, and administration as God bestows upon them. In particular, the laity are called upon to exercise important functions in the Church as members of its governing bodies, both local and central, and of its disciplinary courts.

Women shall be eligible for membership of the Synod, and for membership of Diocesan Councils and any other administrative or governing body in a diocese.

2. The ministry of the laity may be performed by men and women who, in response to God's call, devote their whole time to it, and for whose support the Church must therefore in general make provision. These include both Indian and foreign workers. But a large and increasing part of this work should be undertaken by men and women who, while following their ordinary calling in life, also engage in the work of the Church. Such work may be performed in one or more of the following ways:

(*a*) *Assisting in Pastoral Work.* This includes visiting members of the congregation, especially the sick and erring; meeting them in groups or 'classes' for fellowship and edification, and prayer; having the charge of village congregations; and generally helping the Presbyter in building up the Church. Those who take part in such work should be communicant members solemnly set apart for this special service, and may be known as elders, lay readers, class leaders, lay deacons, deaconesses, &c.

(*b*) *Evangelism.* It is the primary duty of every member of the Church to witness by life and word to Jesus Christ, who came into the world to save sinners. This work of evangelization may be done both individually and by groups, and should include special methods, such as lyrical preaching and the distribution of the scriptures and other evangelistic literature.

(*c*) *Preaching.* Lay persons of gifts and grace should be enlisted for this work, and they may be formed into an order with rules, examinations, and a period of probation. They must be communicant members of the Church, of blameless life, and ever ready to be witnesses to the Master whom they serve. They must act under the direction of the Presbyter in charge of the congregation.

(*d*) The Church has important duties towards its youth, both in preparing them for the time when they make public profession of their faith, and in guiding their subsequent life as full members of the Church. The services of godly persons, and especially of those who have recently become communicants, should be enlisted to help in Sunday Schools, Night Schools, Guilds, Christian Endeavour, and other such societies.

(*e*) *Administration.* The collection and administration of funds and the care of Church property form an important sphere of labour in every congregation. Those who help the Church in these matters may be known as trustees, wardens, treasurers, stewards, elders, lay deacons, &c. Their duties are to raise sufficient funds for the pastorate, to keep the Church buildings and other property in good condition, to help the poor and sick and minister to their needs, and generally to assist the Presbyters in the temporal affairs of the congregation.

(*f*) *Social Service.* Opportunities for social service may be found in visiting hospitals and jails, and in aiding temperance and social purity work, child welfare and health propaganda, village improvement, the boy scout and girl guide movements, and other such activities. The local Church should, whenever possible, co-operate with other organizations engaged in social service.

3. It is desirable that lay persons who are appointed to any office in the Church should be set apart at a service in which they are reminded of the nature and importance of their office, and prayer is offered that they may receive the Holy Spirit to equip them for their work and make them faithful in the discharge of their responsibilities.

4. The Synod or the Diocesan Councils shall make regulations concerning special forms of the ministry of the laity, such as those mentioned in Rule 2. There shall be provision for the regular selection and appointment of these lay workers, and for regular meetings of the clergy and the lay workers in an area for fellowship and consultation.

5. The united Church desires that all its members should constantly bear in mind that their different forms of ministry, both to those within the Church and to those outside it, are only of value for the carrying out of God's purposes in so far as the Divine Spirit is working through those ministries on the hearts of men. The ministry of intercession, therefore, is vital, and it should not only underlie and inspire all those other ministries detailed in this section, but be recognized as one which should constantly be exercised by all members of the Church. Those who have opportunity for other forms of service should not be slack in this service also, and those who are debarred by sickness or other causes from

exercising other ministries should recognize that this ministry of intercession is their special duty and privilege.

The Episcopate

The uniting Churches accept the Presbyteral, Congregational, and Episcopal elements in Church order as necessary parts of the basis of union. They agree that the Episcopate shall be both constitutional and historic, though this agreement is not to be taken as committing them to any particular interpretation.

The meaning in which the uniting Churches thus accept the historic and constitutional Episcopacy is that in the united Church:

(i) The Bishops shall perform their functions in accordance with the customs of the Church, those customs being named and defined in the written constitution of the united Church. They shall include those of pastoral oversight, of teaching, of the supervision of public worship, of ordination of Ministers, and authorization to Ministers to officiate and preach, and of the oversight of the Church. A Bishop will, if required, assist other Bishops in the consecration of persons duly elected or appointed to be Bishops.

(ii) The Bishops shall be elected, both the diocese concerned in each particular case and the authorities of the united Church as a whole having an effective voice in their appointment.

(iii) Continuity with the historic Episcopate shall both initially and thereafter be effectively maintained, it being understood that, as stated above, no particular interpretation of the historic Episcopate, as that is accepted in the united Church, is thereby implied, or shall be demanded from any Minister or member thereof.

(iv) Every ordination of Presbyters shall be performed by the laying on of hands of the Bishop and Presbyter, and all consecrations of Bishops shall be performed by the laying on of hands in which at least three Bishops shall participate. The uniting Churches declare that in making this provision, it is their intention and determination in this manner to secure the unification of the ministry, but that the acceptance of this provision does not involve any judgement upon the validity or regularity of any other form of the ministry, and the fact that other Churches do not follow the rule of episcopal ordination shall not in itself preclude the united Church from holding relations of communion and fellowship with them.

(v) The Bishops of the Church of India, Burma, and Ceylon in the area of union, and the Bishops of the Methodist Church in Southern Asia, together with the new Bishops to be consecrated at the time of union, shall be the first Bishops of the united Church, provided that they accept the Constitution of the united Church. It is, however, recognized that in our divided state the Bishops of the Episcopal Churches which are seeking union through the Round Table Conference do not now possess authority outside their own Churches. In order that the Episcopate of the united Church may be both constitutional and historic, and that the authority of these Bishops may be recognized and exercised throughout the united Church, it is necessary that they should receive authority from those uniting Churches in which they do not now possess it. Therefore at the time of the inauguration of union there shall be a service at which this wider authority will be conferred upon them, and the new Bishops be consecrated. Bishops and Presbyters of all the uniting Churches shall participate in this service.

Polity

1. (i) The Pastorate Meeting shall be presided over by the Pastor and shall meet at least once a year. The whole congregation shall be invited, and the purpose of the meeting shall be to afford an opportunity for acquainting the congregation with matters which it is necessary and profitable for it to know, and also for the election of representatives to the Pastorate Committee.

(ii) The Pastorate Committee, presided over by the Pastor, to consider the general, spiritual, and financial welfare of the local Church and the advancement of the Kingdom of God, and to elect representatives to the next higher court.

(*Note.* After the inauguration of Union it shall still remain possible for local churches to continue their present systems of administration in so far as they do not conflict with the Constitution of the Church.) The detailed constitution of the local Church shall be drawn up by the Synod of the Church after the inauguration of Union.

2. The Diocesan Council, presided over by the Bishop, comprising ministerial and lay delegates.

(*a*) The general welfare of the Church and the evangelization of the diocese, including the selection and training of candidates for the Ministry.

(*b*) The oversight of the theological, educational, and other institutions of the diocese, and the supervision of its property.

(*c*) Election of representatives to the Synod.

(*d*) The provision of arrangements for the allocation and discipline of Ministers.

3. The Synod, consisting of all the Bishops with delegates from the Diocesan Councils. The Synod shall be the supreme supervisory and legislative body of the Church, and its final court of appeal. The arrangements for the election and allocation of Bishops shall be under its direction. It shall make arrangements for institutions serving more than one diocese. It shall deal with the relations of the Church with other Churches.

(*Note.* The Continuation Committee shall draw up proposals for the constitution of the Diocesan Councils and the Synod. It shall also prepare a statement concerning the Faith and Doctrine of the united Church. These proposals shall be submitted through the secretary to the Round Table Conference.)

N.B. 4. *External Relations.* Provision shall be made in the Plan of Union, whereby Church and Mission functions shall be integrated.

Revised by the Round Table Conference, Allahabad, July 23rd and 24th, 1947.

W. MACHIN,
Hon. Sec.

APPENDIX

Resolution of the General Council of the Church of India, Burma, and Ceylon

FEBRUARY 1944

'We, the Bishops, Clergy and Laity of the Anglican Communion in India, Burma, and Ceylon assembled in Council at Nagpur have been burdened with a sense of frustration, as we have considered the failure of twenty-five years of effort to bring union to divided Christians in South India. But in this session there has been given to us a new vision of the unity of Christ's people and new hope as to the means by which that unity can be achieved. It has been laid upon us that we are still depending too much on human contrivance, and that we must learn to trust more fully in God's creative power to do new things and to give to His Church that unity which is according to His will.

'We and those with whom we desire to unite are all one as members of the body of Christ, and through faith in the redemption wrought by God through His only-begotten Son, Jesus Christ; but so long as we remain out of communion with one another we are all defective in spiritual power. This is true in a special way of the ordained ministry. The ministries of all separated communions are by the fact of separation imperfect and limited in authority. As a result of this fact, the witness of us all to Christ is seriously compromised, and the work of setting forward God's purpose for the redemption of all mankind is grievously hindered.

'We acknowledge that in the past we have failed in manifold ways to forward the work of reconciliation. For these sins of the past we earnestly repent and desire to atone; and we desire to express that penitence not only in words, but also in action. We believe that, when separated Communions come together again, their ministries should be united by a solemn act of humility and rededication, in which through the mutual laying on of hands with prayer they seek from God the enrichment of all those ministries.

'If this method of achieving a united ministry commends itself to the mind and conscience of the Churches, those of us who are ordained ministers, bishops and presbyters, desire to present ourselves to those duly authorized in these Communions which are seeking to restore the unity of the body of Christ, that we may receive through the laying on of hands and prayer the spiritual endowment which in separation from them we lack.

'We would earnestly commend this suggestion to our own Communion and also to other Communions who sincerely desire the union of the faithful, asking them to consider prayerfully whether this step is the will of God for us, and whether we may not hope by this means to be brought very much nearer to that perfect reconciliation and union which we all earnestly desire.'

XVI. SOUTH INDIA

[The movement for Union in South India, of which the Scheme of Church Union was the result, began in 1919 with a meeting of thirty-three members of the Church of India, Burma, and Ceylon, and of the South India United Church at Tranquebar—all but two being Indians. The first edition of the Scheme (*vide supra*, Document 139) was published in 1929, and was considered by the Lambeth Conference of 1930 (Document 145, Resolution 40). Since 1929 it has been revised in the light of criticisms and suggestions and has been redrafted, the second edition appearing in 1931; followed by a redraft published in 1936. In 1942 appeared the Seventh Edition (Revised), published by the United Society for Christian Literature. It has now been finally approved by the authorities of the three uniting Churches. The Church of South India was accordingly inaugurated at Madras in a solemn service on September 27, 1947.]

204. The South India Provincial Synod of the Methodist Church. Resolution of Acceptance

JANUARY AND JULY 1943

RESOLUTION passed at the meeting of the Synod on January 28th and 29th, 1943 (the votes being 40 for, 4 against, and 2 neutral).

'1. The Synod with a deep sense of responsibility records its judgement that the Methodist Church in South India should enter into union on the Basis (Parts 1 and 2) of the Proposed Scheme of Church Union in South India as found in the 7th edition, 1942.

'2. The Synod instructs its delegates to convey to the Joint Committee its strong recommendation that in view of misleading interpretations of the Pledge to which currency has been given, there should be printed as an addendum to the Pledge in the Basis of Union, for permanent record, the agreed statement on the meaning of the Pledge issued by the Joint Committee in 1934, with the clarifying addition made in 1935.

'In making this recommendation the Synod recalls that it was on the express acceptance of this agreed statement that the Conference in 1934 gave its judgement that there is nothing in the Scheme contrary to the principles of Methodism, and it is on the same clear understanding of the meaning of the Pledge that the Provincial Synod vote is now given.'

Note. This resolution was endorsed by the Conference at its meeting in July 1943.

205. *Letter from the Archbishop of Canterbury to the Metropolitan of the Church of India, Burma, and Ceylon*

JANUARY 21, 1944

[When the 1936 edition of the Scheme was published the Metropolitan of India referred certain questions arising out of the redraft to the Lambeth Conference Consultative Body in 1938. The general conclusion of the Consultative Body was that except in regard to new provisions which had been introduced into the scheme making it possible for the refusal of the majority of the Bishops to consent to a proposal emanating from the Synod concerning a matter of Faith or Order to be overruled in certain circumstances, the changes introduced since 1930 were not such as to give ground for supposing that the Lambeth Conference of 1940 would wish to reconsider the general approval given in 1930. Further questions were submitted by the Metropolitan of India to the Consultative Body in 1943, arising out of the new and amended edition containing all amendments made by the Joint Committee up to and including October 1941. The general conclusion reached by the Consultative Body was that some of the new modifications were improvements but that taken cumulatively the changes introduced might render acceptance by the Lambeth Conference harder rather than easier; nevertheless the Consultative Body did not think that the substance was so affected as to call for a modification of the reply given in 1938. The Metropolitan of India later submitted two questions to the Metropolitans of the Anglican Communion which are quoted in the Reply of the Archbishop of Canterbury given below.]

LAMBETH PALACE, S.E.

MY DEAR METROPOLITAN,

I duly received your letter in which you put to me, as Metropolitan of the Province of Canterbury, two questions concerning the action of this Province in the event of the inauguration of a united Church of South India in accordance with the Proposed Scheme of Church Union as this is presented in the seventh edition of that Scheme. You asked whether this Province would

(*a*) break off communion with the Church of India, Burma, and Ceylon;

and/or

(*b*) refuse to be in communion with the Church in South India.

I have put these questions before the Diocesan Bishops of the Province of Canterbury in the Upper House of Convocation, and they in turn sought the counsel of the Lower House. You will, of course, understand that our concern was to answer your questions, and to consider the Scheme itself only so far as seemed necessary to that purpose. What I am now conveying to you is, therefore, not to be regarded as a formal Act of Convocation registering approval or disapproval of the Scheme. You will also understand that our answer must be regarded as liable to review if need arises, since it is not yet known what will be the future course either of the proposed United Church or of the relations between it and the Church of India, Burma, and Ceylon. With this understanding I proceed in what follows to express the common mind of the Bishops, who have approved the contents of this statement after receiving a reply from the Lower House to the request for its comment and counsel.

(*a*) As regards the first of the two questions to which we are asked to reply our answer is quite simple: the answer is No. The Church of India, Burma, and Ceylon will, if the Scheme of Union in South India takes effect, lose four of its dioceses; apart from this it will remain unaltered. The Church of India, Burma, and Ceylon is, according to the practice of the Anglican Communion, responsible for deciding, in accordance with the doctrine of the Church and with its knowledge of the special conditions in the area concerned, whether or not to give its sanction to the Scheme.

(*b*) The second question cannot be quite so simply answered. When the Lambeth Conference in 1930 expressed its 'strong desire that, as soon as the negotiations are successfully completed, the venture should be made and the union inaugurated' (Resolution 40 (*c*))[1] it also approved the following description of the resulting situation:

> 'The united Church in India will not itself be an Anglican Church; it will be a distinct Province of the Universal Church. It will have a very real intercommunion with the Churches of the Anglican Communion, though for a time that intercommunion will be limited in certain directions by their rules. Its Bishops will be received as Bishops by these Churches. Its episcopally ordained ministers—a continually increasing number—will be entitled under the usual rules to administer the Communion in the Churches of the Anglican Communion. Its communicants will be entitled to communicate with the Churches of the Anglican Communion, except in cases forbidden by the rules of those Churches. On the other hand no right to minister in the Churches of that Communion will be acquired by those ministers who have not been episcopally ordained.' (Encyclical Letter, p. 27.)

In accordance with that anticipation, and provided that the Scheme as finally adopted does not differ in any point affecting the relation of the Church of England to the Church of South India,

[1] *Vide supra*, Document 145.

from that which is contained in the Seventh Edition of the Scheme, I am conveying the common mind of the Bishops of the Province of Canterbury as finally expressed after considering the comments and counsel of the clergy of the Province as represented by the Lower House of Convocation, when I say that their administrative action will follow these lines:

1. Subject to such rules and customs as are accepted in respect of all communicants in the Province, a communicant member of the united Church would be admissible to Communion in the Churches of the Province.

2. An episcopally ordained minister of the united Church would be qualified to receive the Licence or Permission of a Bishop to officiate, subject, when they apply, to the provisions of the Colonial Clergy Act, and to such rules and customs as are accepted in respect of all ministers in the Province; thus, for example, if he applied for and received such Licence or Permission it would be on the understanding that he should not officiate in non-Anglican Churches except in such ways—e.g. preaching by special invitation on particular occasions—as are permissible or customary for Priests or Deacons of the Church of England.

3. A minister of the united Church who has not received episcopal ordination would not be qualified to receive a Licence or Permission to officiate in the Province, except in such manner as is permitted under the regulations governing the Interchange of Preachers and set out in an Act of Convocation agreed to by both Houses in May, 1943, of which I enclose a copy.[1]

4. No censure would attach to any member, ordained or unordained, of this Province who may be in South India or go thither, if he communicates with the united Church or takes work of any kind in it.

I hope that I have made clear what the position would be.

The united Church would not be a Province of the Anglican Communion, and there would not at this stage be unrestricted intercommunion between it and this Province, but there would be such intercommunion between clergy and laity of the united Church and those of this Province as I have stated.

These provisions represent certain restrictions upon full communion; that is to say, upon complete interchangeability of Ministers

[1] *Vide supra*, Document 173.

and complete mutual admissibility to Communion. We reiterate the hope expressed by the Committee of the Lambeth Conference of 1930 on the Unity of the Church, 'that when the unification within the united Church, contemplated in the Proposed Scheme, is complete, full communion in that sense will be secured between the united Church and the Church in this Province.

Yours very sincerely,

(Signed) WILLIAM CANTUAR:

January 21st, 1944.

206. *The General Council of the Church of India, Burma, and Ceylon. Resolution of Acceptance*

JANUARY 1945

RESOLUTION passed by the General Council meeting on January 23–5, 1945 (carried in the House of Bishops by 6 votes to 4, in the House of Clergy by 38 votes to 10, and in the House of Laity by 31 votes to 7):

That this Council, while reaffirming that the Church of this Province continues to be bound in matters of faith and order by the Constitution, Canons, and Rules of the Church of India, Burma, and Ceylon, finally adopts the *Scheme of Church Union in South India* (seventh edition, *revised*), Parts I and II, in order to permit the dioceses of Madras, Travancore and Cochin, Tinnevelly, and Dornakal to carry out their practically unanimous desire to enter into union with the Methodist and South India United Churches.

207. *The General Assembly of the South India United Church. Resolutions of Acceptance*

SEPTEMBER 1946

RESOLUTIONS passed by the General Assembly of the South India United Church, meeting in September, 1946 (carried by 103 votes to 10, 7 being neutral):

I. The South India United Church agrees to enter into organic union with the South India Province of the Methodist Church and the dioceses of Madras, Dornakal, Tinnevelly, and Travancore and Cochin in the Church of India, Burma, and Ceylon on the basis of the Proposed Scheme of Church Union contained in the latest edition of the *Scheme*, 1942, including the Pledge as accepted by the Joint Committee as part of the Basis of Union, and including the Joint Committee's 1934–5 interpretation thereof.

II. The Assembly authorizes the Joint Committee, as soon as the 1934–5 interpretation of the Pledge is accepted by the Church of India, Burma, and Ceylon, to take all necessary steps to inaugurate the Union at as early a date as possible.

208. *The General Council of the Church of India, Burma, and Ceylon. Resolution of Acceptance*

JANUARY 1947

RESOLUTION passed by the General Council meeting on January 20–2, 1947 (carried in the House of Bishops by 7 votes to 6, in the House of Clergy by 30 votes to 22, and in the House of Laity by 33 votes to 7):

The Council having taken note of Resolution IV, 2 and 4, of the Joint Committee 1946, now accepts the interpretation issued by the Joint Committee in 1934 and amended in 1935, regarding it as wholly in accordance with the Basis of Union which was adopted by the General Council in 1945.

Note on 'The Pledge'

1. The General Council's Resolution of January 22, 1947 has special reference to the Pledge which is incorporated at the end of Section 16 of the *Basis of Union* and runs as follows:

They therefore pledge themselves and fully trust each other that the united Church will at all times be careful not to allow any overriding of conscience either by Church authorities or by majorities, and that it will not in any of its administrative acts knowingly transgress the long-established traditions of any of the Churches from which it has been formed. Neither forms of worship or ritual, nor a ministry, to which they have not been accustomed or to which they conscientiously object, will be imposed upon any congregation; and no arrangements with regard to these matters will knowingly be made, either generally or in particular cases, which would either offend the conscientious convictions of persons directly concerned, or which would hinder the development of complete unity within the united Church or imperil its progress towards union with other Churches.

2. The interpretation of the Pledge issued by the Joint Committee of the Church of India, Burma, and Ceylon, the South India United Church, and the South India Provincial Synod of the Methodist Church in 1934 and amended in 1935 is as follows:

'In view of the questions that have arisen, the Joint Committee thinks it right to state what is in its judgement the meaning of the provisions generally referred to as the Pledge.

'This Pledge applies to the period following the inauguration of the Union when the members of the three Churches, then united in one Church, will be growing together; and the uniting Churches pledge themselves to do all in their power to assist the united Church in its advance towards complete spiritual unity, and towards the time when all the members of the united Church will be willing and able to receive Communion equally in all its Churches.

'Further they pledge themselves that because of the Union no congregation shall be deprived of forms of worship or a ministry to which it has been accustomed, but every honest endeavour will be made by the authorities of the united Church that neither forms of worship or ritual, nor a ministry to which they have not been accustomed or to which they conscientiously object, shall be imposed upon any congregation. But the Committee does not understand the Pledge to imply that the fact that a minister of the united Church has previously been a minister of either an episcopal or a non-episcopal Church will itself debar him from appointment to or working in any congregation of the united Church where that congregation desires it.

'Further the intention of the uniting Churches is that there shall be no infringement of the liberty of conscience which every worshipper and every minister now enjoys, and that in the united Church all alike will be free to worship and to teach according to their conscience, only so that nothing be done to break the fundamental unity of the Church.

'The Joint Committee further wishes to urge upon the negotiating Churches that while the purpose for which these provisions have been inserted in the Basis of Union will not be fulfilled unless the real scope and effect of the Pledge be understood by all parties, that purpose will be entirely defeated if detailed interpretations of the Pledge and precise statements of its application to particular future and hypothetical cases are demanded; and it appeals to the negotiating Churches to act in this matter in the full spirit of the declaration that freedom of opinion on debatable matters and mutual respect for differences of opinion and practice can be safeguarded, not by the framing of detailed regulations but by assurances given and received in a spirit of confidence and love.'

(*Note*. This interpretation had not been before the General Council of the Church of India, Burma, and Ceylon, as an accepted part of the scheme, when it passed its Resolution adopting the scheme in 1945.)

3. The Joint Committee in December 1946 adopted the following Resolution which is referred to in the Resolution of the General Council of the Church of India, Burma, and Ceylon in its Resolution of January 22, 1947.

i. The Joint Committee is of opinion that the interpretation of the Pledge which it gave in 1934–5, rightly understood, provides adequate safeguards against coercion.

ii. The Joint Committee approves the following statement: 'It is understood that during the period of unification congregations will ordinarily continue to be served by the ministries to which they are accustomed, except where pastoral needs obviously demand other arrangements. The duly constituted authority within the united Church shall be the sole judge of the urgency of such pastoral needs.'

iii. But the Joint Committee does not consider that this statement (ii) should be added to the Interpretation of the Pledge, as two of the Churches have already voted upon the Scheme as containing the Interpretation without this addition.

iv. The Joint Committee endorses the Report of the Continuation Committee, section 2 (*c*), viz: 'A question having been raised as to the meaning of the italicized words in the following sentence of the 1934–5 Interpretation: "The Committee does not understand the Pledge to imply that the fact that a minister of the united Church has previously been a minister of either an episcopal or a non-episcopal Church will itself debar him from appointment to or working in any congregation of the united Church *where that congregation desires it*", the Joint Committee understands this to mean:

(*a*) such appointments would not be made if a congregation objects on conscientious grounds, and

(*b*) as stated in ii. 9 of the Governing Principles of the Church, that "every pastorate shall have an opportunity of expressing its judgement as to the appointment of its pastor", while the responsibility for making the appointment remains with the duly constituted authority of the united Church.'

XVII. IRAN

209. Proposed basis for the union of the Episcopal and Presbyterian Churches in Iran

1945

[Discussions began in 1912. Proposals for a united Church in Persia approved by a Presbyterian and Anglican Inter-Church Conference at Isfahan in 1927 were noted by the Lambeth Conference 1930 (Resolution 41).[1] Further discussions took place—and correspondence followed between Bishop J. H. Linton, his successor, Bishop W. J. Thompson, and the Archbishop of Canterbury. Various modifications have been made. The proposed basis is a draft proposed by the Inter-Church Union Committee, but not formally accepted in detail by the Churches concerned. The Committee decided to publish the draft in 1945 with a view to arousing increased interest and constructive criticism.]

PREFACE

THE Evangelical (Presbyterian) Church in the North of Iran and the Anglican Episcopal Church in the South are the fruit of the work of the Board of Foreign Missions of the Presbyterian Church of the U.S.A. and the Church Missionary Society respectively. These two societies mutually agreed from the first to adopt a policy of co-operation whereby the respective areas of their mission activities were defined. From the beginning a very happy relationship has existed between the two Missions and this is reflected in the spirit of co-operation and fellowship between the two Churches. But this has only emphasized the need and increased the desire for a more formal and organic unity.

The Presbyterian Church gradually took shape in the North and in 1934 was formally organized into three presbyteries under one central Council. This was later recognized by the Church and Mission Board in America as an Independent Church with powers to develop its own life and organization. At the same time the Episcopal Church in the South was taking shape, and eventually it was organized as a separate diocese in 1912, the bishop being directly responsible to the Archbishop of Canterbury in ecclesiastical matters.

The desire for the unity and independence of the Church in Iran has been evident from the beginning. The question of church union was formally discussed at an inter-church conference as early as

[1] *Vide supra*, Document 145, Resolution 41.

1912. Since then the matter has been constantly under review. In 1940 an Inter-Church Union Committee was formed to which both churches elected representatives. This Committee was asked to draw up plans for the Constitution of a United Church for consideration. The Committee has met periodically and in 1942 drew up draft proposals which were submitted to the Churches. These were in principle accepted by both churches, but criticisms of various kinds were made. These have been very carefully considered by the Committee and the original draft has been modified and expanded in various ways in the light of these criticisms and of the experience of the last few years.

The Committee feel that the time has come when the proposals should be more widely known and studied. Not only should all the members of both churches be more fully informed about them, but they should be made available to a larger circle of friends outside Iran. The Committee have, therefore, decided to print them in a more permanent and readily accessible form in both English and Persian.

We are, however, anxious that it should be clearly understood by all that these proposals are only a draft agreed to by the Committee and that they have not yet been formally accepted in detail by the authoritative bodies of either church. But the main lines of the scheme have been approved. We hope that the greater publicity we now propose to give to them will result in increased interest and in constructive criticisms which will enable us to improve and complete the scheme. It will be obvious to all who read this draft that there are still many matters which have to be included in any final Constitution, but the present draft, we believe, indicates the way in which God is leading our churches to unite. We invite all Christians to unite with us in praying that God will guide us into a fuller understanding of His Will for us in this matter.

Our indebtedness in many directions and specially to the South India Scheme for Church Union will be obvious to all who have studied that scheme. It was natural and inevitable that we should follow along the lines so carefully worked out in India. That we have in a few places ventured to take a different line, is largely due to the matured consideration which the whole subject has latterly been given in many parts of the world by which we have been able to profit. God is leading His Church throughout the world to a new realization of the tragic loss of spiritual life and power due to our unhappy divisions. As our fellowship together deepens and widens so the world will recognize the Spirit of Christ in us. 'By this shall all men know that ye are my disciples if ye have love one to another.'

W. J. THOMPSON, Bishop in Iran, *Chairman.*
REV. J. ELDER, *Secretary.*
REV. JOLYNOOS HAKIM.
REV. A. NAKHOSTEEN.
REV. M. REZAVI.
RABI S. KHOOBYAR.
AGA A. NAKHOSTEEN.

DRAFT OF THE PROPOSED CONSTITUTION FOR THE UNION OF THE PRESBYTERIAN AND ANGLICAN EPISCOPAL CHURCHES IN IRAN

INTRODUCTION

WE believe the following considerations, among others, should impel our two Churches in Iran to move as rapidly as possible toward the ultimate goal of corporate union.

1. That such a union would be the carrying out of God's will as expressed in the prayer: 'That they all may be one . . . that the world may believe that Thou hast sent me.'

2. That as we are all spiritually one as members of the body of Christ, this union should find outward expression in a United Church.

3. That our present division is a cause of weakness to the Spiritual life of the Churches and a cause of stumbling to those who are outside.

4. That while co-operation without union is effective to a degree in the first presentation of the Gospel to men, it breaks down later in the task of building up the Church.

5. That the spiritual life of the Church when united would be richer in fellowship through a closer sharing of experience and viewpoints.

6. That the urgency of our need for union is being brought home to us by modern developments in Iran resulting in closer contacts with one another, while recent developments abroad have confronted the Church everywhere with new and powerful enemies in the face of which our divisions are an increasing danger.

7. That the Spirit of God is evidently drawing Christians together all over the world as witnessed by the many and varied efforts for reunion. This is a movement of the Spirit which should strengthen our faith that we are in line with God's will in working for this goal in Iran.

1. *The Name of the Church*

The Church shall be called 'The Church of Christ in Iran'.

2. *The Church and Its Membership*

The Church of Christ in Iran acknowledges that the Church is the Body of Christ and its members are the members of His Body; that those are members according to the will and purpose of God who have been baptized into the name of the Father and of the Son and of the Holy Spirit, and receiving the calling and grace of God with faith, continue steadfast therein, maintaining their vital union with the Head of the body, Jesus Christ, by the same faith, through the various means of grace which He has provided in His Church.

3. *The Faith of the Church*

The Church of Christ in Iran holds the faith which the Church has ever held in Jesus, and in accordance with the revelation of God which He has made, being himself God incarnate, it worships one God in Trinity and Trinity in unity. It accepts the Holy Scriptures of the Old and New Testaments as containing all things necessary to salvation and as the ultimate standard of faith. It accepts the Apostles' Creed and the creed commonly called the Nicene, as valuable in witnessing to and safeguarding the faith which is continually confirmed in the spiritual experience of the Church of Christ, and requires no other statement of faith for a basis of union.

4. *The Sacraments in the Church*

The Sacraments of Baptism and Holy Communion being directly ordained by Christ shall be officially recognized in the Church of Christ in Iran as means of grace through which God works in us. This will not preclude the use of other rites such as Confirmation and Admission to Communion.

5. *The Ministry in the Church*

The Church of Christ in Iran believes that the Church is a royal priesthood of believers and all its members have direct access to

God. All have their various shares in the commission and authority of the whole Church, and therefore they all have duties to perform in order that the priestly work of the Church may be fulfilled.

The Church of Christ in Iran also believes that the Ministry is a gift of God through Christ to His Church which he has given for the perfecting of the life and service of all its members, that God Himself calls men into the Ministry through His Holy Spirit, and that their vocation is to bring sinners to repentance and to lead God's people in worship, prayer, and praise, and through pastoral ministrations, the preaching of the Gospel and the administration of the Sacraments (all these being made effective through faith), to assist men to receive the saving and sanctifying benefits of Christ and to fit them for service; and it believes that in ordination God, in answer to the prayers of His Church, bestows on and assures to those whom He has called and His Church has accepted for any particular form of the Ministry, a commission for it and the grace appropriate to it.

The Church of Christ in Iran recognizes three distinct forms of ordained Ministry, viz. the Diaconate, the Presbyterate, and the Episcopate.

6. *The Congregation in the Church of Christ in Iran*

Subject to the provisions of the Constitution and to such general regulations thereunder as may be issued in any matter by the Church as a whole or a regional Council, every congregation of the Church shall, with its pastor, be responsible for maintaining its own spiritual life and purity of doctrine, and for the proclaiming of the Gospel to those outside the Church. It shall elect a body of Ruling Elders or Pastorate Committee from amongst its own members. These are the representatives of the congregation chosen for the purpose of exercising government and discipline in conjunction with the pastor or minister. They shall assist and co-operate with the Minister in providing services of worship in the local church, and the reception and disciplining of members of the Church. They may be set aside for their service by the laying on of hands by the Minister if so be desired.

7. *The Diaconate*

The Church of Christ in Iran accepts the diaconate as part of the historic ministry of the church, and accepting the New Testament account of its origin recognizes that the ministry of the diaconate may be undertaken for life by persons who have been accepted for the same by the diocesan authorities and have received due training.

Persons who have been selected as candidates for the presbyterate shall ordinarily, after undergoing the necessary theological training, serve for a period of one or two years as a deacon.

The functions of a Deacon in the Church of Christ in Iran shall include the following: assisting the presbyter in the administration of the Lord's Supper and in other services of the Church; administering of baptism; ministering in the temporalities of the Church; giving succour to the poor, the needy, and the sick; instructing of children and catechumens in the faith; preaching the Word; and generally assisting in pastoral and evangelistic work.

Deacons shall be set apart for their ministry by the laying on of hands by the bishop of the diocese. No person shall be made a deacon until he has attained to the age of 23 years.

8. *The Presbyterate*

The Church of Christ in Iran believes that presbyters are specially called and commissioned by God to be dispensers of His Word and Sacraments, to declare His message of pardon to penitent sinners, to build up the members of the Church in their most holy faith, and, through the councils of the Church and otherwise, to share with the bishops and lay members in its government and in the administration of its discipline.

It is the rule of the Church of Christ in Iran that none except presbyters and bishops have the right to celebrate the Holy Communion.

9. *The Episcopate*

The Church of Christ in Iran accepts and will maintain the historic Episcopate in a constitutional form. But this acceptance does not commit it to any particular interpretation of episcopacy or to any particular view or belief concerning orders of the ministry, and it will not require the acceptance of any such particular view or interpretation as a necessary qualification for its ministry. Whatever differences there are, however, the Church of Christ in Iran agrees that, as Episcopacy has been accepted in the Church from early times, it may in this sense fitly be called historic. Any additional interpretations, though held by individuals, are not binding on the Church of Christ in Iran.

The meaning in which the Church of Christ in Iran thus accepts an historic and constitutional Episcopacy is that in it:

i. The bishops shall perform their functions in accordance with the customs of the Church, those functions including pastoral oversight, teaching, supervision of public worship, ordination of ministers and authorization of ministers to officiate and preach, and the oversight of the discipline of the Church, which functions are more fully set forth in another section of this constitution.

ii. The bishops shall be elected. Only those who have been ordained as presbyters shall be eligible for election. The Diocese concerned, through its Diocesan Council and other duly appointed diocesan elections, shall elect the man they desire to be appointed and consecrated as their bishop. The Presiding Bishop may submit one or two names of presbyters outside the diocese for the consideration of the diocese along with any other names under consideration. The name of the elected person shall be submitted to the House of Bishops for confirmation, if after due examination they be convinced of his suitability in soundness of doctrine and purity of life. If the Diocesan Council so desire they may submit more than one name to the Bishops, leaving the final choice with them.

iii. A bishop shall be appointed to the Episcopal charge of a diocese for a limited period of time. At the end of this period he may be reappointed to the same or another diocese on conditions laid down later in this constitution. (See note below.)

iv. Continuity with the historic Episcopate will be effectively maintained.

v. Every ordination of presbyters shall be performed by the laying on of hands by the Bishops and presbyters. The consecration of bishops at the inauguration of the union shall be performed by the laying on of hands of at least three bishops and three presbyters. Subsequently, all consecration of bishops shall be performed by the laying on of hands of at least three bishops after presentation of the person to be consecrated to the Presiding Bishop by two delegated presbyters from the diocese to which he is appointed.

The Church of Christ in Iran believes that in all ordinations and consecrations the true Ordainer and Consecrator is God, who in response to the prayers of His Church and through the words and acts of its representatives, commissions and empowers for the office and work to which they are called, the persons whom it has selected.

In making this provision for Episcopal ordination and consecration the Church of Christ in Iran declares that it is its intention and determination in this manner to secure the unification of the ministry but that this does not involve any judgement upon the validity or regularity of any other form of the ministry, and the fact that other Churches do not follow the rule of Episcopal ordination will not in itself preclude it from holding relations of communion and fellowship with them.

Note. In regard to the appointment of bishops (iii above) it is proposed that upon the inauguration of the United Church half of the House of Bishops shall be appointed to their diocese for five years and half of them for eight years. Thereafter each appointment shall be for a period of eight years, or until the person concerned shall reach the age of retirement, whichever comes first.

The reappointment of bishops to their diocese shall require at least a majority of 75 per cent. of those present and voting of each of the electing bodies.

The retiring age for bishops shall be 65, but they may be invited by the Church to continue in office for a further period of service not exceeding five years.

10. *The Worship of the Church of Christ in Iran*

The Church of Christ in Iran will aim at conserving for the common benefit whatever of good has been gained in the separate history of those Churches from which it has been formed, and therefore in its public worship will retain for its congregations freedom either to use historic forms or not to do so as may best conduce to edification and to the worship of God in spirit and in truth.

No forms of worship which before the union have been in use in either of the uniting Churches shall be forbidden in the Church of Christ in Iran, nor shall any wonted forms be changed or new forms introduced into the worship of any congregation without the agreement of the pastor and the congregation arrived at in accordance with the conditions laid down in this Constitution.

Subject to these conditions, and to the provisions of this Constitution and any special regulations which may hereafter be issued by the authorities under the Constitution with regard to the services of ordination and consecration and the essential elements or central parts of other services, especially those of Baptism, Holy Communion, and Marriage, every pastor and congregation shall have freedom to determine the forms of their public worship.

11. *Unity in Ministry and Life within the Church of Christ in Iran*

The first act of the newly consecrated bishops of the Church of Christ in Iran shall be to commission by the laying on of hands all of the ordained Ministers of both the uniting churches for service in the Church of Christ in Iran. Such a Commission does not imply re-ordination or a repudiation of the validity of the orders of either Church as real ministries of the Word and Sacraments, but rather an extension of ministerial authority which is conferred on all concerned by the fact of union.

We suggest that the formula to be used at the time of commissioning might be as follows:

> 'Receive the Holy Spirit for the work of a presbyter in the Church of God, both for the continuance of that work which thou hast done hitherto and for the performance of that work which is now committed unto thee by the laying on of our hands. Take thou authority to preach and teach the Word, to fulfil the Ministry of reconciliation and to minister Christ's sacraments in the congregations whereunto thou shall be further called and lawfully appointed; and see that thou do all these things in brotherly partnership with God's fellow workers whom in this union of Churches He has made thine.'

The Church of Christ in Iran recognizes that the act of union has initiated a process of growing together into one life and of advance towards complete spiritual unity. But it is convinced that this can only take place on the basis of freedom of opinion and practice. The Church of Christ in Iran therefore pledges itself that it will not in any of its administrative acts knowingly transgress the long-established traditions of either of the Churches from which it has been formed. Neither forms of worship nor ritual, to which they have not been accustomed, or to which they conscientiously object, will be imposed upon any congregation; and no arrangements with regard to these matters will knowingly be made, either generally or in particular cases, which would either offend the conscientious convictions of congregations directly concerned, or which would hinder the development of complete unity within the Church or imperil its progress towards union with other Churches.

12. *Relations with Other Churches*

The Church of Christ in Iran desires to be permanently in full communion and fellowship with the two Churches with which its constituent groups have had such communion and fellowship.

Any communicant member of any Church with which the Church of Christ in Iran has relations of fellowship shall be at liberty to partake of the Holy Communion in any church of the Church of Christ in Iran, and any minister of such a church shall be free as a visitor to minister or celebrate the Holy Communion in any church of the Church of Christ in Iran if he is invited to do so.

The Church of Christ in Iran will also gladly accept invitations to send delegates as visitors to the assemblies or other representative bodies of the Churches through whose labours its constituent groups have come into being, and will seek, by interchange of visiting delegates or such other means as may be available, to promote and maintain brotherly relations with other Churches.

The Church of Christ in Iran, as a part of the Church Universal, is prepared to give full weight to the pronouncements of bodies representative of the whole Church, and would desire to take part in the deliberations and decisions of an Oecumenical Council if such should in the mercy of God be some day called together; and in particular will desire to unite with the newly founded World Council of Churches at the earliest opportunity.

13. *Autonomy of the Church of Christ in Iran*

The Church of Christ in Iran, while retaining all spiritual fellowship with the parent churches, shall become fully autonomous upon completion of its organization and the consecration of its first bishops, and thus no foreign ecclesiastical authority shall have jurisdiction or control, direct or indirect, in or over the United Church.

14. *Relations of Ministers and Members of the Church of Christ in Iran with Other Churches*

None of the ministers or members of the Church of Christ in Iran shall because of the union forgo any rights with regard to intercommunion and intercelebration which they possessed before the union.

Every minister of the Church of Christ in Iran who was ordained outside of its area shall be at liberty to retain the ecclesiastical status (e.g. connexion with a home presbytery) which he had before the union in the Church in which he was ordained, subject to such arrangements between the Church of Christ in Iran and any of the Churches concerned as may be found necessary, and provided that he shall not by any such arrangement be released from the obligations of his position as a minister of the Church of Christ in Iran.

Every minister of the Church of Christ in Iran shall be at liberty to exercise any ministry in a Church outside its area which he was entitled to exercise before the union, provided that that Church permit him to do so.

Every minister of the Church of Christ in Iran shall be at liberty to minister and celebrate the Holy Communion in any church of a Church with which either of the Uniting Churches have enjoyed relations of fellowship, if he is invited to do so.

In all these, as in other matters, the Church of Christ in Iran desires to avoid on the one hand any encouragement of licence or condonation of breaches of Church comity and fellowship, and on the other hand any unchristian rigidity in its regulations or in their application.

15. *Organization of the Church of Christ in Iran*

At the time of inauguration the Church of Christ in Iran shall be organized into 4 Dioceses each of which shall be under the supervision of a bishop and a Diocesan Council, this Council to consist of all clergy in charge of congregations and other presbyters and lay representatives elected by the Parishes or organized congregations, the laity having a majority in such Councils.

The whole Church of Christ in Iran shall be directed by a Central Synod or Council consisting of a House of Bishops and an Assembly consisting of clerical and lay members elected by the Diocesan Councils.

The definition of 'Parish' and other terms, the method of elections, the Powers of the various Bodies, and other matters are still to be determined.

XVIII. THE WORLD CONFERENCE ON CHURCH, COMMUNITY, AND STATE, OXFORD, 1937

[The World Conference on Church, Community, and State which met at Oxford from July 12 to July 26, 1937, was prepared by the Universal Christian Council for Life and Work, which owed its origin to the Stockholm Conference of 1925. It comprised 425 members from some 120 churches. The joint presidents were: The Archbishop of Canterbury (Cosmo Gordon Lang), Archbishop Germanos, The Archbishop of Upsala (Erling Eidem), the Bishop of Dornakal (V. S. Azariah), Professor W. Adams Brown, and Pastor Marc Boegner. The full Report of the Conference was published under the title *The Churches Survey Their Task* (London, George Allen and Unwin, 1937).]

210. The Oecumenical Church

[*Extract from the Report on the Universal Church and the World of Nations*]

A SPECIAL ground of faith and courage amid the perplexities of our age is that the Christian Church is becoming truly oecumenical. The missionary movement of the past century carried forward the sense of world mission inherent in the Biblical records, making the bounds of the Christian community co-extensive with the habitable globe. This movement has been the principal sign that the Church was alive to the God-given vision of the Church Universal. Moreover the Churches are realizing anew that the Church is one. We say this in full recognition of the fact that between many of the Churches which we represent there is a lack of true fellowship, and that the Church of Rome is not represented in our midst. At the same time, the emergence in different parts of the world of political systems usurping the role of Churches, and demanding the absolute allegiance of men and women, is awakening in Christians in every land a deepened loyalty to Christ and the Church and a fresh sense of their need of solidarity in Christ.

It is important to bear in mind in this connexion the fundamental distinction between 'oecumenical' and 'international'. The term 'international' necessarily accepts the division of mankind into separate nations as a natural if not a final state of affairs. The term 'oecumenical' refers to the expression within history of the given unity of the Church. The one starts from the fact of division and the other from the fact of unity in Christ. The thought and action of the Church are international in so far as the Church must operate in a world in which the historical Christian bodies share with the rest of mankind the division into national and racial groups. They are oecumenical in so far as they attempt to realize the Una Sancta, the fellowship of Christians who acknowledge the one Lord.

This fact of the oecumenical character of the Church carries with it the important consequence that the Church brings to the task of achieving a better international order an insight that is not to be derived from ordinary political sources. To those who are struggling to realize human brotherhood in a world where disruptive nationalism and aggressive imperialism make such brotherhood seem unreal, the Church offers not an ideal but a fact, man united not by his aspiration but by the love of God.

True oecumenicity therefore must be the goal of all our efforts. Churches must not simply be tolerant one towards another but concerned about unity one with the other. Very especially at a time when in parts of the world 'some members of the Body suffer', and others are still weak, must the privileged and stronger members remember the words: 'Bear ye one another's burdens and so fulfil the law of Christ.'

Moreover, lack of unity conflicts seriously with the ultimate and supreme purposes of the Church. These purposes are, and must remain, to proclaim the Gospel of God's love in Jesus Christ to all mankind, to administer the Sacraments, to fulfil the Christian ideal of fellowship, and to guide the souls of her children in the ways of holiness. No other activity in which she may engage can be a substitute for these. For the Church is supremely concerned with persons, and world problems have their roots ultimately in the hearts of persons who 'must be born again'. She must speak therefore in the name of God to the individual men and women who make up the nations, and announce to them, in language they can understand, the news of the world's Saviour. As the greatest need of the world is new men, and the Church's chief opponents in our time aspire to change the very structure of human nature in those whom they control, the Church of Christ throughout the world should work unceasingly for human renewal and the cure of souls, in His name and through His strength 'who maketh all things new'.

At the same time the Church has a concern with civilization in general. With penitence on the one hand, because of the share of responsibility belonging to many of her members for the present state of the world, with thanksgiving on the other, because she has been herself under God the source of some of the chief treasures that the world possesses, the Church must recognize her concern with the secular order. With her members active in every sphere of life, resident in every land, owing allegiance to every form of State, the Church is concerned with the whole world, and the whole of life within it. The Christian Church, acknowledging Christ's work of redemption, possesses a unique insight into the problems of human relationship. Knowing man and 'what is in man' Christians will not be elated with un-Christian hope; knowing Christ and what is 'in Christ' they will not be cast down with un-Christian despair. There comes a call to the Church to face in the light of Christ all the facts that may be gathered from every quarter, and thereafter, in the spirit and through the grace of Christ, to work for the manifestation of the new divine order which appeared in the Cross and Resurrection of the Son of God.

XIX. THE SECOND WORLD CONFERENCE ON FAITH AND ORDER, EDINBURGH, 1937

[The Second World Conference on Faith and Order, which met at Edinburgh from August 3 to August 18, 1937, was prepared for by the Continuation Committee of the Lausanne Conference. It was attended by some 443 delegates, representing 123 churches. The President was Archbishop William Temple, the Vice-Presidents were Dr. A. E. Garvie, Bishop Aulén, Pastor Marc Boegner, Archbishop Germanos, and Dr. J. Ross Stevenson; and Canon Leonard Hodgson was the General Secretary. The Conference adopted the following unanimous Report.]

REPORT OF THE CONFERENCE: SUBMITTED FOR THE CONSIDERATION OF THE PARTICIPATING CHURCHES

211. *Chapter I: Introduction*

Ten Years' Progress

LOOKING back to the first great Conference on Faith and Order held in Lausanne in 1927, we thankfully recognize the real progress made since then in the field of Church union.

Its detailed history is written in the book, *A Decade of Objective Progress in Church Unity, 1927–36*,[1] which was prepared for us under the direction of the Commission on the Church's Unity in Life and Worship. We cannot better open this Report than by offering a factual summary of the most important steps taken during the last ten years in every continent of the world.

The specific unions or approaches to union which the decade has witnessed have sometimes concerned Churches in different nations, as, for example, those between the Anglican Communion on the one side and the Old Catholic Churches of Europe and the Churches of the Orthodox Communion on the other; but they have generally been confined to Churches within their several nations. A special complication has been experienced in connexion with mutual approaches among the younger Churches, particularly in the Orient and in Africa, the control of which still rests partially with parent Churches in the older Christian lands.

[1] By H. Paul Douglass, D.D. New York: Harper and Brothers, 1937. Price $1.50.

The total number of active unity movements is impressive. Nearly half of them have occurred in North America, a fact which reflects the exceptionally large number of previous divisions needing to be healed. And nearly as many are to be found in Asia as in Europe, a fact to be explained in part by the immense pressure of non-Christian civilizations which forces the Churches together, and in part by the practical necessities of the situation. The majority of the achieved unions have thus occurred between Churches not previously sundered by the profounder differences of theological or cultural tradition; so that, in the main, unity has as yet been fully reached only in the easier situations.

Moreover, the group of movements towards unity which marks the period represents very different stages of progress. Some have only reached the stage of vague or tentative exploration. Others have gone as far as definite negotiations regarding terms and conditions of union. Still others, as in the recent conversations between the Church of England and the Church of Scotland and the associated Churches in both countries, have suffered indefinite postponement. Some have even had to be abandoned. A somewhat larger number has been consummated. It is a matter for great satisfaction to be able to record that all unions which have been in existence long enough to be tested have been distinctly successful in the eyes of those primarily concerned.

The schemes attempted illustrate all the usual meanings of the word unity. Some schemes have sought and some have secured mutual recognition between Churches, and thus have laid the basis for intercommunion. As an example we may quote the agreement establishing full intercommunion between Churches of the Anglican Communion and the Old Catholic Churches. An agreement has happily been reached and ratified between the Church of England and the Church of Finland, and negotiations are in progress with the Churches of Latvia and Estonia. Other Churches have been content with more or less complete federation. About three-quarters of all the cases recorded, however, have contemplated the actual corporate union of two or more previously separate bodies. This is exemplified in such conspicuous instances as the reunion of the Scottish Presbyterian Churches in 1929 and that of the English Methodists in 1932, as the union of three Churches in Canada in 1925, as the formation of the Church of Christ in China in 1927 combining Baptist, Congregational, Methodist, Presbyterian and Reformed Churches, United Brethren, the United Church of

Canada, and independent Chinese Churches founded by six English-speaking nations. There are to be borne in mind also the contemplated unions of the French Reformed Churches and of the chief Methodist Churches of the United States. All these cases significantly change former ecclesiastical structure and constitute single Churches.

Many of the great denominational types of Churches represented in the Faith and Order Movement have been involved in these recent developments. Some have been primarily interested in the realization of a particular form or kind of unity. Others have limited themselves to the uniting of bodies of the same religious type and tradition. But highly significant unions in the United States, Canada, and China have brought into single communions Churches of very divergent traditions and polity; so that the record of the immediate past does not suggest any necessity for waiting upon unions of denominational families before wider union is attempted.

Obviously any estimate of the very varied forms of mutual approach depends upon the kind of unity one believes to be important and on the true objective. Schemes of a denominational kind might in some cases prove in a few years' time to have strengthened confessional consciousness and so to have postponed oecumenical union by widening the gulfs between the large Churches thus created. Some may see in most of the recent movements only minor cases mainly remedying, on a local or regional scale, certain practical disadvantages of disunion. Intercommunion has not been widely extended during the decade; and no union has been consummated between a Church of radically 'Catholic' and one of radically 'Evangelical' tradition. While, then, the significance of the progress made must not be overstated, the trend towards unity is nevertheless marked both in magnitude and in character. It is widespread throughout the world. It occurs in a wide variety of forms. It is vital, relevant to actual situations. It is making increasing appeal to the heart and conscience of all Christian men.

212. *Chapter II: The Grace of our Lord Jesus Christ*

With deep thankfulness to God for the spirit of unity, which by His gracious blessing upon us has guided and controlled all our discussions on this subject, we agree on the following statement and recognize that there is in connexion with this subject no ground for maintaining division between Churches.

(i) *The Meaning of Grace*

When we speak of God's grace, we think of God Himself as revealed in His Son Jesus Christ. The meaning of Divine grace is truly known only to those who know that God is Love, and that all that He does is done in love in fulfilment of His righteous purposes. His grace is manifested in our creation, preservation, and all the blessings of this life, but above all in our redemption through the life, death, and resurrection of Jesus Christ, in the sending of the holy and life-giving Spirit, in the fellowship of the Church, and in the gift of the Word and Sacraments.

Man's salvation and welfare have their source in God alone, who is moved to His gracious activity towards man not by any merit on man's part, but solely by His free, out-going love.

(ii) *Justification and Sanctification*

God in His free out-going love justifies and sanctifies us through Christ, and His grace thus manifested is appropriated by faith, which itself is the gift of God.

Justification and Sanctification are two inseparable aspects of God's gracious action in dealing with sinful man.

Justification is the act of God, whereby He forgives our sins and brings us into fellowship with Himself, who in Jesus Christ, and by His death upon the Cross, has condemned sin and manifested His love to sinners, reconciling the world to Himself.

Sanctification is the work of God, whereby through the Holy Spirit He continually renews us and the whole Church, delivering us from the power of sin, giving us increase in holiness, and transforming us into the likeness of His Son through participation in His death and in His risen life. This renewal, inspiring us to continual spiritual activity and conflict with evil, remains throughout the gift of God. Whatever our growth in holiness may be, our fellowship with God is always based upon God's forgiving grace.

Faith is more than intellectual acceptance of the revelation in Jesus Christ; it is whole-hearted trust in God and His promises, and committal of ourselves to Jesus Christ as Saviour and Lord.

(iii) *The Sovereignty of God and Man's Response*

In regard to the relation of God's grace and man's freedom, we all agree simply upon the basis of Holy Scripture and Christian experience that the sovereignty of God is supreme. By the sovereignty of God we mean His all-controlling, all-embracing will and purpose revealed in Jesus Christ for each man and for all mankind. And we wish further to insist that this eternal purpose is the expression of God's own loving and holy nature. Thus we men owe our whole salvation to His gracious will. But, on the other hand, it is the will of God that His grace should be actively appropriated by man's own will and that for such decision man should remain responsible.

Many theologians have made attempts on philosophical lines to reconcile the apparent antithesis of God's sovereignty and man's responsibility, but such theories are not part of the Christian Faith.

We are glad to report that in this difficult matter we have been able to speak with a united voice, so that we have found that here there ought to be no ground for maintaining any division between Churches.

(iv) *The Church and Grace*

We agree that the Church is the Body of Christ and the blessed company of all faithful people, whether in heaven or on earth, the communion of saints. It is at once the realization of God's gracious purposes in creation and redemption, and the continuous organ of God's grace in Christ by the Holy Spirit, who is its pervading life, and who is constantly hallowing all its parts.

It is the function of the Church to glorify God in its life and worship, to proclaim the Gospel to every creature, and to build up in the fellowship and life of the Spirit all believing people, of every race and nation. To this end God bestows His grace in the Church on its members through His Word and Sacraments, and in the abiding presence of the Holy Spirit.

(v) *Grace, the Word, and the Sacraments*

We agree that the Word and the Sacraments are gifts of God to the Church through Jesus Christ for the salvation of mankind. In both the grace of God in Christ is shown forth, given and through faith received; and this grace is one and indivisible.

The Word is the appointed means by which God's grace is made known to men, calling them to repentance, assuring them of forgiveness, drawing them to obedience and building them up in the fellowship of faith and love.

The Sacraments are not to be considered merely in themselves, but always as sacraments of the Church, which is the Body of Christ. They have their significance in the continual working of the Holy Spirit, who is the life of the Church. Through the sacraments God develops in all its members a life of perpetual communion lived within its fellowship, and thus enables them to embody His will in the life of the world; but the loving-kindness of God is not to be conceived as limited by His sacraments.

Among or within the Churches represented by us there is a certain difference of emphasis placed upon the Word and the sacraments, but we agree that such a difference need not be a barrier to union.

(vi) *Sola Gratia*

Some Churches set great value on the expression *sola gratia*, while others avoid it. The phrase has been the subject of much controversy, but we can all join in the following statement: Our salvation is the gift of God and the fruit of His grace. It is not based on the merit of man, but has its root and foundation in the forgiveness which God in His grace grants to the sinner whom He receives to sanctify him. We do not, however, hold that the action of the Divine grace overrides human freedom and responsibility; rather, it is only as response is made by faith to Divine grace that true freedom is achieved. Resistance to the appeal of God's out-going love spells, not freedom, but bondage, and perfect freedom is found only in complete conformity with the good and acceptable and perfect will of God.

213. Chapter III: The Church of Christ and the Word of God

(i) *The Word of God*

We concur in affirming that the Word of God is ever living and dynamic and inseparable from God's activity. 'In the beginning was the Word, and the Word was with God, and the Word was God.' God reveals Himself to us by what He does, by that activity by which He has wrought the salvation of men and is working for their restoration to personal fellowship with Himself.

He calls and fashions His chosen people and speaks His Word to His prophets and apostles, interpreting to them the meaning of His action. In the fullness of time the word, the Eternal Son of God, is manifested in Christ our Lord, the Incarnate Word, and His redeeming work, that is, in His words and deeds, in His life and character, in His suffering, death, and resurrection, culminating in the gift of the Spirit and in the life which He gives to the Church which is His body.

This divine revelation is addressed to man in the wholeness of his personality, and is apprehended by faith.

We are at one in asserting the uniqueness and supremacy of the revelation given in Christ, in whose Name alone salvation is offered to the world. But when we turn from this to the question whether we can come to know God through other and partial revelations we find differences which demand further study and discussion. None of us holds that there is a revelation *out*side Christ which can be put on the same level as the revelation *in* Christ. But while some are prepared to recognize a *præparatio evangelica* not only in Hebrew but also in other religions, and believe that God makes Himself known in nature and in history, others hold that the only revelation which the Church can know and to which it should witness is the revelation in Jesus Christ, as contained in the Old and New Testaments.

(ii) *Holy Scripture and Tradition*[1]

A testimony in *words* is by divine ordering provided for the revelation uttered by the *Word*. This testimony is given in Holy Scripture, which thus affords the primary norm for the Church's teaching, worship, and life. We discern a parallel, though an imperfect one, between the inspiration of Holy Scripture and the incarnation of the Word in Our Lord Jesus Christ: in each there is a union, effected by the Holy Spirit, between the divine and the human, and an acceptance, for God's saving purpose, of human limitations. 'We have this treasure in earthen vessels.' We are all convinced that this conception of the revelation cannot be shaken by scientific Bible research. But if it is conscious of its true nature, such research can render the Church important services in bringing about a right interpretation of the Scripture, provided that the freedom needed for carrying out its work is not denied to it.

Further, there is matter for fuller discussion in the problem of the tradition of the Church and its relation to Holy Scripture. By tradition is meant the living stream of the Church's life. Thus the Orthodox East, but not it alone, allows that there may be wide-

[1] *Vide infra*, Document 216.

spread opinions which, as being contrary to Scripture, cannot be considered to have the true authority of tradition, but it does not exclude from tradition some beliefs which do not rest explicitly on Scripture, though they are not in contradiction with it.

We are at one in recognizing that the Church, enlightened by the Holy Spirit, has been instrumental in the formation of the Bible. But some of us hold that this implies that the Church under the guidance of the Spirit is entrusted with the authority to explain, interpret, and complete (*συμπληροῦν*) the teaching of the Bible, and consider the witness of the Church as given in tradition as equally authoritative with the Bible itself. Others, however, believe that the Church, having recognized the Bible as the indispensable record of the revealed Word of God, is bound exclusively by the Bible as the only rule of faith and practice and, while accepting the relative authority of tradition, would consider it authoritative only in so far as it is founded upon the Bible itself.

We all agree that the Christian Church is constituted by the eternal Word of God made man in Christ and is always vitalized by his Holy Spirit. On the other hand the divine task given to the Church is to proclaim and bear witness to this Word throughout the world by its preaching, its worship, and its whole life.

(iii) *The Church: Our Common Faith*

We are at one in confessing belief in the Holy Catholic Church. We acknowledge that through Jesus Christ, particularly through the fact of His resurrection, of the gathering of His disciples round their crucified, risen, and victorious Lord, and of the coming of the Holy Spirit, God's almighty will constituted the Church on earth.

The Church is the people of the new covenant, fulfilling and transcending all that Israel under the old covenant foreshadowed. It is the household of God, the family in which the fatherhood of God and the brotherhood of man is to be realized in the children of His adoption. It is the body of Christ, whose members derive their life and oneness from their one living Head; and thus it is nothing apart from Him, but is in all things dependent upon the power of salvation which God has committed to His Son.

The presence of the ascended Lord in the Church, His Body, is effected by the power of the one Spirit, who conveys to the whole fellowship the gifts of the ascended Lord, dividing to every man severally as He will, guides it into all the truth and fills it unto all the fullness of God.

We all agree that Christ is present in His Church through the Holy Spirit as Prophet, Priest, and King. As Prophet He reveals the divine will and purpose to the Church; as Priest He ever liveth to make intercession for us, and through the eternal sacrifice once offered for us on Calvary, He continually draws His people to the Most High; and as King He rules His Church and is ever establishing and extending His Kingdom.

Christ's presence in the Church has been perpetual from its foundation, and this presence He makes effective and evident in the preaching of the Word, in the faithful administration of the Sacraments, in prayer offered in His name, and through the newness of life whereby He enables the faithful to bear witness to Himself. Even though men often prove faithless, Christ will remain faithful to the promise of His presence, and will so continue till the consummation of all things.

In their apprehension of this Faith different persons lay a different emphasis on one or another aspect. Some lay greater stress on the perpetual and abiding Presence of Christ in His Body and with His people, while others lay greater stress on the fact that Christ is present only where His word is truly preached and received by faith.

A point to be studied is in what degree the Christian depends ultimately for his assurance that he is in vital touch with Christ upon the possession of the ministry and sacraments, upon the Word of God in the Church, upon the inward testimony of the Holy Spirit, or upon all of these.

(iv) *The Church: Agreements and Differences*

The Church, then, is the body of those on whom the call of God rests to witness to the grace and truth of God. This visible body was, before the Lord came, found in Israel and it is found now in the new Israel to which is entrusted the ministry of reconciliation. To this visible body the word 'Ecclesia' is normally applied in the New Testament, and to it the calling of God belongs. It is the sphere of redemption. Apart from the Church man cannot normally attain full knowledge of God nor worship Him in truth.

Different Churches differ in their use of the term 'church'. Some would apply the term not only to the visible redeemed and redemptive community, but also to the invisible company of the fully redeemed; for only when the word is used in this sense would it be right to say *extra ecclesiam nulla salus*. But the invisible Church is no ideal Platonic community distinct from the visible Church on earth. The invisible Church and the visible Church are inseparably connected though their limits are not exactly coterminous. Others regard the use of the term 'church' with reference to this invisible company of true Christians known only to God as misleading and unscriptural. To speak of this invisible body as the true Church conveys the disastrous suggestions that the true Church need not be visible and that the visible Church need not be true. We all, however, recognize that the number of those whom God has brought into newness of life and joy in the Holy Ghost, and who have made personal response to the forgiving love of God, has limits hidden from human vision and known only to God.

Different Churches hold different views as to the basis of Church membership. Some would hold that all who have been baptized and have not by deed or word repudiated their heritage belong to the Church and are to be regarded as members. Others would confine membership to those who have made an open profession of faith in Christ and in whose lives some measure of the spirit of Christ may be discerned.

There are other important differences in this connexion, some of which will be discussed in other chapters of this Report.[1]

(v) *The Church and the Kingdom of God*

The Gospel of Jesus Christ bears witness to the reality both of the Church and of the Kingdom of God.

The Church rejoices in the Kingdom of God as present whenever man obeys the will of God. But the Church always looks with glad expectation to the consummation of the Kingdom in the future, since Christ the King, Who is present and active in the Church through the Holy Spirit, is still to be manifested in glory. The Kingdom of God realizes itself now in a veiled form, until its full manifestation when God shall be all in all.

Agreeing in this faith we are not yet of one mind about (*a*) the relationship of the Church to the Kingdom, and (*b*) the extent to which the Kingdom is made known here and now.

Some stress the kinship between the Church and the Kingdom, others the distinction between them. Some lay emphasis on the actual presence of the Kingdom within the Church and the continuity of the two, holding that the coming of the Kingdom can be seen in the progress of the Church in this world and the work

[1] *Vide infra*, Document 216.

wrought through believers, or even through all men of goodwill the world over. Others lay emphasis on the Kingdom that is to come in glory; and others again think of the Kingdom as the ever-increasing reign of the righteousness and the love of God as manifested in Jesus Christ in every realm of life.

Again, some hold that the progress of the Kingdom can already be seen in this world; others hold that the Church knows the Kingdom by faith only, since the victory of Christ is still hidden from the world and is destined to remain hidden until the end of this age.

In some Churches these differing conceptions are felt to be of great moment, and act as a barrier to full intercourse, while in others they form no such obstacle but are held side by side without interfering with complete communion.

(vi) *The Function of the Church*

The function of the Church is to glorify God in adoration and sacrificial service and to be God's missionary to the world. She is to bear witness to God's redeeming grace in Jesus Christ in her corporate life, to proclaim the good news to every creature, and to make disciples of all nations, bringing Christ's commandments to communities as well as to individuals. In relation to those who belong to her fellowship or who are placed under her influence, the function of the Church is through the ministry of the Word and the Sacraments, and through Christian education, to make them into convinced Christians conscious of the reality of salvation. The needs of individual souls call for pastoral care and for a fellowship in the things of the Spirit through which the members provoke one another to good works, and to walk worthily of their calling, by true friendship, mutual help, and consolation, and the exercise of loving discipline. She is to intercede for all her members, especially for those who suffer for their faith, and for all mankind.

The Church must proclaim the righteousness of God as revealed in Jesus Christ and thus encourage and guide her members to promote justice, peace, and goodwill among all men and through the whole extent of life. The Church is thus called to do battle against the powers of evil and to seek the glory of God in all things, looking to the day when His Kingdom shall come in the fullness of its power.

(vii) *The Gift of Prophecy and the Ministry of the Word*

We are agreed that the presence and inspiration of the Holy Spirit are granted to His chosen instruments to-day, and especially to those called to be ministers of the Word of God. Not only in the corporate life and the teaching of the Church as a whole, but in each of its members according to his ability and calling, the Holy Spirit has come to dwell. Indeed all perfect and abiding revelation given to us in Christ our Lord would certainly have perished from the world had there been no inspired men to record it and to preach it in every age. This revelation does not belong only to the past; it is also an ever-present word by which God speaks directly to the listening soul.

Moreover all manifestations of the Spirit are manifestations of God's divine activity. It is here that prophecy finds its place in the Church's corporate life. In Christ all the truth of God's redemptive purpose for men is fully and sufficiently contained, but every age has its own problems and its own difficulties, and it is the work of the Spirit in every age to apply the one truth revealed in Christ to the circumstances of the time. Moreover, as past experience shows, these new applications bring to the Church a new understanding of the truth on which they rest. The Spirit may speak by whomsoever He wills. The call to bear witness to the Gospel and to declare God's will does not come to the ordained ministry alone; the Church greatly needs, and should both expect and welcome, the exercise of gifts of prophecy and teaching by laity, both men and women. When prophetic gifts appear it is for the Church not to quench the spirit or despise prophesyings but to test these prophesyings by their accordance with the abiding truth entrusted to it, and to hold fast that which is good.

(viii) '*Una Sancta*' *and our Divisions*

Everything which the New Testament teaches concerning the Church presupposes its essential unity. But we, as we confess our faith in the one Church, are conscious of a profound cleavage between that faith and the conditions of the present time.

We acknowledge that all who accept Jesus Christ as Son of God and their Lord and Saviour, and realize their dependence upon God's mercy revealed in Him, have in that fact a supernatural bond of oneness which subsists in spite of divergences in defining the divine mystery of the Lord. We rejoice that this sense of kinship is now drawing Christians nearer to each other, and that in many partial ways a foretaste of full fellowship between severed communions is even now being sought and found.

But we believe that the divisions of Christendom in every land are such as to hamper the manifestation of the unity of Christ's body. We deplore this with all our hearts; and we desire the Conference to summon members of the Churches to such penitence that not only their leaders, but the ordinary men and women who hear their message, may learn that the cause of Christian unity is implicit in God's word, and should be treated by the Christian conscience as an urgent call from God.

214. Chapter IV: The Communion of Saints

'Wherefore seeing we also are compassed about with so great a cloud of witnesses, let us lay aside every weight, and the sin which doth so easily beset us, and let us run with patience the race that is set before us, looking unto Jesus the author and finisher of our faith.'—Heb. xii. 1–2.

We use the term 'communion of saints' as meaning that all who are 'in Christ' are knit together in one fellowship through the Holy Spirit. This conception, which is found repeatedly in the Scriptures, occurs as a phrase of the Apostles' Creed, and gives expression to a precious truth for all Christians. With some, the phrase is regarded as synonymous with the Holy Catholic Church. For others, it expresses a quality of the Church which is realized only in so far as its members mutually share all the blessings which God bestows. For others, it is the description of a quality of life in those who are in grace. The communion of saints is not always regarded as coextensive with the Church. For the Orthodox and certain other Churches and individual believers it means fellowship not only with living and departed Christians but also with the holy angels, and, in a very special sense, with the Blessed Virgin Mary.[1]

In this connexion the way in which we should understand the words 'all generations shall call me blessed' was considered. No agreement was reached, and the subject requires further study.

The words 'the communion of saints' (κοινωνία τῶν ἁγίων) express certain well-defined phases of the Christian Gospel and of the doctrine of the Church.

In the New Testament the word 'saints' is applied to all the baptized. The term is further applied to the patriarchs, prophets, or martyrs of the Old Covenant and to those who, believing in

[1] These last hold that the mother of our Lord, designated as *Theotokos* (God-bearer), the ever-Virgin, should be venerated as the highest of all saints and angels, and of all creation. In addition to the general recognition of the Communion of Saints, they venerate particular saints who are honoured by the Church, and ask their intercession and that of angels before God.

Christ, laid down their lives for Him before they could receive baptism. In every case, the saints are those who are devoted to God, who yield themselves as instruments to His sovereign will. They are saints, not by virtue of their own merits, but through the forgiving grace and love of God.

There are Churches which hold that the communion is not as between individuals as such, but as between those who are being sanctified by God in His Church. Their unity is not merely the sum total of individuals, but it is a spiritual solidarity which has reality only in so far as they are in Christ, and thereby in His Church.

There are also those who interpret the word *ἁγίων* as neuter as well as masculine. For them the phrase means sharing in holy things, i.e. the means of grace. They emphasize right relations to holy things as the principal mark of the holiness of the faithful.

There are others who regard the Word of God and the Holy Spirit as the sole source of the communion of saints, and at the same time would emphasize righteousness and holiness of life. They would also stress the sacredness and value of the individual's personality. While doing so, they would guard against the evils resulting from an over-emphasized individualism by insisting on the corporate nature of the fellowship in Christ. Since the term 'saints' is almost always in the plural in the Scriptures, so it is believed that there is no true sainthood apart from the saintly community.

We are agreed that the communion of saints most certainly involves the mutual sharing of both spiritual and temporal blessings on the part of all living Christians. We believe that this mutual sharing should transcend all racial, political, social, and denominational barriers, in the spirit of Gethsemane and the Cross. Such, for example, is the fellowship of those associated in any truly Christian oecumenical movement. Therein we have experienced a very real, though not complete, communion of saints. Therein we humbly believe we experience the presence and power of the Holy Spirit.

Any conception of the communion of saints which is confined to the Church on earth alone is defective. Many further see in the communion of saints an affirmation of the unbroken communion between the living and departed in Christ. They believe themselves to be in communion with the departed and express this in their worship. They rejoice to think that there is a growing consciousness among Christians of nearness to the redeemed in the unseen world, refusing to believe that death severs the communion of those on earth with those departed.

For some, it is sufficient to leave their departed ones with God, being linked with them through Christ. Others regard it as a Christian privilege and duty to pray for the departed. Still others, conscious of the living presence, guardianship, and help of the saints, ask their prayers before God.

We all agree that we ought to remember with thankfulness those who as followers of Christ witnessed a good confession in their day and generation, thereby winning victories for Christ and His Kingdom.

We wish to make it clear that 'the communion which the saints have with Christ does not make them in any wise partakers of the substance of His Godhead, or to be equal with Christ in any respect'. In no circumstances should the cherishing of this doctrine veil or shadow the sufficient and only mediatorship of Jesus Christ as our Lord and Redeemer. Neither must this honouring of the saints descend to superstition or abuse.

A right understanding of the doctrine of the communion of saints will help us to realize more vividly both that we are in this life members one of another, and that

> 'We are come unto mount Sion, and unto the city of the living God, the heavenly Jerusalem, and to an innumerable company of angels, to the general assembly and church of the firstborn, which are written in heaven, and to God the Judge of all, and to the spirits of just men made perfect, and to Jesus the mediator of the new covenant.'—Heb. xii. 22–4.

215. Chapter V: The Church of Christ: Ministry and Sacraments

(i) *The Authority for the Sacraments*

1. We are agreed that in all sacramental doctrine and practice the supreme authority is our Lord Jesus Christ Himself.

2. All the Churches have based their sacramental doctrine and order upon their belief that,[1] according to the evidence of the New

[1] Many preferred the original wording of this clause which ran '. . . have based their sacramental doctrine and order upon the evidence of the New Testament that . . .'.

Testament, the sacraments which they accept were instituted by Christ Himself. We are agreed that Baptism and the Lord's Supper occupied from the beginning a central position in the Church's common life, and take their origin from what was said and done by Jesus during His life on earth. Sacramental teaching and practice, therefore, are rightly founded upon the record of the New Testament.

3. The sacraments are Christ's gifts to His Church, which is not a static society but a living and growing organism and communion, guided by the Holy Spirit into all truth.[1]

4. The Holy Spirit enables the Church, walking by faith in its risen Lord, to interpret Holy Scripture as expressing the living Word of God to every age, and to exercise a stewardship of its tradition concerning the sacraments.

5. All Church tradition regarding the sacraments ought to be controlled and tested by Scripture.[2]

(ii) *The Nature of the Sacraments*

1. The sacraments are given by Christ to the Church as outward and visible signs of His invisible grace. They are not bare symbols, but pledges and seals of grace, and means whereby it is received.

2. Grace is bestowed in the sacraments within the fellowship of the Church by the personal action of Christ upon the believer. Faith[3] is therefore a necessary condition for the effectual reception of grace.

[1] Scholars differ in their views of the passages of Scripture relating to the institution of the sacraments by our Lord. Many of the Conference believe that no one who recognizes the ministry and the sacraments as Christ's gifts to His Church should be excluded from a united Church on the ground that he does not stand for one particular view of the historical origin of the holy ordinances and the ecclesiastical offices.

[2] The Orthodox and some others would wish to add: 'All the Sacraments can be founded upon Holy Scripture as completed, explained, interpreted, and understood in the Holy Tradition by the guidance of the Holy Spirit residing in the Church.'

Anglican members observe: 'The Church of England, while recognizing the authority of the Church to decree rites and ceremonies, forbids it to ordain anything contrary to the Scriptures, but limits the necessity of Scripture sanction to articles of faith in things necessary to salvation.'

[3] Baptist delegates desire this clause to run: 'Faith on the part of the recipient is therefore . . . .'

3. God's gracious action is not limited by His sacraments.[1]

4. It is our Lord Jesus Christ who through the Holy Spirit accomplishes every sacrament, and the action of the minister of the Church is only instrumental.

5. The Sacraments are celebrated by the minister, not in virtue of any personal right of his own, but as minister of the Church.

6. Regarding the obligation of the sacraments and the questions whether and in what way they are to be deemed necessary to salvation there is divergence of doctrine among us. We think that some further mutual understanding and agreement on those points is required as a condition of full union.

(iii) *The Number of the Sacraments*

The Orthodox Church, the (Assyrian) Church of the East, the (Coptic) Egyptian-Orthodox Church, the Syrian Orthodox and Armenian Churches, and the Old Catholic Churches, and many individual believers, as well as the Roman Catholic Church, hold that there are seven sacraments, but the Protestant Churches accept only two, Baptism and the Eucharist. The Anglican Church has never strictly defined the number of the sacraments, but gives a pre-eminent position to Baptism and the Lord's Supper as alone 'generally necessary to salvation.'

The Society of Friends and the Salvation Army observe no sacraments in the usual sense of that term.[2]

The number of the sacraments largely depends upon the definitions of the term 'sacraments' as given by various Churches. In most of the Protestant Churches there are such solemn religious acts as correspond more or less closely with some or all of the five other sacraments which are taught by the Roman, Orthodox, Old Catholic, and other Churches. And even though the name 'sacrament' be refused they are nevertheless *instituta Dei utilia,* as the second Helvetic Confession puts it.

Most of us agree that the question of the number of the sacraments should not be regarded as an insurmountable dividing line when we strive to attain to a united Church.

[1] Orthodox delegates and some others desire to exclude from the reference of this proposition cases in which failure to receive the sacraments is due to contempt or culpable negligence, since sacraments are divinely instituted means of grace generally necessary for salvation.

[2] *Vide infra,* Document 216.

The divergence between the practice of the Society of Friends and the Salvation Army on the one hand, and that of other Churches on the other, admittedly presents serious difficulties, but we trust that even here the Holy Spirit will show us His will.

(iv) *Validity*

1. We agree that the sacraments practised by any Christian Church which believes itself to be observing what Christ appointed for His Church are means of grace to those who partake of them with faith.

2. Confusion has sometimes been introduced by the use of the term 'valid' in the two following senses:

(*a*) It is sometimes used synonymously with 'efficacious', so that the term 'invalid' would imply that a sacrament has no spiritual value and is not a means of grace.

(*b*) It is sometimes used to imply that the sacrament has been correctly performed.[1]

In so far as Christians find themselves obliged by loyalty to Christ and to His Church to judge that the sacraments practised by other Christians are invalid, or doubtfully valid, they should, in the cause of Christian truth and charity, do all in their power to see that the precise meaning of their judgement, and the grounds on which they are obliged to make it, are clearly understood.

Many of us are of opinion, and desire to record our belief, that, although it is the duty of a Church to secure that sacraments should be performed regularly and canonically, yet no judgement should be pronounced by any Church denying the 'validity' of the sacraments performed by any Christian Church which believes itself to be observing what Christ appointed for His Church.

A special difficulty in regard to union arises from a great difference in doctrine which must not be under-estimated. Those Churches which adhere to the doctrine of the Church from the age of the Great Councils to the Reformation regard it as one of the conditions for the validity of any sacrament except baptism (and in some cases, marriage) that it should be performed by a validly ordained or consecrated minister. Thus to them the validity of Holy Order is one of the indispensable conditions of the validity of other sacra-

[1] The Conference is indebted to Canon Quick for submitting a note on this subject, which will be printed in the full record of the proceedings of the Conference.

ments. On the other hand some other Christians do not hold ordination to be a sacrament of Christ's institution, yet hold that an ordained minister is the proper minister of the Eucharist. Other Christians again hold that ordination is a sacrament, but do not hold it to be an essential condition of the validity of other sacraments, that they should be ministered by a validly ordained presbyter or bishop.

3. We believe that every sacrament should be so ordered that all may recognize in it an act performed on behalf of the universal Church.

4. To this end there is need of an ordained ministry recognized by all to act on behalf of the universal Church in the administration of the sacraments.

Note. The Orthodox delegates submit the following statement:

Validity. As regards the validity of Sacraments the Orthodox delegates would like to confine themselves only to the following statement: According to the Orthodox doctrine valid Sacraments are only those which are (1) administered by a canonically ordained and instituted minister and (2) rightly performed according to the sacramental order of the Church.

They regard it therefore as unnecessary to accept any other document on this matter presented by the Conference.

(v) *Baptism*

Baptism is a gift of God's redeeming love to the Church; and, administered with water in the name of the Father, the Son, and the Holy Spirit, is a sign and seal of Christian discipleship in obedience to our Lord's command.[1] It is generally agreed that the united Church will observe the rule that all members of the visible Church are admitted by Baptism.

[1] Baptist delegates desire to add as follows: As regards the above statement which has been passed by their brethren who practise infant baptism, the Baptists could accept it as applying to the baptism of believers, i.e. of those who are capable of making a personal confession of faith. In practising the baptism of believers only they hold that they are maintaining the practice of baptism as it is found in the New Testament in the Apostolic Church, and also the principle which is laid down on page 27 of the Report of Commission III, to this effect, viz.: 'The necessary condition of receiving the grace of a sacrament is the faith of the recipient.' They believe that children belong to God and that no rite is needed to secure His grace for them. This statement of the Baptists was accepted also by a representative of the Disciples of Christ on behalf of that body.

In the course of discussion it appeared that there were further elements of faith and practice in relation to Baptism about which disagreement existed. Since the time available precluded the extended discussion of such points as baptismal regeneration, the admission of unbaptized persons to Holy Communion,[1] and the relation of Confirmation to Baptism, we are unable to express an opinion how far they would constitute obstacles to proposals for a united Church.

(vi) *The Eucharist*

1. We all believe that Christ is truly present in the Eucharist, though as to how that presence is manifested and realized we may differ. Every precise definition of the presence is bound to be a limiting thing, and the attempt to formulate such definitions and to impose them on the Church has itself been the cause of disunity in the past. The important thing is that we should celebrate the Eucharist with the unfailing use of bread and wine, and of prayer, and of the words of institution, and with agreement as to its essential and spiritual meaning.

If sacrifice is understood as it was by our Lord and His followers and in the early Church, it includes, not His death only, but the obedience of His earthly ministry, and His risen and ascended life, in which He still does His Father's will and ever liveth to make intercession for us. Such a sacrifice can never be repeated, but is proclaimed and set forth in the eucharistic action of the whole Church when we come to God in Christ at the Eucharist or Lord's Supper. For us, the secret of joining in that sacrifice is both the worship and the service of God; corporate because we are joined to Christ, and in Him to each other (1 Cor. x. 16–17); individual, because each one of us makes the corporate act of self-oblation his own; and not ceremonial only, but also profoundly ethical, because the keynote of all sacrifice and offering is: 'Lo! I come to do Thy will, O God.' We believe also that the Eucharist is a supreme moment of prayer, because the Lord is the celebrant or minister for us at every celebration, and it is in His prayers for God's gifts and for us all that we join. According to the New Testament accounts of the institution, His prayer is itself a giving of thanks; so that the Lord's Supper is both a *verbum visibile* of the divine grace, and the supreme thanksgiving (*eucharistia*) of the people of

[1] For most Churches this is not an open question, since Baptism is regarded as the only and necessary means of admission to the Church.

God. We are throughout in the realm of Spirit. It is through the Holy Spirit that the blessing and the gift are given. The presence, which we do not try to define, is a spiritual presence. We begin from the historical fact of the Incarnation in the power of the Holy Spirit, and we are already moving forward to the complete spiritual reality of the coming of the Lord and the life of the Heavenly City.[1]

(vii) *Ministry*

A

The consideration of this subject took its start from the Report prepared by Commission III on the Ministry and Sacraments.

The following statements derived in substance from that Report are accepted by the Conference as providing a broad foundation for a common understanding of the nature and functions of the ministry.

I. The ministry was instituted by Jesus Christ, the Head of the Church, 'for the perfecting of the Saints . . . the upbuilding of the body of Christ', and is a gift of God to the Church in the service of the Word and sacraments.

II. This ministry does not exclude but presupposes the 'royal priesthood', to which all Christians are called as the redeemed of Jesus Christ.

III. Ordination to the ministry, according to New Testament teaching and the historic practice of the Church, is by prayer and the laying on of hands.

IV. It is essential to a united Church that it should have a ministry universally recognized.

It must be acknowledged, however, that even in connexion with these statements, different interpretations are to be reckoned with.

[1] The Conference is indebted to the Bishop of Lincoln for submitting a note on this subject, which will be printed in the full record of the proceedings of the Conference.

Orthodox delegates desire to add the following statement:

Eucharist: (*a*) The Orthodox Church believes and teaches that in the Sacrament of the Holy Eucharist, which is the extension of the only and once offered sacrifice of our Lord, the offered gifts by virtue of the consecration are changed (*metaballontai*) into the very Body and the very Blood of our Lord Jesus Christ, and given to the faithful for the remission of sins and life everlasting.

(*b*) The Holy Eucharist can be celebrated only by a validly ordained minister.

Certain other Churches and delegates would associate themselves with the Orthodox in making a somewhat similar statement.

For example, while all would agree that the ministry owes its origin to Jesus Christ and is God's gift to the Church, there are differences of judgement regarding the sense in which we may say that the ministry was 'instituted' by our Lord.

Again, those who agree in accepting the laying on of hands as the form of ordination differ on the meaning to be attached to the rite, or on the question by whom it should be administered.

Further fundamental differences of interpretation arise in connexion with the doctrine of Apostolic Succession. In Episcopal Churches it has been thought of both as the succession of bishops in the principal sees of Christendom, handing down and preserving the Apostles' doctrine, and as a succession by laying on of hands. From early times this double succession has been associated with the stewardship of the sacraments, and is regarded by certain Churches as constituting the true and only guarantee of sacramental grace and right doctrine. This view is represented by the statement formulated by the delegates of the Orthodox Church at Lausanne:

> 'The Orthodox Church, regarding the ministry as instituted in the Church by Christ Himself, and as the body which by a special charisma is the organ through which the Church spreads its means of grace such as the sacraments, and believing that the ministry in its threefold form of bishops, presbyters and deacons can only be based on the unbroken Apostolic Succession, regrets that it is unable to come, in regard to the ministry, into some measure of agreement with many of the Churches represented at this Conference; but prays God that He, through His Holy Spirit, will guide to union even in regard to this difficult point of disagreement.'

Substantially the same view finds another expression in the following statement offered on behalf of the Old Catholic Church:

> 'The Old Catholics maintain that Episcopacy is of apostolic origin, and that it belongs to the essence of the Church. The Church is the bearer of the ministry. The ministers act only by the commission of the Church. The ministry is received, administered, and handed on in the same sense and in the same way as the Apostles handed it down to the Church. The Apostolic Succession means the inseparability of Church and ministry and the continuity of both.'

Certain other Churches of the East and some Anglicans would wish to be associated with one or other of the above statements.

Other Anglicans would interpret the Succession in a more general way to mean the transmission from generation to generation of the authority of ministerial oversight over both clergy and laity in the Church, and they regard it as both a symbol and a bond of unity.

In communions of the Presbyterian and Reformed tradition the view is held that the true Apostolic Succession is manifested in a succession of ordination by presbyteries duly constituted and exercising episcopal functions, and in the succession of presbyters in charge of parishes, with special emphasis on the true preaching of the Word and the right administration of the Sacraments. Thus the following statement was presented by Presbyterian delegates:

> 'Presbyterian delegates desire to have it noted that the conception of the ministry held by their Churches is founded on the identity of "bishops" and "presbyters" in the New Testament; that ordination is not by individual presbyters, nor by groups of presbyters, but only by "presbyters orderly associated" in courts exercising episcopal functions; that a presbyterian succession in orders has been maintained unbroken; and that the functions of the diaconate in the New Testament have been performed not only by those named deacons, but also in some measure by the lay eldership, which in addition to a responsible share in the government and discipline of the Church in all its courts, assists in the dispensing of charity, the visitation of the people, and the distribution of the elements at Holy Communion.'

Other communions, while unaccustomed to use the term 'Apostolic Succession,' would accept it as meaning essentially, or even exclusively, the maintenance of the Apostles' witness through the true preaching of the Gospel, the right administration of the Sacraments, and the perpetuation of the Christian life in the Christian community.

In every case Churches treasure the Apostolic Succession in which they believe.

B

In its brief consideration of the form which the ministry might take in the united Church of the future, the Conference started from the following formula in the Report of the Lausanne Conference:

'In view of (1) the place which the Episcopate, the Councils of Presbyters, and the Congregation of the faithful, respectively had in the constitution of the early Church, and (2) the fact that episcopal, presbyteral and congregational systems of government are each to-day, and have been for centuries, accepted by great communions in Christendom, and (3) the fact that episcopal, presbyteral and congregational systems are each believed by many to be essential to the good order of the Church, we therefore recognize that these several elements must all, under conditions which require further study, have an appropriate place in the order of life of a reunited Church, and that each separate communion, recalling the abundant blessing of God vouchsafed to its ministry in the past, should gladly bring to the common life of the united Church its own spiritual treasures.'

The acceptance of the 'historic Episcopate' carries with it the acceptance of the threefold ministry of bishops, presbyters, and deacons. Many would hold that such acceptance does not require any one dogmatic determination of the doctrine concerning the ministry, while for some this would be requisite. But all who value the 'historic Episcopate' hold that it should not be interpreted apart from its historical functions.

In a united Church the intimate association of the presbyters in council with the bishop, and of the laity with both, in the government of the Church, should be conserved or restored. Thus the Episcopate would be both constitutional and representative of the whole Church.

If the ministry of the united Church should sufficiently include characteristic elements from the episcopal, presbyteral, and congregational systems, the present adherents of those systems would have recognized each other's places in the Church of God, all would be able to find a spiritual home in the united Church, and the doctrine of the Apostolic Succession would, upon a common basis of faith, attain to the fullness which belongs to it by referring at once to the Word, to the ministry and the sacraments, and to the life of the Christian community.

It should, however, be recognized that there are members of the Conference who are not persuaded that it is God's will that the one spiritual life of the undivided Church should be expressed through any one form of government, but would find place side by side for Churches of differing form of government, and within or beside the more formally organized body would include freer societies like the Friends and the Salvation Army.

The foregoing suggestions are put forward in the knowledge that they contain features which at the present stage may be unacceptable to some Churches on both wings of the Movement, but we are confident that, where the will to unite exists, the Holy Spirit will enable the Churches in coming years to improve and develop these first tentative suggestions.

We are alike called of God to pray and to labour by every means for the promotion of this common aim, recognizing that the future or ultimate form to be assumed by the united Church must depend not only on the experience of the past, but above all, upon the continued direction of the Holy Spirit.

216. *Chapter VI: The Church's Unity in Life and Worship*

(i) *Our Premise and Our Goal*

WE take as the premise of our findings and our recommendations the already existing and growing spiritual unity, experienced by Christians as love of one another, understanding of one another, and respect for one another. We believe that no visible unity, acceptable to God and to the people of God, can be achieved save on the foundation of this spiritual unity. We believe that our common experience of spiritual unity derives from the fundamental faith that the Church is the body of Christ, and is, therefore, in principle and ideal, one. In trying to envisage the goal of our endeavours, we are not seeking to create something new; rather we are attempting to discover under the guidance of the Holy Spirit the full nature of the Church created by God in Christ.

Our goal is to realize the ideal of the Church as one living body, worshipping and serving God in Christ, as the fulfilment of our Lord's prayers and of our prayers.

(ii) *The Several Conceptions of Church Unity*

(*a*) *Co-operative Action*

The unity which we seek may be conceived as a confederation or alliance of Churches for *co-operative action.*

In all areas where common purposes and tasks exist, such action is already widely possible without violation of conscience. Church 'federations' are the most common expressions of such unity, and one of the most hopeful paths to understanding and brotherly relations. We believe federation, so construed, is a promising approach to more complete forms of unity. We do not share the fears, often expressed, that 'federation' in this sense will obscure the goal of a fuller unity or postpone its attainment. The experience of many Churches in many lands forbids such fears, since they run counter to the facts.

We recognize that federations for co-operative action should not be construed as examples of 'federal union'. Certain of our members wish to be recorded as believing that 'federal union' is not merely the most we can achieve, but also the most that we should desire.

We are agreed that co-operative action between Churches unable to achieve intercommunion or to look towards corporate union, and compelled by fidelity to conscience to remain separate bodies with separate loyalties, is not our final goal, since co-operative action in itself fails to manifest to the world the true character of the Church as one community of faith and worship, as well as of service.

(*b*) *Intercommunion*

A second aspect of Church unity is commonly indicated by the term '*intercommunion*'. This is the fullest expression of a mutual recognition between two or more Churches. Such recognition is also manifested in the exchange of membership and ministrations.

We regard sacramental intercommunion as a necessary part of any satisfactory Church unity. Such intercommunion, as between two or more Churches, implies that all concerned are true Churches, or true branches of the one Church.

We think that it should be pointed out that the word 'intercommunion' has at present several different connotations. In the fullest sense it means a relation between two or more Churches in which the communion of each is open to all members of the other at all times. This is to be distinguished from relations in which the communion of one Church is 'open' to members of other Churches without complete reciprocal recognition, and still more from the occasional welcoming of members of other Churches by a Church whose normal rule would exclude them. We believe that 'regularity' and 'mutuality' belong to the full meaning of intercommunion. When this term 'intercommunion' is used in discussion of Church unity, its meaning should be clearly defined.

We must note also the occasions on which at a gathering of Christian people united in a common enterprise, a Church has invited all who have full status in their own Churches to receive the Holy Communion according to the rite of the inviting Church. This has occurred both at Oxford and at Edinburgh during the Conferences held this year. It is to be distinguished both from 'intercommunion' and 'open communion' as usually understood, and from such 'joint celebration' as took place at Jerusalem in 1928.

(*c*) *Corporate Union*

The third form in which the final goal of our movement may be expressed presents, from the standpoint of definition, the greatest difficulties. It is commonly indicated by such terms as 'corporate union' or 'organic unity'.

These terms are forbidding to many, as suggesting the ideal of a compact governmental union involving rigid uniformity. We do not so understand them, and none of us desires such uniformity. On the contrary, what we desire is the unity of a living organism, with the diversity characteristic of the members of a healthy body.

The idea of 'corporate union' must remain for the vast majority of Christians their ideal. In a Church so united the ultimate loyalty of every member would be given to the whole body and not to any part of it. Its members would move freely from one part to another and find every privilege of membership open to them. The sacraments would be the sacraments of the whole body. The ministry would be accepted by all as a ministry of the whole body.

Our task is to find in God, to receive from God as His gift, a unity which can take up and preserve in one beloved community all the varied spiritual gifts which He has given us in our separations. Such a living community, like all that lives, cannot be a construction; life can come only from life; the visible unity of the Body of Christ can issue only from the Living God through the work of the life-giving Spirit.

While we do not conceive of the 'corporate union', which we seek from God, as a rigid governmental unity, we find it difficult to imagine that unity, as it would exist between Churches within the same territory, without some measure of organizational union. At the same time, we can hardly imagine a corporate union which should provide for the relative autonomy of the several constituent parts in entire neglect of the 'federal' principle.

In particular, and with immediate reference to the existing world situation, we do not believe that a Church, 'corporately' united, could be an effective international community without some permanent organ of conference and counsel, whatever might be the authority and powers of that organ.

(iii) *The Forms of Likeness Basic for Church Unity*

1. *Likeness in Faith or Confession as a Basis for Unity*

(*a*)[1] Likeness in faith or confession is not necessary for co-operative action, but we find that essential unity in faith or confession is a necessary basis for (*b*) full intercommunion and for (*c*) corporate union.

Such essential unity in faith would be sufficiently expressed for many of the Churches represented in this Conference by such a statement as the following:

> We accept as the supreme standard of the faith the revelation of God contained in the Holy Scriptures of the Old and New Testaments and summed up in Jesus Christ.
>
> We acknowledge the Apostles' Creed and the Creed commonly called the Nicene, as witnessing to and safeguarding that faith, which is continuously verified in the spiritual experience of the Church and its members—remembering that these documents are sacred symbols and witnesses of the Christian faith rather than legalistic standards.
>
> We further affirm that the guidance of God's Holy Spirit did not cease with the closing of the canon of the Scripture, or with the formulation of the creeds cited, but that there has been in the Church through the centuries, and still is, a divinely sustained consciousness of the presence of the living Christ. (*Note.* Known in the Orthodox Church as the Holy Tradition.)
>
> Finally, we are persuaded, in the classical words of one of the non-confessional communions, that 'God has yet more light to break forth from His Holy Word' for a humble and waiting Church. We Christians of this present age should therefore seek the continued guidance of the Spirit of the Living God, as we confront our troubled time.

Some of the Churches represented in the Conference hold that Scripture is not only the supreme but the sole standard and source of Christian faith; they reject any suggestion of the equivalence of

[1] These letters in subsection (iii) refer to the three headings in subsection (ii) above.

Scripture and tradition and any implication that the ancient creeds contain a sufficient interpretation of the Scriptural faith. Some of these Churches regard certain later confessions as possessing an importance and authority at least equal to that of the ancient creeds.[1]

(*Note.* We call attention here to the following statement in Section IV of the Lausanne Report:

> 'It is understood that the use of these Creeds will be determined by the competent authority in each Church, and that the several Churches will continue to make use of such special Confessions as they possess.' (*Faith and Order*, edited by H. N. Bate, p. 467.)

The Orthodox and certain other Churches can accept the Nicene Creed only in its uninterpolated form without the *filioque* clause, and those Churches and others hold that the 'Holy Tradition' must be acknowledged as a standard and source of the faith complementary to, though wholly consonant with, the revelation in Scripture.

2. *Likeness in Non-sacramental Worship*

(*a*) Likeness in non-sacramental worship is not necessary for co-operative action.

(*c*) In the non-sacramental worship of God the Father, Son, and Holy Spirit, we are agreed that there is little remaining occasion for maintaining the existing divisions between our Churches, and much common ground already exists for further unity.

We are all united, in such worship, in the use of the Holy Scriptures. We are further united in common prayer, which may be expressed in the spoken word, through silence, or by employment of the sacred treasures of Christian literature, art, and music. In this worship we all stand before God in adoration of His majesty, bringing to Him our own needs and the needs of our fellows. We wait for His grace in the forgiveness of our sins and for the restoration of our spirits through renewed communion with Him, and we dedicate ourselves to His service and the service of all mankind.

3. *Likeness in Sacramental Faith and Practice*

(*a*) Co-operative activities do not require likeness in doctrine and administration of the sacraments.

(*b*) For Intercommunion.

(i) Some of us hold that Churches which within their own

[1] *Vide supra*, Document 213.

order practise the two Gospel sacraments can freely allow intercommunion between their respective members.

(ii) Others hold that no such intercommunion can take place until their Churches have agreed as to the validity of each other's ministrations of these, to them, essential sacraments.

(*c*) For full corporate union it will be necessary to reconcile the differences between Churches which insist, some upon two sacraments, some upon seven, and some upon no formal sacraments whatsoever.

The sacrament of the Lord's Supper (or Eucharist) is the Church's most sacred act of worship. Unity in sacramental worship requires essential unity in sacramental faith and practice.

The Society of Friends, in the silence of its meetings, seeks without formal sacraments the Real Presence of Him who suffered death that mankind might have life.[1]

In this connexion we find much cause for encouragement in (i) the liturgical movement on the Continent, and among the non-liturgical Churches in many other lands, and (ii) the increasing opportunities allowed for silence, and for spontaneity, among those who use traditional liturgies. In this matter the distinction between liturgical and non-liturgical forms of worship is a diminishing occasion for division.

4. *Likeness of Orders as a Basis for Unity*

(*a*) Lack of likeness of orders is no obstacle to co-operative action.

For (*b*) full intercommunion and (*c*) corporate union it will be necessary to reconcile the differences between Churches which hold (i) that a ministry in the threefold form of bishops, priests, and deacons was instituted in the Church by Christ; (ii) that the historic episcopate is essential for corporate union; (iii) that a ministry was instituted by Christ in which bishops as distinct from presbyters are not essential; (iv) that no specially ordained ministry whatsoever is required by the conception of the Church.

5. *Likeness in Polity as a Basis for Unity*

(*a*) Likeness in polity is not necessary for co-operative action.

(*c*) With reference to corporate union most of us endorse the following statement from Section V of the Lausanne Report:[2]

[1] *Vide supra*, Document 215.

[2] This assumption as regards episcopacy is not accepted by large sections of Free Church opinion.

'In view of (1) the place which the episcopate, the council of presbyters, and the congregation of the faithful, respectively had in the constitution of the early Church, and (2) the fact that episcopal, presbyteral, and congregational systems of government are each to-day, and have been for centuries, accepted by great communions in Christendom, and (3) the fact that episcopal, presbyteral, and congregational systems are each believed by many to be essential to the good order of the Church, we therefore recognize that these several elements must all, under conditions which require further study, have an appropriate place in the order of life of a reunited Church.' (*Faith and Order*, p. 469.)

It will be noted that the above statements assume a substantial likeness, already existing or conceded in theory, with respect to faith, confession, worship, polity.

It will be further noted that there is a marked unlikeness, whether as a matter of existing practice or as a matter of rival doctrines, when we are considering sacraments and orders.

(iv) *Obstacles to Church Unity*

1. *Obstacles which are restricted to 'Faith' and 'Order'*

We find that the obstacles most difficult to overcome consist of elements of 'faith' and 'order' combined, as when some form of Church government or worship is considered a part of the faith.

But we are led to the conclusion that behind all particular statements of the problem of corporate union lie deeply divergent conceptions of the Church. For the want of any more accurate terms this divergence might be described as the contrast between 'authoritarian' and 'personal' types of Church.

We have, on the one hand, an insistence upon a divine givenness in the Scriptures, in orders, in creeds, in worship.

We have, on the other hand, an equally strong insistence upon the individual experience of Divine grace, as the ruling principle of the 'gathered' Church, in which freedom is both enjoyed as a religious right and enjoined as a religious duty.

We are aware that between these extremes many variations exist, expressed as well in doctrine as in organization, worship, and types of piety. These variations are combinations of the two contrasted types of Church to which we have referred.

We do not minimize the difficulties which these contrasted types of Church present to our Movement, nor are we willing to construe them as being due mainly to misunderstandings or to sin.

It is our hope and prayer that through the guidance of the Holy Spirit they may, in God's good time, be overcome.

Meanwhile it is our duty to attempt by study to enter still more sympathetically into the experience of others, and to 'keep the unity of the Spirit in the bond of peace'.

We suggest that the full range of the contrast between the two types of Church to which we have been referring, is in no wise covered by the antithesis of episcopal and non-episcopal orders.

This contrast may be expressed in many other terms. The problem of the authority of Scripture and the modes of its interpretation is the most classical instance.[1]

2. *Obstacles not restricted to 'Faith' and 'Order'*

(*a*) Obstacles which are, in part, theological or ecclesiastical, and, in equal part, sociological or political.

Such obstacles are met in the case of a national Church which hallows the common life of a given people, but is at the same time exposed to the perils of an exclusive provincialism or of domination by a secular state.

Frequently renewed testimony, given at this Conference, makes it plain that the Churches of the mission field are grievously hindered in their efforts to solve problems of this order so long as they remain unsolved in the 'home' lands.

(*b*) Obstacles which are due mainly to historical factors.

We have, in Western Christendom, many separations which are the result of the divided secular history of Europe.

We have, in the Near and Middle East, certain conspicuous examples of religiously isolated communities, whose isolation is primarily due to their loyalty to an ancient heritage which goes back to earliest Christian times and often to lands far off from those in which they now exist.

(*c*) Obstacles which are of 'cultural' origin.

In Churches which already enjoy substantial agreement upon matters of faith and order, and which may be said to stand upon common ground as representatives of one or other of the two contrasted types of Church, the prospect of corporate union is by no means clear or assured.

[1] *Vide supra*, Document 212.

These Churches are not conscious of any obstacles to such union because of mutually exclusive doctrines. They are, however, kept apart by barriers of nationality, race, class, general culture, and more particularly, by slothful self-content and self-sufficiency.

(v) *What can we do to move towards the Unity we should seek ?*

The unity we seek is not simple but complex. It has two aspects: (*a*) the inner spiritual unity known in its completeness to God alone; and (*b*) the outward unity which expresses itself in mutual recognition, co-operative action, and corporate or institutional unity. The concrete proposals here brought forward may be regarded as next steps toward the realization of the unity which the Churches should seek. Some of these proposals are of concern to individual communions, others of concern to groups of communions in certain countries or other areas, and still others may be considered as of oecumenical or world-wide range.

1. *Need of Wider Knowledge*

In view of the admitted fact that a principal hindrance to Christian and Church unity is the widely prevailing ignorance, apathy, and inertia on the whole subject of unity, we earnestly advocate the launching and conduct in various communions of an adequate educational oecumenical programme. To this end simple, and also more elaborate, outlines of study of interesting and relevant aspects of the Christian union movement should be prepared and introduced.

Existing books on the principles of the world-wide Christian movement, now commonly called 'oecumenism', though valuable, are, as a rule, too technical for general use. So much depends on a widespread understanding of this subject that special material should be produced for the general Church membership. For instance, a series of small volumes about the various communions, giving the facts which are most distinctive, significant, and of living interest, would meet a very real need in many countries. There is a place, moreover, for carefully planned articles in the more influential magazines. Current oecumenical developments must also receive more systematic attention in both the religious and the secular press. It is at this point—the failure to educate the rank and file of the lay membership, both men and women—that so many co-operative and union schemes break down or fail to advance.

In this connexion we warmly approve the proposal, already discussed in several quarters, that an authoritative, Christian, oecumenical review should be undertaken, preferably under the auspices of such oecumenical Church organization as may follow the Oxford and Edinburgh Conferences.

2. *Theological Education*

It is to be desired that theological colleges, faculties, or seminaries should make provision in the curriculum for instruction of the future ministry in all that pertains to the drawing together of the various Christian communions, with special reference to the more significant developments and plans of present-day oecumenical movements. The chairs dealing with doctrine should include instruction in the doctrines and life, not only of the Church to which each institution is attached, but also of other communions. Chairs of Church History, Liturgics, Symbolics, and Missions should deal with the history and work of all branches of Christendom. In certain centres this can be achieved by joint action on the part of several colleges. Moreover, in addition to instruction through lectures and seminar work, intervisitation on the part of students of the colleges of different communions should be encouraged. The valuable work of the Oecumenical Seminar in Geneva will be found suggestive, as also the activities of the Student Christian Movements in the theological colleges and seminaries.

3. *Cultivation of the Spirit of Unity*

The spreading of the spirit of Christian oecumenical fellowship needs not only the conscious communication of knowledge and ideas, but the fostering of such attitudes and spiritual experience as will lead to the desire for unity. While this is true of old and young alike, it is peculiarly desirable that in the processes of Christian education this principle should be borne in mind.

4. *Research Groups*

The plan followed in Holland, France, Victoria (Australia), and also in other countries of forming societies of theologians and other scholars for more profound study and research in the problems of oecumenism might well be followed in other countries, possibly through the agency of existing institutions.

5. *Special Times of Prayer*

The practice in some countries, for example, Norway, of setting apart one Sunday each year for special prayer for the oecumenical movement is worthy of wide observance. Since 1920 the world-wide observance of the eight days before Pentecost (Whit Sunday) as a special time of prayer for the unity of Christ's Church has been fostered by the Faith and Order Movement. Moreover, we draw attention to the suggestion of Pastor Wilfred Monod, endorsed by many others, that when the Holy Communion is celebrated the officiating minister should use words in prayer or in preaching which will help worshippers to identify themselves with the whole Christian fellowship in the act of communion.

6. *Mutual Church Aid*

The practice of the early Christian Church, which is being followed so helpfully to-day by the European Central Office for Inter-Church Aid, the Russian Church Aid Fund, and by certain individual communions, of affording mutual help to suffering or weaker Churches of other communions, is not only an expression of the spirit of Christ but also an invaluable means of fostering oecumenical education and fellowship.

7. *Spiritual Preparation*

A precursor to many very significant Church union movements has been prolonged and pronouncedly spiritual preparation, including united movements for prayer, and joint participation in such Christian tasks as evangelism and meeting great moral and social needs. Of this there are conspicuous examples in India, China, Japan, and Korea, as well as in the West. The recent united Preaching Mission in a score or more of the leading cities of America, and other united evangelistic campaigns, not only afford convincing demonstrations of unity but also have been the means of generating the spirit of unity and creating a temper which finds the continuance of division intolerable.

The Conference urges on all the Churches the desirability of organizing and participating in efforts of evangelism in co-operation with Christians of other communions, both as a means of bearing effective witness before the multitudes who are detached from Christianity and as a means of expressing and strengthening that unity in the Gospel which binds together in spiritual fellowship those who own allegiance to different Churches.

8. *Principles of Co-operation*

It is widely recognized that sound policies of co-operation in all spheres of Christian action have done much to facilitate the drawing together of the Christian Churches. Such co-operation between Christian bodies, if it is to be truly effective, must have regard to certain guiding principles and governing considerations drawn from experience already accumulated in many countries.

Among these attention is called to the following:

(1) In determining the sphere of co-operation due regard is paid to the objects to be achieved, namely:

(*a*) to meet real and recognized need;

(*b*) to obviate conflict and unnecessary waste;

(*c*) to accomplish important results which cannot be secured as well, if at all, by the co-operative agencies working separately.

(2) At the very beginning of the undertaking the various bodies joining in the co-operative arrangement enter into an understanding as to objectives, scope, direction, assignment of responsibilities, support, and all else vital to the success of the undertaking, and this understanding is set forth with clarity in writing.

(3) The co-operative agency possesses only such power as the co-operating bodies confer upon it.

(4) The plan of organization is made as simple as is compatible with achieving the desired results.

(5) Everything is done openly and in consultation.

(6) There is a sincere determination to understand the viewpoints and the distinctive characteristics of the different units, and willingness to accept what others have to give.

(7) Wherever co-operation is undertaken it is carried through so thoroughly as to create the confidence on which further developments must depend.

(8) No large venture of co-operation can proceed to high success without adequate financial resources, but it is believed that those will be forthcoming if the other conditions here emphasized are met.

(9) The leaders are on their guard lest in their own lives there be manifested or tolerated those things which tend to destroy co-operation or to make impossible true Christian unity; for example, ignorance and prejudice, hazy thinking and vague statements, selfish ambition and jealousy, suspicion and lack of frankness, intriguing and disloyalty.

(10) The prime consideration to be borne constantly in mind by all engaged in the work of co-operation is that of rendering

Christ-like service. First and last in point of importance is the recognition of the Lordship of Jesus Christ, and the conviction that He Himself wills co-operation and unity.

9. *Fellowships of Unity*

Springing up in different parts of the world are fellowships of unity which are exerting an influence out of all proportion to their number. The Association of Unity inaugurated by the late Peter Ainslie is an illustration. Other examples are the Friends of Reunion in Great Britain, the Anglican and Eastern Churches Association, and the Fellowship of St. Alban and St. Sergius. Still another is the Fellowship of Unity in Egypt. This fellowship holds each year great united meetings of members of several communions, Eastern and Western, provides lectures on various aspects of the religious life and practices of the Churches, furnishes articles for the press dealing with oecumenical questions, and arranges for parties to visit different Churches at special times and seasons for the study of different forms of worship. The Churches have hardly begun to explore the possibilities of realizing a more vital understanding and a deeper unity through acquaintance with each other's modes and experiences of worship. Much might be done by introducing the best-known hymns of one Church or confessional group into the service of others.

The Conference asks the Continuation Committee to take this matter into consideration, and to take steps to promote the study of liturgical questions by the appointment of a commission or by what other method seems best.

10. *Regional Conferences*

We believe the time has come when in our various countries there should be held regional conferences similar to those held at Oxford and Edinburgh. In certain of the larger countries there might well be held in different areas a series of more intimate consultations, or retreats, of Church leaders, or other specialized groups.

11. *Youth Movements*

A most reassuring feature of the oecumenical movement is the growing keen interest in the subject being manifested by the Student Christian Movements and other Christian youth organizations. This interest should be fostered in every possible way. We commend heartily the World Christian Youth Conference planned for the year 1939.

12. *Increase of Intercourse*

We draw attention to the multiplying examples of exchange of membership, of interchange of pulpits, and of intercommunion on the part of the different Churches in all parts of the world, and, subject to proper understanding and regulation, believe that these practices should be encouraged.

Where occasional communion is admitted in the practice of a Church but is not formally recognized by its law, it is desirable that, where principles permit, this apparent incongruity should be removed as soon as possible in order to avoid misunderstanding, both on the part of the recipient and of members of the communion extending the invitation. Where hesitancy still remains because of this ambiguity or for any reason, the communicants of one Church, whether ministers or laymen, should be encouraged to be present, even if they do not participate, at the sacraments of other Churches. And such presence should be regarded as an act of common worship expressing the measure of spiritual unity already attained.

We feel moved to say in this connexion that neither those who press for intercommunion nor those who feel obliged to oppose it should condemn the others, but should in all ways respect one another's consciences; but all Christians should be saddened by every hindrance to the fellowship of full communion with all sincere disciples of our Lord.

13. *Plans for Church Union*

It is recommended that communions represented at the present Conference should consider the desirability of setting up effective standing commissions for the study of the oecumenical questions, for fostering mutually helpful relations with other communions, and for conducting conversations with other communions leading toward Church union.

It is highly desirable, in countries where conditions are favourable and the time seems ripe, that those communions which already enjoy a considerable measure of mutual understanding, fellowship, and co-operation should proceed without undue delay to the stage of official negotiations, or at least of conversations, and in particular should produce, as soon as may be, a preliminary or provisional draft scheme of union for submission to their constituencies.

14. *Needs of Special Areas*

In certain regions circumstances make a special demand on the Churches for co-operative action. One type of problem is presented by areas where there has been a sudden marked increase in population, or where there have been created entirely new communities through the operation of rehousing schemes. This calls for united action on the part of different Churches, and the absence of such action is likely to lead to bitterness, strife, and wasted effort. To deal with such situations it is suggested that the Churches, where their principles permit, should set up permanent comity or international commissions to review, recommend, and guide the location of new Churches. Such a plan will avoid the danger of congregations being created which have a local unity, but are cut off from the contacts and resources afforded by membership in a wider communion. Similar action may be possible in the numerous centres where, owing to a decrease of population, more Churches exist than the populations need or can support. There are other problems presented in other areas which are susceptible of similar treatment.

15. *Territorial and Oecumenical Unity*

A problem calling for far-sighted policy is that presented in areas where, when union is under discussion, it becomes necessary for a Church to choose between, on the one hand, entering into a unity with other denominations within the same national boundary, and, on the other hand, maintaining connexions with other Churches of its own order throughout the world. Experience shows that the injury done to the Christian cause by the multiplicity of separate Churches within a given area is so great that the territorial unity of Churches should normally be regarded as desirable where it can be accomplished without violating the principles of the Churches concerned. It must, however, be recognized that the ideal of a territorially or nationally united Church is accompanied by certain dangers. Therefore we urge that in developing Church union on the territorial basis every care should be taken to preserve in nationally constituted Churches a sense of oecumenical relationship, and to maintain such relationship in every possible way. For example, the United Church of Canada not only has united three communions into one united Church, but also maintains affiliations with the oecumenical bodies to which the three uniting communions belonged.

16. *The Older and Younger Churches*

The Churches and Mission Boards of the West have a great responsibility to discharge in regard to union movements among the younger Churches. Even where the younger Churches are autonomous, they will naturally seek counsel and encouragement from the older Churches to which under God they owe their origin. While it is right and proper for the older Churches to place at the disposal of younger Churches what they most value in doctrine, worship, and order, it must be recognized as a fundamental necessity that in all matters both older and younger Churches should be free to follow the leading of the Spirit of God as it is apprehended by them.

The Conference has heard, with deep appreciation, of movements towards Church union in many parts of the world. It regards the scheme for Church union in South India, about which three Churches are now negotiating, as deserving of particular attention and study, because in it an attempt is being made to include within a united Church communions holding to the episcopal, the presbyteral, and the congregational principles. The importance of prayerful study of this scheme is further shown by the fact that union negotiations based on its principles are in progress in other parts of the world. In dealing with this and with similar cases the Churches of East and West alike may be called upon for great acts of trust.

17. *The Council of Churches*

This Conference as well as the World Conference held at Oxford have approved in principle the proposal that the Churches should form a Council of Churches. Some members of this Conference desire to place on record their opposition to this proposal, but we are agreed that if the Churches should adopt it, the Council should be so designed as to conserve the distinctive character and value of each of the Movements represented in the two Conferences. To this end it is desirable that, while freedom should be exercised in the formation of special committees, the Churches as such should come together on the basis of the doctrine of the Incarnation. The largest success of the plan depends upon securing adequate representation of every communion.

XX. THE WORLD MEETING OF THE INTERNATIONAL MISSIONARY COUNCIL

TAMBARAM, NEAR MADRAS, DECEMBER 12–29, 1938

[The World Meeting was attended by 471 members from 69 different countries. The Chairman was Dr. John R. Mott, and the joint Secretaries were Dr. A. L. Warnshuis and the Rev. William Paton. The Conference did its work by means of various sections, the Reports of which were adopted by the Council, after discussion in plenary sessions. The following is the Report of the section on Co-operation and Unity. See *The World Mission of the Church*, pp. 151–5 (International Missionary Council, 1939).]

217. Co-operation and Unity

REPORTS from all parts of the world show a truly remarkable development of co-operation within the Christian Church since the Edinburgh Conference of 1910. For this we thank God. While we are deeply humbled by the lack of unity in the Church, and by serious limitations even in the practice of co-operation, we nevertheless wish to place on record the fact that the co-operation thus far achieved has led to a great increase of mutual understanding and trust. Through partnership in our Master's work we have entered into a fuller appreciation of the heritage and riches of spiritual experience of one another, and a unity of spirit unknown before. This unity of spirit has made us realize more fully how gravely our outward divisions are hindering the extension of the Kingdom of God, and indeed are stultifying our message of the love of God as the great reconciling force in a world that desperately needs it. We have found that there are many ranges of Christian service which can be undertaken and successfully carried through only in co-operation with one another. We have had evidence that results have been achieved which humanly speaking could not have been secured by separate action.[1] It is our deep and joyous conviction that in our advance along this path we have been led by God Himself and that He has put the seal of His blessing on our co-operative service.

We therefore urge the continuance and further extension of co-operation in fields and in types of work where it is imperfectly

[1] For instances of this, reference may be made to *Co-operation and the World Mission*, by Dr. J. R. Mott.

practised. At present, co-operation in institutional work absorbs most of the men and money and time available for co-operative activities. Such institutions are outstanding examples of the indispensability of joint effort for effective working. We also rejoice in the wide variety of other forms of co-operation, but there is need for a great extension of it in such fields as those of theological education, religious education, the production and distribution of Christian literature, many forms of social service, and supremely in the Church's primary task of evangelism. Efforts should also be made to bring within the co-operative movement branches of the Church which have hitherto held aloof from it, and whose abstention, we believe, means weakness and spiritual loss to the Church as a whole.

We desire to lay special stress on the urgency of the need for co-operation in the vital matter of Church discipline. An agreed practice among the churches is needed in regard to the treatment of Christians who are under discipline. It is imperative that there should be common action with regard to marriage customs and other practices, which are bound up with the social structure of the people to whom the Gospel is presented. Unless a common standard and common action can be maintained here, Christian levels of family life and social relationship must deteriorate.

We would also emphasize the necessity of joint planning for the whole Christian enterprise in any given area in order that the field may be wisely covered and unnecessary duplication and waste avoided.

In these matters we believe that the National Christian Councils and similar organizations have a most important part to play. We recognize with thankfulness the value of the service they are rendering in many parts of the world and urge that they should receive the fullest possible support. We also recommend that such organizations should be brought into being in regions where they do not already exist.

In recommending an extension of the field of co-operative work we would suggest that, especially in institutions, care should be taken to foster loyalty to the visible Church of Christ. We also feel that it is of prime importance that such institutions should not be carried on apart from the growing indigenous church and unrelated to its life: it is essential that in the control and direction of policy, and in the relating of institutions to the whole Christian enterprise, the Church should have an influential share. We recommend that the organization of existing co-operative enterprises should be reviewed in the light of this principle.

We believe that co-operation is in line with the will and purpose of God and that it is thus essentially Christian. We would urge that not only between churches in each field, but also in the relations between the older and the younger churches co-operation be regarded as the governing principle. In some cases eagerness to co-operate among the younger churches is thwarted by a too rigid control from abroad, and we cannot too strongly urge that such rigidity of control in this and in other matters must be relaxed if the younger churches are to grow into fullness of Christian life and experience and service. Further, while we rejoice in the growth of co-operation at the home base of Christian missions we would emphasize the need of its further development both for its own sake and because it would avoid the multiplication of cumbrous and wasteful machinery on the field.

We have heard with interest of the proposed formation of the World Council of Churches. We look forward with confidence to the part which the younger churches will play in the future work of the Council. We trust that in the application of the constitution care will be taken to ensure that the membership of the Council is genuinely representative of indigenous leadership. In welcoming the appearance of this Council we consider that the distinctive service and organization of the International Missionary Council should be maintained. It is of particular importance that nothing should be done to undermine the confidence in the International Missionary Council that has been built up during so many years.

While we are profoundly thankful for the growth in brotherly love and understanding that has come with increased co-operation, and while we are convinced of the need for its yet further extension, there are certain parts of the Christian obligation which in our judgement demand more than a co-operative basis. In particular it has been found that in most cases co-operation in the great evangelistic task stops at the point where pastoral care is needed for the building up of the Church. We can act together in the presentation of the Gospel to men and in the winning of them to the Christian faith; but there is evidence that in the next necessary stage co-operation breaks down owing to divided church loyalty. From this standpoint therefore, as well as from the growing spirit of unity that has resulted from common working at a common task, has come in many fields a deep and a growing conviction that the spirit of God is guiding the various branches of His Church to seek for the realization of a visible and organic union. We recognize that not all share this conviction, and we respect their views; but for many it has become the dominant concern and care. They find in it the verification in experience of the deep purpose of God as expressed in our Lord's high-priestly prayer for the oneness of His followers 'that the world may believe that Thou hast sent Me'.

We recognize with thankfulness several notable achievements of organic Church union in various parts of the world during recent years. We would associate ourselves fully with the judgement of the Edinburgh Conference on Faith and Order. This said that the scheme for Church union in South India in which three churches are now negotiating 'deserves particular attention and study because in it an attempt is being made to include within a united Church communions holding to the episcopal, the presbyteral and the congregational principles. The importance of prayerful study of this scheme is further shown by the fact that union negotiations based on its principles are in progress in other parts of the world.'

The following statement has been drawn up by the representatives of the younger churches in this section and expresses their unanimous view. We most earnestly commend it to the prayerful consideration of all the churches.

The representatives of the younger churches in the section desire to make the following statement:

> 'During the discussion it became abundantly clear that the divisions of Christendom were seen in their worst light in the mission field. Instances were cited by the representatives of the younger churches of disgraceful competition, wasteful overlapping, and of groups and individuals turned away from the Church because of the divisions within. Disunion is both a stumbling-block to the faithful and a mockery to those without. We confess with shame that we ourselves have often been the cause of thus bringing dishonour to the religion of our Master. The representatives of the younger churches in this Section one and all gave expression to the passionate longing that exists in all countries for visible union of the churches. They are aware of the fact of spiritual unity; they record with great thankfulness all the signs of co-operation and understanding that are increasingly seen in various directions; but they realize that this is not

enough. Visible and organic union must be our goal. This, however, will require an honest study of those things in which the churches have differences, a widespread teaching of the common church membership in things that make for union and venturesome sacrifice on the part of all. Such a union alone will remove the evils arising out of our divisions. Union proposals have been put forward in different parts of the world. Loyalty, however, will forbid the younger churches going forward to consummate any union unless it receives the whole-hearted support and blessing of those through whom these churches have been planted. We are thus often torn between loyalty to our mother churches and loyalty to our ideal of union. We, therefore, appeal with all the fervour we possess, to the missionary societies and boards and the responsible authorities of the older churches, to take this matter seriously to heart, to labour with the churches in the mission field to achieve this union, to support and encourage us in all our efforts to put an end to the scandalous effects of our divisions, and to lead us in the path of union—the union for which our Lord prayed, through which the world would indeed believe in the Divine Mission of the Son, our Lord Jesus Christ.'

XXI. THE WORLD COUNCIL OF CHURCHES

(IN PROCESS OF FORMATION)

[At a meeting attended by thirty-five officers of the various branches of the Oecumenical movement and other church leaders, and held at Westfield College, Hampstead, in July 1937, the following proposal was adopted:

'That, with a view to facilitating the more effective action of the Christian Church in the modern world, the movements known as "Life and Work" and "Faith and Order" should be more closely related in a body representative of the Churches and caring for the interests of each movement.'

This proposal was submitted to the Oxford (Life and Work) and Edinburgh (Faith and Order) Conferences of 1937 and approved in principle by each, with a particular reservation on the part of the Edinburgh Conference. A Committee of fourteen (seven from each Conference) was appointed, which summoned a larger and more representative body of seventy-five church leaders, who met at Utrecht, from May 9 to May 12, 1938, and drew up the following Constitution, which was adopted by the Committee of Fourteen at its meeting on May 13, 1938, and, with a Note attached at the end of the Constitution, by the Continuation Committee of Faith and Order at Clarens, September 1938. Archbishop William Temple was elected chairman of the Provisional Committee which has carried on the work since that date and has made preparations for the first Assembly of the World Council of Churches to be held at Amsterdam from August 22 to September 5, 1948. Following the death of Archbishop Temple in 1944, five Joint Presidents were appointed, namely: Dr. Marc Boegner (Acting Chairman), Dr. J. R. Mott, Archbishop Germanos, the Archbishop of Canterbury (Geoffrey Francis Fisher), and the Archbishop of Upsala (Erling Eidem).

Dr. W. A. Visser 't Hooft has held the office of General Secretary from the first. The Headquarters are at 17 Route de Malagnou, Geneva. The subject of the Amsterdam Conference is 'Man's Disorder and God's Design'. By January 1948 one hundred and thirty-three Churches had joined the World Council. The Constitution will be presented to the Council at Amsterdam for approval.]

218. Constitution for the World Council of Churches[1]

(In Process of Formation)

SEPTEMBER 1938

I. *Basis*

THE World Council of Churches is a fellowship of Churches which accept our Lord Jesus Christ as God and Saviour. It is constituted for the discharge of the functions set out below.

[1] The official translations are:
Ökumenischer Rat der Kirchen
Conseil Œcuménique des Églises
Κοινωνία τῶν 'Εκκλησίων.

II. *Membership*

All Churches shall be eligible for membership in the World Council which express their agreement with the basis upon which the Council is founded.

After the Council has been organized the application of Churches to become members shall be considered by the Assembly or its Central Committee as it may be advised by national or confessional associations of Churches.

Note. Under the word 'Churches' are included such denominations as are composed of local autonomous churches.

III. *Functions*

The functions of the World Council shall be:

(i) To carry on the work of the two world movements for 'Faith and Order' and for 'Life and Work'.

(ii) To facilitate common action by the Churches.

(iii) To promote co-operation in study.

(iv) To promote the growth of oecumenical consciousness in the members of all Churches.

(v) To establish relations with denominational federations of world-wide scope and with other oecumenical movements.

(vi) To call world conferences on specific subjects as occasion may require, such conferences being empowered to publish their own findings.

Note: In matters of common interest to all the Churches and pertaining to Faith and Order, the Council shall always proceed in accordance with the basis on which the Lausanne (1927) and Edinburgh (1937) Conferences were called and conducted.

IV. *Authority*

The World Council shall offer counsel and provide opportunity of united action in matters of common interest.

It may take action on behalf of constituent Churches in such matters as one or more of them may commit to it.

It shall have authority to call regional and world conferences on specific subjects as occasion may require.

The World Council shall not legislate for the Churches; nor shall it act for them in any manner except as indicated above or as may hereafter be specified by the constituent Churches.

V. *Organization*

The World Council shall discharge its functions through the following bodies:

(i) An Assembly which shall be the principal authority in the Council, and shall ordinarily meet every five years. The Assembly shall be composed of official representatives of the Churches or groups of Churches adhering to it and directly appointed by them. It shall consist of not more than 450 members who shall be apportioned as is provided hereafter. They shall serve for five years, their term of service beginning in the year before the Assembly meets.

The membership shall be allocated provisionally as follows:

85, representing the Orthodox Churches throughout the world, allocated in such manner as they may decide;

110, representing the Churches of the Continent of Europe, allocated in such manner as they may decide;

60, representing the Churches of Great Britain and Eire, allocated in such manner as they may decide;

90, representing the Churches of the United States of America and Canada, allocated in such manner as they may decide;

50, representing the Churches of Asia, Africa, Latin America, and the Pacific Islands, to be appointed by them as they may decide;

25, representing the Churches of South Africa, Australasia, and areas not otherwise represented, to be appointed by them, such places to be allocated by the Central Committee;

and, not more than 30 members representing minority Churches, which in the judgement of the Central Committee are not granted adequate representation by the above provisions of this section, such Churches to be designated by the world confessional organizations.

The Assembly shall have power to appoint Officers of the World Council and of the Assembly at its discretion.

The members of the Assembly shall be both clerical and lay persons—men and women. In order to secure that approximately one-third of the Assembly shall consist of lay persons, the Central Committee, in consultation with the different areas and groups, shall suggest plans to achieve this end.

(ii) A Central Committee which shall consist of not more than 90 members designated by the Churches, or groups of Churches, from among persons whom these Churches have elected as members of the Assembly. They shall serve from the beginning of the Assembly meeting until the next Assembly, unless the Assembly otherwise determine. Any vacancy occurring in the membership of the Central Committee shall be filled by the Churches or group of Churches concerned. This Committee shall be a Committee of the Assembly. The Assembly shall have authority to modify the allocation of members of the Central Committee as herein provided, both as to the manner and as to the ratio of the allocation.

The membership shall be allocated provisionally as follows:

17, of whom at least 3 shall be lay persons, representing the Orthodox Churches throughout the world, allocated in such manner as they may decide;

22, of whom at least 5 shall be lay persons, representing the Churches of the Continent of Europe, allocated in such manner as they may decide;

12, of whom at least 4 shall be lay persons, representing the Churches of Great Britain and Eire, allocated in such manner as they may decide;

18, of whom at least 5 shall be lay persons, representing the Churches of the United States of America and Canada, allocated in such manner as they may decide;

10, of whom at least 2 shall be lay persons, representing the Churches of Asia, Africa, Latin America, and the Pacific Islands, to be appointed by them as they may decide;

5, of whom at least 2 shall be lay persons, representing the Churches of South Africa, Australasia, and areas not otherwise represented, to be appointed by them, such places to be allocated by the Central Committee;

and, not more than 6 Members representing minority Churches, which in the judgement of the Central Committee are not granted adequate representation by the above provisions of this section, such Churches to be designated by the world confessional organizations.

The Central Committee shall have the following powers:

(*a*) It shall, between meetings of the Assembly, carry out the Assembly's instructions and exercise its functions, except that of amending the Constitution or modifying the allocation of its own members.

(*b*) It shall be the finance committee of the Assembly, formulating its budget and securing its financial support.

(*c*) It shall name and elect its own Officers from among its members and appoint its own secretarial staff.

(*d*) The Central Committee shall meet normally once every calendar year, and shall have power to appoint its own Executive Committee.

Quorum. No business, except what is required for carrying forward the current activities of the Council, shall be transacted in either the Assembly or the Central Committee unless one-half of the total membership is present.

VI. *Appointment of Commissions*

The World Council shall discharge part of its functions by the appointment of Commissions. These shall be established under the authority of the Assembly, whether they be actually nominated by the Assembly or by the Central Committee acting under its instructions. The Commissions shall, between meetings of the Assembly, report annually to the Central Committee which shall exercise general supervision over them. The Commissions may add to their membership clerical and lay persons approved for the purpose by the Central Committee.

In particular, the Assembly shall make provisions by means of appropriate Commissions for carrying on the activities of 'Faith and Order' and of 'Life and Work'. There shall be a Faith and Order Commission which shall conform to the requirements of the Second World Conference on Faith and Order, held at Edinburgh in 1937 (see below).

VII. *Other Oecumenical Christian Organizations*

World Confessional Associations and such Oecumenical Organizations as may be designated by the Central Committee may be invited to send representatives to the sessions of the Assembly and of the Central Committee in a consultative capacity, in such numbers as the Central Committee shall determine.

VIII. *Amendments*

The Constitution may be amended by a two-thirds majority vote of the Assembly, provided that the proposed amendment shall have been reviewed by the Central Committee, and notice of it sent to the constituent Churches not less than six months before the meeting of the Assembly. The Central Committee itself, as well as the individual Churches, shall have the right to propose such amendment.

Note: The requirements of the Second World Conference on Faith and Order, held at Edinburgh in 1937, referred to above, are the following:

(*a*) That the World Council's Commission on Faith and Order shall, in the first instance, be the Continuation Committee appointed by this Conference.

(*b*) In any further appointments made by the Council to membership of the Commission on Faith and Order, the persons appointed shall always be members of the Churches which fall within the terms of the Faith and Order invitation as addressed to 'all Christian bodies throughout the world which accept our Lord Jesus Christ as God and Saviour'.

(*c*) The work of the Commission on Faith and Order shall be carried on under the general care of a Theological Secretariat appointed by the Commission, in consultation with the Council and acting in close co-operation with other secretariats of the Council. The Council shall make adequate financial provision for the work of the Commission after consultation with the Commission.

(*d*) In matters of common interest to all the Churches and pertaining to Faith and Order, the Council shall always proceed in accordance with the basis on which this Conference on Faith and Order was called and is being conducted.

(*e*) The World Council shall consist of *official* representatives of the Churches participating.

(*f*) Any Council formed before the first meeting of the General Assembly shall be called Provisional, and the Assembly, representing all the Churches, shall have complete freedom to determine the constitution of the Central Council.

219. *Letter from the Archbishop of York (William Temple) to the Cardinal Secretary of State*

FEBRUARY 10, 1939

[There is some uncertainty as to the date on which this letter was posted. A pencil note on the copy at the office of the World Council in Geneva reads 'Sent off March 14, 1939'.]

TO THE CARDINAL SECRETARY OF STATE

BISHOPTHORPE
YORK
10 February 1939

MAY IT PLEASE YOUR EMINENCE,

THE Provisional Committee constituted in connexion with the World Council of Churches now in process of formation desires to submit to the Holy See the information that such a Council is being established in accordance with the Constitution set out in the enclosed paper.

The project has its origin, as the accompanying memorandum explains, in the history and experience of the 'Life and Work' Movement and of the 'Faith and Order' Movement.

We understand from previous communications which have passed in connexion with World Conferences held under the auspices of those Movements that the Church of Rome would not desire to be formally associated with the Council. But it seems to us required by courtesy that we should inform the Holy See of what is being done. We hope that it may be permissible to exchange information with agencies of the Church of Rome on matters of common interest and that we should have the help from time to time of unofficial consultation with Roman Catholic theologians and scholars. Such sharing in our activities as Roman Catholics may be ready to undertake will be cordially welcomed by us as a manifestation of fellowship in Christ. At a time when all that Christians hold in common is menaced by forces of demonic power we venture to hope that we may have the benevolent sympathy of our Roman Catholic brethren as we attempt to recall men to the faith and obedience of the Lord Jesus Christ as the one hope for the salvation of the world.

With assurances of profound respect I am, my Lord Cardinal,

Your Eminence's brother and servant,

WILLIAM EBOR:
Archbishop of York.
Primate of England and Metropolitan.
Chairman of the Provisional Committee.

220. *Reply from the Cardinal Secretary of State for the Archbishop of York (William Temple)*

JULY 12, 1939

[The following is the text of the reply from the Cardinal Secretary of State to the Archbishop of York's inquiry, sent through the Apostolic Delegate to Great Britain. It was transmitted to the Archbishop by the Apostolic Delegate in a letter dated July 21, 1939.]

SECRETARIATE OF STATE OF HIS HOLINESS

From the Vatican, 12th July, 1939

YOUR EXCELLENCY,

THE Anglican Archbishop of York sent me on the 4th July a letter in which he informs me that there is in preparation a 'World Council of Churches'. The above-named Prelate, although aware, as he himself mentions, that the Roman Church is not desirous of formally associating itself with the initiative above mentioned, nevertheless wishes to inform the Vatican, as an act of courtesy, of what is happening.

He would also be glad to know, seeing that formal co-operation by the Vatican is not possible, if it could be hoped that there might be an exchange of information with agencies of the Roman Church, and the possibility of recourse, for consultation, to Catholic theologians.

I would ask Your Excellency in my name to explain to the writer that there is no obstacle in the way of consultation with the Bishops and the Apostolic Delegate. Likewise there is nothing in the way of an exchange of confidential information with Catholic theologians, who will, naturally, make reply in their own name.

Your Excellency will have the goodness to add that the Cardinal Secretary of State has not replied directly to the letter, but, as is the custom, has informed the Representative of the Holy See in England, and given him the necessary instructions.

With the expression of my sincere high regard, I am,

Your Excellency's servant,

L. CARD. MAGLIONE

221. Statement by the Provisional Committee of the World Council of Churches on the Function of the World Council

APRIL 25, 1947

[The following statement was adopted by the Provisional Committee at its meeting at Buck Hill Falls, Pennsylvania, U.S.A., on April 25, 1947.]

THE World Council of Churches, composed of Churches which acknowledge Jesus Christ as God and Saviour, owes its existence to the desire of its member Churches to express their unity in Him. The Council seeks to promote this unity among its members and to serve them as an organ whereby they may bear witness together to their common faith and co-operation in matters requiring united action. The Council does not aim, however, to usurp the functions which belong to its constituent members, nor in any way to control or legislate for these bodies. Moreover, while earnestly seeking the co-operation and unity of all the Churches that accept its basis, the Council disavows any thought of becoming a single unified church structure dominated by a centralized administrative authority.

The Christian unity for which the Council stands is of a different order. It strives after a unity in which Christians and Christian Churches, joyously aware of their oneness in Jesus Christ their Lord, and pursuing an ever fuller realization and expression of that oneness, shall in times of need give help and comfort to one another, and at all times inspire and exhort one another to live worthily of their common membership in the Body of Christ.

With respect to public pronouncements, the Council regards it as an essential part of its responsibility to address its own attention in the realm of thought or action 'not as having dominion of their faith, but as helpers of their joy'. The Council further considers itself responsible to Jesus Christ, the Head of the Church, to seek to know the Will of God upon important issues which radically affect the Church and society, and thereafter, in the name of Christ, in dependence upon the Holy Spirit, and in penitence and faith, to call upon Churches, governments, or men in general, as the situation may require, to deal with a given historical issue, in the name of Christ and in the light of God's revelation in Jesus Christ the Lord.